Cyber Breach Response That Actually Works

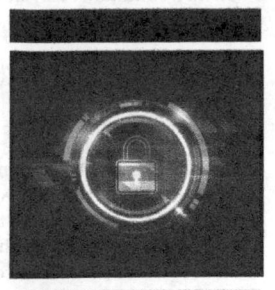

Cyber Breach Response That Actually Works

Organizational Approach to Managing Residual Risk

Andrew Gorecki

WILEY

About the Author

Andrew Gorecki is a cybersecurity professional with experience across various information technology and cybersecurity disciplines, including network and security engineering, data management, cybersecurity operations, and incident response.

Andrew has provided cybersecurity consulting services across various industry sectors in the United States, the United Kingdom, and other European countries. Andrew developed a strong interest in incident response while working as a cybersecurity consultant in the U.K. Following his interest, Andrew joined the X-Force Incident Response and Intelligence Services (X-Force IRIS) competency of IBM Security in the U.S. to work in incident response full-time.

As of this writing, Andrew manages a team of incident response consultants within X-Force IRIS. In addition to his managerial responsibilities, Andrew leads investigations into large-scale breaches for Fortune 500 organizations and consults on building and optimizing incident response programs.

Andrew takes a holistic approach to incident response by focusing on the end-to-end business process, facilitating cross-functional engagements, and helping clients build capabilities based on sound risk management principles.

About the Technical Editors

Adam Brand has spent most of his career focused on helping organizations improve their security programs. Over the years, he has also helped untangle complex malware found in breaches, led breach response efforts, and identified unknown attackers through threat hunting engagements. At the time of writing, Adam is a Managing Director with a large consulting firm in the cybersecurity strategy and governance group.

Adam has worked with dozens of clients throughout his career on both proactive and reactive cybersecurity projects. While he can and often does delve into the technical details, his key to success is often helping position technical challenges or information in ways nontechnical executives can understand in order to take action.

An active public speaker and security community participant, Adam has spoken at dozens of industry conferences over the years. Furthermore, Adam has developed an active interest in skillsets focused on medical device security, and currently works with both device manufacturers and healthcare providers to help improve patient safety.

Rhodes Gregory Taylor-Broun is a security operations center and computer incident response professional with decades of hands-on experience and several industry certifications. Greg holds the SANS Advanced Penetration Testing and Exploit Writing (GXPN), SANS Certified Intrusion Analyst (GCIA), and Certified Information Systems Security Professional (CISSP) certifications. He has worked on a wide variety of information security incidents and high-profile data breaches, and he brings real-world, hands-on experience to bear when working in the field. Greg calls San Diego home with his wife and daughter, where he runs a meetup for digital forensicators and incident responders, sharing his knowledge freely with the community.

Acknowledgments

Writing this book has been both hard and rewarding. I am grateful to everyone who contributed to this book and made it possible. I want to thank my colleagues and friends for their invaluable contributions, especially Kurt Rohrbacher, Warren Stramiello, Matthew Sullivan, Pavle Culum, Markus Schober, Phil Harrold, Chris Sperry, Matt DeFir, John Dwyer, and David Porco.

I also want to thank Himanshu Wickramasinghe, who introduced me to cybersecurity, mentored me over the last several years, and guided me on the consulting path.

A very special thanks to Adam Brand and Greg Taylor for reviewing the book and providing valuable suggestions, as well as the Wiley team, especially Gary Schwartz and Jim Minatel.

Finally, this book would not be possible without the support of my wife Marie. I want to thank her for support, encouragement, and sacrifices that allowed me to make this book a reality!

— Andrew Gorecki

Contents at a Glance

Contents

Foreword

It is often said that air traffic controllers have the most stressful job in the world. Being able to coordinate the safe takeoff and landing of dozens of commercial airliners, each carrying hundreds of passengers per day, all while dealing with a myriad of externalities, including the weather, ground control, controlled and noncontrolled airspaces, regulators like the FAA, flight crews, and airport operators, must seem like an impossible task. That is why in the United States, air traffic controllers must undergo a series of background checks and psychological exams, a rigorous training program, and certification testing, all before they ever set foot in a control tower.

If air traffic controllers have the most stressful job, cybersecurity incident responders might be a close second. As an incident responder, you're responsible for performing technical forensic investigations of highly complex environments as well as ensuring that the response team is maintaining its composure and working toward a common goal of mapping the full extent of attacker activity and eliminating their access to the network. It requires producing answers to questions that do not have an easy answer. It demands a deep level of technical knowledge in addition to a militaristic ability to lead a team toward a common objective. A responder must also consider the potential ramifications of a breach that may only surface much further down the line and take measures to protect the organization involved in the scenario, however improbable, that events unfold in such a way. It is part art form, part science.

When I interview people for incident responder positions, I often ask candidates to describe a situation where they were able to thrive under adverse conditions, because they will absolutely find themselves in an even more difficult position as an incident responder. During a cyber-security breach, stress levels are at their peak, people fear for their jobs and for the survival of their business, and in some circumstances, even fear for the physical safety of the general public. Attacks against critical infrastructure are not unheard of and seem to become even more prevalent as time goes on. In addition to the high-stress environment, financial budgets and higher-level business objectives undermine every step of the process. If you're not prepared to have the CEO of a Fortune 500 company channel his or her anger and frustration by yelling at you, you might not be cut out for the job. It is for these reasons that most incident responders do not stay in the field for very long. They move on to other roles and apply their experience in a proactive way to prevent organizations from experiencing their worst day. A responder with 10 years of experience is considered a relic.

All of this helps to explain why I always believed that there was no manual for how to do incident response, no textbook you could give to an inexperienced responder that tells them everything they need to know to be able to respond to incidents. The cybersecurity industry does not have a standard training curriculum and testing process to admit new entrants into the field, like the aviation industry has for air traffic controllers. Incident response is one of those things that you can truly learn only by doing, and you can only succeed after you have failed several times. It is baptism by fire, and the anointed need no other teacher.

That's why this book is so ambitious—it is an attempt to bring order to an inherently chaotic process. Over the past several years that Andrew and I have worked together, I have learned that he has a knack for reading complex situations, digesting critical information, and building structure around the process that allows various elements to operate more efficiently. Most responders get so "into the weeds" in trying to solve the immediate problem that they don't have either the time or the ability to step back and consider the bigger picture. Andrew has taken his experience and engineered a framework for doing incident response more effectively. Take his advice and run with it—and if even one paragraph of this book helps your organization avoid the worst-case scenario in a cybersecurity incident, you'll know who to thank.

—Kurt Rohrbacher

Introduction

Cybersecurity has taken the media by storm in recent years, and cyber-attacks are now headline news, from destructive ransomware attacks that impact manufacturing plants to data breaches that involve Fortune 500 companies.

Organizations have experienced notable disruptive cyberattacks in recent years. A ransomware attack on a global shipping company, A. P. Møller – Mærsk, wiped out their entire IT infrastructure across 600 sites in 130 countries. As a result of the cyberattack, Maersk had to rebuild their entire infrastructure in a heroic effort over 10 days. The total losses are estimated to have cost Mærsk up to $300 million.[1]

The National Health Service (NHS) in the U.K. incurred a cost of £92 million ($120 million) as a result of the WannaCry ransomware outbreak in June 2017. The cyberattack also resulted in the cancellation of 19,000 appointments.[2]

There are also numerous examples of data breaches resulting in significant financial losses, damage to brand reputation, and fines imposed by regulators. One of the most significant data breaches in recent years was the Equifax breach that led to the disclosure of personal data of 145 million U.S. consumers, including Social Security numbers, credit card information, addresses, and birth dates.[3]

As businesses and other organizations increase their digital footprint and online presence, the need to secure their information assets is more critical than ever before. The Ponemon Institute's Cost of a Data Breach Study (2019) determined an average cost of a data breach across various industries was $3.92 million.[4] Furthermore, the World Economic Forum identifies cyberattacks as the fifth top risk in terms of likelihood and the seventh top risk in terms of impact.[5]

Many organizations are increasingly concerned about their exposure to cyberattacks. Businesses exist to generate value for their shareholders, and cyberattacks ultimately impact the bottom line. Even nonprofit organizations can suffer severe financial consequences as the result of a cyberattack.

In my consulting engagements, I have observed that cyber risk has become a frequent topic of board-level conversations, and enterprises increasingly perceive exposure to cyberattacks as a business issue. To address cyber risk, organizations build information security programs to protect critical assets and reduce risk to an acceptable level. As residual risk is inevitable, incident response is a critical control in the risk management process that allows organizations to address the aftermath of an incident, reduce the impact of a cyberattack, and restore the affected assets to a fully operational state.

An effective cyber breach response program is like a fire department. Organizations design a set of capabilities based on their needs and requirements, build an incident response team, acquire the necessary technology, and operationalize those capabilities. When the inevitable happens, the affected stakeholders can call the fire department, who might be able to extinguish the fire before the real damage is done, or at least reduce the amount of damage.

The benefits of developing an effective cyber breach response program include the following:

Minimize the impact of cyberattacks. The sooner an organization detects and responds to a cyberattack, the lesser the impact to business operations, brand reputation, and financial standing.

Decrease the cost of response. Effective incident response helps organizations decrease the overall attacker dwell time on their network, leading to a decreased cost of response. *Dwell time* is the time a threat actor remains on your network from the initial compromise to eradication.

Prevent enterprisewide incidents. Undetected intrusions can swiftly progress into enterprisewide incidents within weeks. The response effort is usually proportional to the time an attacker dwells on the network. Furthermore, enterprisewide incidents usually require disruptive remediation and can impact the bottom line of the victim organization.

Improve security posture. Incident response is an iterative process, with evaluation being one of its core components. The lessons-learned outcome can help organizations improve their policies, controls, and the incident response process itself. This approach ultimately leads to an enhanced security posture and cyber resilience.

Ensure compliance. Specific regulations and standards require organizations to have incident response capabilities, including an incident response plan.

Enhance service quality. Information technology is a business enabler, and its mission is to provide value to the business. The role of information security, on the other hand, is to protect that value. By building incident response capabilities, organizations can minimize the impact of cyberattacks on their services and core business functions, leading to overall better service quality to internal and external clients.

Who Should Read This Book

I have written this book for anyone who is looking for an authoritative source of information on building and managing a cyber breach response program, including senior cybersecurity managers and chief information security officers (CISOs).

This book is also a valuable source of information for executive leaders, business and technology professionals, legal counsel, risk managers, and other stakeholders who have an active interest in cyber breach response in their organizations or who are planning to transition into a career in this field.

In this book, I explain cyber breach response concepts in a clear, concise, and technology-agnostic language that anyone with a grasp of fundamental cybersecurity and risk management concepts can understand.

How This Book Is Organized

I organized this book into six chapters that provide a comprehensive discussion of various topics relating to cyber breach response. I designed the book to serve both as a guide for building cyber breach response programs from scratch and as a reference guide for organizations that strive to grow and evolve their capabilities. Although the book consists of progressive chapters, each chapter provides stand-alone content that the reader can reference. Where appropriate, I also direct the reader to other chapters for specific information.

Chapter 1: Understanding the Bigger Picture This chapter defines cyber breach response and discusses foundational concepts. It starts with a brief overview of the threat landscape and discusses drivers for cyber breach response and their role within an overall cybersecurity program. A discussion of the critical building blocks of a sound cyber breach response strategy concludes this chapter.

Chapter 2: Building a Cybersecurity Incident Response Team Chapter 2 discusses the various considerations that organizations need to take into account when building an incident response team. The topics in this chapter include incident response competencies and functions, team models, skills, the hiring and retaining of talent, and cross-functional team development. A brief discussion on outsourcing considerations concludes this chapter.

Chapter 3: Technology Considerations in Cyber Breach Investigations This chapter focuses on building the technical capabilities necessary to support incident response investigations. The chapter starts with a discussion on general considerations for sourcing incident response technology. Then it progresses into a discussion on data acquisition in on-premises and virtualized environments, including cloud computing. The final two sections discuss sources of network data and log management solutions.

Chapter 4: Crafting an Incident Response Plan Chapter 4 starts with a discussion on the incident response lifecycle. Then it dives into various incident management concepts before concluding with a discussion on post-incident activities and continual improvement.

Chapter 5: Investigating and Remediating Cyber Breaches This chapter takes an in-depth look at a methodology that incident responders employ during investigations. It discusses topics such as digital forensics and data analysis, cyber threat intelligence, malware analysis, threat hunting, and reporting. This chapter also discusses evidence types before concluding with a discussion on remediating cyber breaches.

Chapter 6: Legal and Regulatory Considerations in Cyber Breach Response Chapter 6 discusses how the legal and regulatory landscape impacts cyber breach investigations. It goes in-depth into considerations that organizations need to keep in mind to establish a defensible protocol for the handling of digital evidence. The chapter concludes with a brief discussion on data privacy considerations in investigations.

How to Contact Wiley or the Author

You can contact the author at andrew@agorecki.net.

If you believe you have found an error in this book, and it is not listed on the book's page at www.wiley.com, you can report the issue to our customer technical support team at support.wiley.com.

Notes

1. "NotPetya Ransomware Attack Cost Shipping Giant Maersk Over $200 Million," *Forbes*, August 16, 2017, www.forbes.com/sites/ leemathews/2017/08/16/notpetya-ransomware-attack-cost- shipping-giant-maersk-over-200-million/#21c48af04f9a.

2. "WannaCry cyber attack cost the NHS £92m as 19,000 appointments cancelled," *The Telegraph*, October 11, 2018, www.telegraph .co.uk/technology/2018/10/11/wannacry-cyber-attack-cost-nhs- 92m-19000-appointments-cancelled.

3. Federal Trade Commission, Equifax Data Breach Settlement, January 2020, www.ftc.gov/enforcement/cases-proceedings/refunds/ equifax-data-breach-settlement.

4. IBM Security, "How much would a data breach cost your business?" www.ibm.com/security/data-breach.

5. World Economic Forum, The Global Risks Report 2019, 14th Edition, www.weforum.org/reports/the-global-risks-report-2019.

Understanding the Bigger Picture

Organizations across all industries increasingly rely on digital information to execute their business processes and support core business functions. Digital information that is of value to enterprises is also often a valuable and appealing target for threat actors. As a result, it requires protection in the same way as assets do in the physical world. Organizations implement safeguards to minimize risk arising from internal and external factors that might have a detrimental impact on their business. Cyber breach response plays a vital role in this process.

Building an effective cyber breach response program starts with strategy. *Strategy* is a process that allows organizations to achieve a vision and ensure that everyone is working toward the same goal. It enables this by providing a sense of direction and helping enterprises set measurable goals. A sound strategy also allows organizations to align capabilities to business objectives and manage residual risk when other controls fail.

This chapter discusses relevant foundational cybersecurity concepts, explains drivers for cyber breach response, and discusses the critical building blocks of strategy relating to cyber breach response.

Evolving Threat Landscape

Cyber breach response is typically a part of a more comprehensive cyber-security program. Enterprises build cybersecurity programs to manage cyber risk and to ensure that they can continue business operations during significant cyber events. This section discusses the cyberattack lifecycle and the different types of threat actors who pose a threat to enterprises.

Identifying Threat Actors

The cyber threat intelligence (CTI) community coined the term *threat actor* to describe an individual or a group who is responsible for cyberattacks or who poses a threat to an organization. Cybersecurity professionals and business stakeholders often use the term *attacker* or *adversary* instead. I use these terms interchangeably throughout this book.

Digital information has inherent risks associated with it. The World Economic Forum ranks cyberattacks as the fifth top risk in terms of likelihood and the seventh top risk in terms of impact.[1] The majority of medium-sized and large enterprises rely on critical digital assets that threat actors seek to exploit for a variety of purposes.

Historically, individuals and small groups engaged in hacking for notoriety or even fun. Their tactics typically focused on exploiting vulnerabilities in perimeter security in order to gain unauthorized access to computer networks. However, the rise of hacktivism, advanced persistent threats (APTs), and organized cybercrime have significantly increased cyber risk. The following list discusses common threat actor types and their motivations:

Advanced Persistent Threats *Advanced persistent threats*, also referred to as *nation-state actors*, are sophisticated threat actors who work on behalf of nation-states and foreign intelligence agencies, typically engaging in social espionage and stealing foreign intellectual property. What truly differentiates APTs from other threat actors is seemingly unlimited resources and substantial funding. APT actors target specific organizations with clear objectives in mind. For example, the Chinese state-sponsored espionage group APT41 has targeted organizations in 14 countries over 7 years, and their operations have been consistent with Chinese national policy priorities.[2] Another key differentiator is that APTs often create custom malware that they tailor for the target. The meaning of APT has blurred in recent years, and it is not uncommon for cybersecurity professionals to use the term to refer to advanced cybercrime adversaries.

Organized Cybercrime   Organized cybercrime has been on a steep rise over the last several years.[3] According the Federal Bureau of Investigation (FBI), its Internet Crime Complaint Center (IC3) received 351,937 complaints in 2018, as compared to 288,012 complaints in 2015.[4] With no geographic boundaries and the ability to stay anonymous, the Internet is a very attractive place for cybercriminals. The Internet made it possible for traditional crimes, such as theft or fraud, to evolve into cybercrime and maximize profits in the shortest time possible.[5] Organized cybercriminals have become increasingly sophisticated and often specialize in certain aspects of cybercrime. It is also not uncommon for cybercriminals to leverage models such as malware-as-a-service or pay-per-infection. Cybercriminals exploit organizations for financial gain in numerous ways. Examples include stealing intellectual property and other highly confidential information, stealing financial information and payment card data, planting ransomware, and cyber extortion through distributed denial-of-service (DDoS) attacks.

Insider Threats   *Insider threats* come from within an organization and are particularly dangerous to enterprises due to the amount of trust their employers give them. Another concern is the level of access insider threats have to valuable digital assets. Examples of insider threats include current and former employees, contractors, and even business partners who have inside information or access to digital assets. The industry also coined the term *unintentional insider threat* to describe individuals who unintentionally cause damage—for example, by sharing passwords or leaving sensitive documents in plain view.[6]

Hacktivists   *Hacktivism* is a blend of computer hacking and activism. Hacktivists use technology and cyberattacks to draw attention to their ideology and political, social, or religious views. Common targets of cyber hacktivists may include corporations, government agencies, or any other entities that hacktivists consider or perceive as corrupt or not aligned with their ideology. Hacktivist attacks can cause severe disruption to enterprises. For example, a cyber hacktivist group may launch a DDoS attack against the victim or deface their website and leave a visible message to draw attention to the hacktivist's ideology. An example of a notable hacktivist attack is "Operation Tunisia," where the Anonymous group with the help of Tunisian hackers took down eight government websites using DDoS attacks in support of the Arab Spring movement in 2010.[7] It is also worth mentioning that hacktivist attacks have dropped nearly 95 percent since 2015.[8]

Script Kiddies   *Script kiddies* are the least sophisticated threat actor discussed thus far. They lack programming knowledge and computer expertise of their own. Instead, they use scripts, open source software tools, and other freely available hacking tools to launch cyberattacks. In some cases, script kiddies may be experimenting with a tool that they downloaded from the Internet without being aware that they are launching a cyberattack. There are plenty of freely available tools and tutorials on the Internet that script kiddies can leverage.

In many cases, script kiddies are just a nuisance to organizations. However, their actions can also negatively impact enterprises. For example, a script kiddie may unleash a DDoS attack that could cause interruption of applications or use social engineering toolkits to steal sensitive data from employees, even if the attack is relatively unsophisticated. Also, script kiddies commonly engage in cyberstalking and cyberbullying. Cyberstalking and cyberbullying refer to the stalking and bullying that occurs by means of electronic communications technologies, often over the Internet.

Cyberattack Lifecycle

Some threat actors operate predictably, and the threat intelligence community created models to describe their operations. A *cyberattack lifecycle* is a sequence of steps that typically more sophisticated attackers move through to attain their goals. The threat intelligence community sometimes classifies those steps into two categories: preparation and execution. Understanding a cyberattack lifecycle is essential because breaking one of the stages can prevent a threat actor from attaining their goals. Cyber breach response plays a vital role in this process.

Various organizations have created their own models of the cyberattack lifecycle, such as the Lockheed Martin Cyber Kill Chain[9] or the MITRE ATT&CK framework.[10] This book discusses the *cyberattack preparation and execution frameworks* that IBM X-Force Incident Response and Intelligence Services (X-Force IRIS) created to provide a conceptual representation of how sophisticated threat actors prepare and execute their attacks against a target. I chose this model because it clearly distinguishes between the preparation and execution phases of a cyberattack. It also incorporates additional steps, such as building an infrastructure for an attack that other approaches lack. Another crucial differentiator of the model is that it incorporates the idea of an attack "feedback loop." The attacker feedback loop allows for continuous engagement and refinement by the attacker to reach their objectives. This approach is more consistent with real-life incidents where threat actors adjust their operations in response to detection in order to remain in a compromised environment.

The threat intelligence community uses the concept of *tools, tactics, and procedures (TTPs)* to define behavioral characteristics that describe how threat actors operate. The term *TTPs* also refers to tactics, techniques, and procedures. However, in the context of cyber breach response, the terms are interchangeable. I discuss this concept in-depth in Chapter 5.

The X-Force IRIS cyberattack preparation and execution frameworks characterize threat data and communicate threat intelligence. These frameworks explain the full range of activities that occur before and during an actual compromise. This process provides incident responders and threat intelligence analysts with a model they can use to track data, conduct peer review research, and communicate analysis with greater clarity and consistency.

IBM X-Force IRIS Cyberattack Preparation and Execution Frameworks

---

Cyberattack Preparation Framework

The cyberattack preparation framework addresses activities that threat actors execute before the initial comprise.

The X-Force IRIS cyberattack preparation framework consists of eight phases, beginning with the determine objective phase and ending with the launch attack phase, where the attacker determines whether the attack resulted in a successful compromise or not. Between those initial and final phases, the attacker has several options to design an attack and may use any combination of the prepare attack phases. Upon determining the success or failure of the launch attack phase, the attacker will either move on to the execution framework in the case of success, or revise, change, or cancel the attack plan in the case of a failure.

IBM X-Force IRIS Cyberattack Preparation and Execution Frameworks

---

Each phase within the preparation framework describes unique activities that an attacker can execute to prepare a cyberattack:

- **External reconnaissance:** Determine a target and perform research on the target to identify exploitable access points.

- **Align TTPs to target:** Identify and determine TTPs necessary to conduct a successful attack.

- **Infrastructure:** Build a command and control (C2) infrastructure to access and control malware planted on the victim's network.

- **Malware and software tools:** Prepare an attack toolset necessary to launch and carry out the attack.

When all of the prerequisites are in place, an attacker launches an attack using either direct or indirect methods. A *direct attack* refers to a situation where the attacker directly compromises the target. In contrast, an *indirect attack* involves an intermediary step. For example, an attacker may choose to compromise a third-party website or launch a supply-chain attack.

The operational security component underpins the entire preparation process. It represents the actions that an attacker takes to remain undetected. Examples include using obfuscation techniques, hiding their infrastructure behind different network addresses, or performing a reconnaissance from a different network. Finally, there is a feedback loop from the preparation process that allows attackers to revise and adjust their strategies.

Cyberattack Execution Framework

The cyberattack execution framework addresses activities that attackers execute after a successful compromise and focuses on access to the compromised environment, as well as expanding that access to attain the attacker's objectives, as depicted in Figure 1.1.

The X-Force IRIS cyberattack execution framework includes the phases that occur after the attacker moves through the key phases of the X-Force IRIS cyberattack preparation framework, and successfully gains access to at least one host within a network, or has logged in to one or more user account.

IBM X-Force IRIS Cyberattack Preparation and
Execution Framework

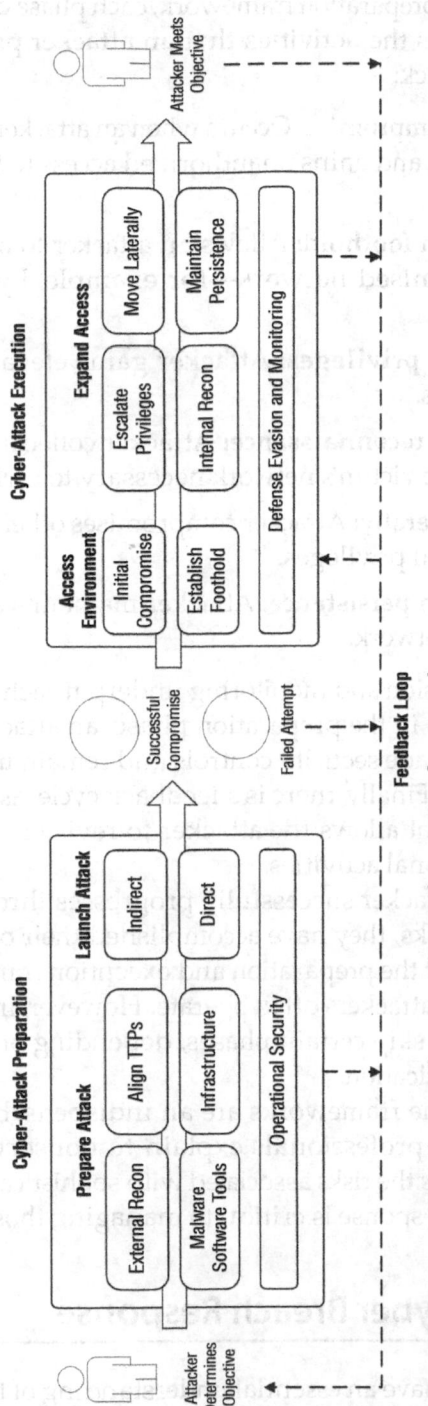

Figure 1.1: X-Force IRIS cyberattack preparation and execution frameworks

As with the preparation framework, each phase of the execution framework describes the activities that an attacker progresses through to execute an attack:

- ▪ **Initial compromise:** Occurs when an attacker successfully executes an attack and gains unauthorized access to the victim's system or network.

- ▪ **Establish foothold:** Allows an attacker to maintain access to the compromised network—for example, by planting backdoor malware.

- ▪ **Escalate privileges:** Attacker gains elevated access to system resources.

- ▪ **Internal reconnaissance:** Attacker collects internal information about the victim's network necessary to carry out the attack.

- ▪ **Move laterally:** Attacker compromises other systems and acquires additional privileges.

- ▪ **Maintain persistence:** Attacker maintains access to the compromised network.

Defense evasion and monitoring underpin each phase of the *execution* framework. As in the preparation phase, an attacker takes operational measures to evade security controls and remain undetected on the victim's network. Finally, there is a feedback cycle, as with the preparation framework, that allows the attacker to revisit some of the stages and execute additional activities.

When an attacker successfully progresses through all the stages of both frameworks, they have accomplished their objectives. It is vital to emphasize that the preparation and execution frameworks model demonstrates how attackers often operate. However, in practice, an attacker may choose to skip certain phases, depending on their objectives and level of sophistication.

That said, the frameworks are an indispensable tool that can help cybersecurity professionals explain to nonsecurity personnel and business leaders the risks associated with sophisticated attackers and why cyber breach response is critical to managing those risks.

Defining Cyber Breach Response

Now that you have an essential understanding of threat actors and how they operate, it is time to explain some crucial cyber breach response terms. There is a great deal of confusion in the cybersecurity community when it comes to terminology. At times, even seasoned professionals incorrectly use basic terms relating to cyber breach response. This section discusses the basic terminology of cyber breach response and articulates important differences between fundamental concepts.

Events, Alerts, Observations, Incidents, and Breaches

It is essential to understand the difference between events, alerts, observations, incidents, and breaches in order to avoid confusion and to ensure an appropriate response. Although these terms may be obvious to cybersecurity professionals, cyber breach response also includes business and technology stakeholders who may not be familiar with essential terms relating to cyber breach response. The following paragraphs explain the difference between these terms.

Events

An *event* is a change in the state of a computer system.[11] Systems and software applications change their state frequently in the course of their operations. For example, a state change occurs when a user authenticates into a system in order to perform some activities and the system captures the state change information in a log. This behavior is normal, and the generated log data provides a chronological record of system activities. For example, in my experience it is not uncommon for a medium-sized domain controller to generate more than 20,000 events a day, or for a demilitarized zone (DMZ) firewall to generate more than 70,000 events a day.

Some events may be indicative of an adverse activity that threatens the confidentiality, integrity, or availability of a computer system, including software applications and digital information that the system handles. For example, an *adverse event* occurs when a system or a software application generates errors in response to an unauthorized activity, such as an attempt to exploit a vulnerability.

Alerts

Organizations often use the terms *event* and *alert* interchangeably. However, there is a significant difference between them. An *alert* is a notification that a particular adverse event has occurred and may be indicative of a cybersecurity incident. Administrators configure systems and tools to trigger alerts when a specific event or a series of events occurs.

For example, an administrator might configure an alert in a security information and event management (SIEM) tool for conditions such as a high number of failed authentication events within a short period associated with a particular user account.

Over the years, cybersecurity vendors and the open source community have developed systems and tools that inspect data in motion and data at rest to alert on adverse events, and in some cases to prevent them. For example, network-based *intrusion detection systems (IDSs)* inspect network traffic and trigger alerts for events that match patterns of known attack vectors.

Observations

Observations is a term that is associated with events. Some organizations collect significant amounts of data, such as security events, social media data, email, data gathered through honeypots, and web crawling data, among others. By processing the data and applying algorithms to it, enterprises can generate observations that they can consume to identify patterns and formulate a threat hypothesis. For example, an organization may create an observation in the form of a graph diagram that shows particular malware connecting to a specific C2 domain that is associated with a phishing email address. Observations augment CTI capabilities, can help make informed decisions regarding defenses, and are invaluable in incident response investigations.[12]

Incidents

An adverse event becomes a *cybersecurity incident* when it either negatively impacts or poses an imminent threat to the confidentiality, integrity, or availability of a digital asset. Organization also often classify explicit or implied security policy violations as cybersecurity incidents. There is no one universal definition of when an event becomes a cybersecurity incident. Enterprises need to establish criteria such as impact and urgency to determine when to declare a cybersecurity incident. Various noncommercial organizations established incident classification taxonomies that enterprises can adopt and customize to their needs. For example, the European Union Agency for Cybersecurity, or ENISA, created a reference incident taxonomy that consists of the following classifications:[13]

- ■ Abusive Content
- ■ Malicious Code

- Information Gathering
- Intrusion Attempts
- Intrusions
- Availability
- Information Content Security
- Fraud
- Vulnerable
- Other

The taxonomy also includes specific examples and a description for each of these incident categories.

Furthermore, depending on the combination of the criteria, organizations typically declare cybersecurity incidents at different levels of severity to ensure that they allocate the necessary resources to response. Chapter 4 discusses incident management in detail, and it explains the criteria that organizations typically use to assign a severity level to a cybersecurity incident.

Breaches

A cybersecurity breach is a type of an incident. A *cybersecurity breach* occurs when an attacker gains unauthorized access to a computer system, software application, or digital data. All cybersecurity breaches are incidents. However, not all incidents are cybersecurity breaches. For example, an attacker might perform a password brute-force attack against a critical server that causes performance issues. If the attacker does not gain unauthorized access to the server as a result of the attack, the incident does not qualify as a breach. Another example is a DDoS attack that leads to an availability incident but not unauthorized access.

It is critical to emphasize that a *cybersecurity breach* is not synonymous with the term *data breach*. A *data breach* is a legal term that refers to unauthorized disclosure of sensitive information. A data breach often occurs when an attacker gains unauthorized access to highly confidential data. In other words, a data breach occurs when an attack impacts data confidentiality but not data integrity or data availability. Data privacy officers and other legal professionals interpret various laws and regulations and closely work with incident responders to determine whether a data breach has occurred as a result of a cyberattack. Consequently, incident responders and other stakeholders with no expertise in data privacy laws and regulations should abstain from using the term during investigations to minimize the risk of legal exposure. I typically advise clients to use the term *significant event* or *incident* instead.

What Is Cyber Breach Response?

Cyber breach response is a set of business, technical, and cybersecurity capabilities that allow organizations to address and manage a cybersecurity breach in an organized and orchestrated manner according to business priorities. The goal of cyber breach response is to reduce the attacker dwell time on the compromised network and prevent further damage to the enterprise. *Dwell time* refers to the time that an attacker remains on the compromised network from the initial compromise to the time when the organization eradicates the attacker from their environment.

An effective cyber breach response program aligns people, processes, and technology in a way that helps organizations achieve this goal. Response to a cybersecurity breach spans multiple organizational functions that provide expertise in their functional areas, including cybersecurity, information technology, legal counsel, senior management, corporate communications, risk management, or human resources (HR), among other functions. As part of building a cyber breach response program, organizations enact appropriate policies and create a response plan to ensure coordination and orchestration of activities at all levels of the organizational hierarchy.

A term similar to cyber breach response is *incident response*. As discussed in the previous section, not all incidents result in cybersecurity breaches. When an enterprise detects an incident, it is not always obvious whether the attacker gained unauthorized access to a digital asset. Incident responders need to perform an investigation to determine the impact associated with the incident, including any evidence of unauthorized access to systems, software applications, or digital data that the enterprise protects. In simple terms, incident response is the de facto industry term[14] and has a wider scope than cyber breach response.

Throughout this book, I use the term *incident response* when talking about incident investigations in a general sense. I use the term *cyber breach response* to refer exclusively to responding to confirmed cybersecurity breaches.

Identifying Drivers for Cyber Breach Response

As part of outlining a strategy, enterprises need to identify internal and external drivers for a cyber breach response program.

Clearly identified drivers provide stakeholders with the information that they need to build a business case and socialize the necessity for cyber breach response with executive leaders and other key stakeholders.

This section discusses common considerations that directly shape the requirement for cyber breach response.

Risk Management

Risk management is a coordinated set of activities designed to direct and control an organization with regard to risk.[15] This approach focuses on the continuous process of identifying, evaluating, and treating cyber risk in order to ensure that it remains at an acceptable level. This process also includes managing residual risk when other controls fail. Cyber breach response is a vital function in addressing that residual risk.

Conducting Risk Management

Not all digital information requires the same level of protection against cyber threats. To determine the right level of protection, organizations must perform a risk assessment and apply risk treatment strategies to ensure that cyber risk remains at an acceptable level.

The objective of *risk management* is to manage the inherent risk associated with information technology and increase cyber resilience. As part of risk management, organizations implement controls to prevent certain types of cyberattacks and adequately respond to cyber events in order to minimize their impact on business operations. Residual risk is the remaining risk once an organization has applied controls to reduce the inherent risk associated with information technology.

Over the years, various risk management methodologies have emerged both in the private and public sectors to help enterprises manage cyber risk, such as the International Organization for Standardization and the International Electrotechnical Commission (ISO/IEC) 27005, National

Institute of Standards and Technology (NIST) Risk Management Framework (RMF), and Control Objectives for Information and Related Technology (COBIT) 5 from the Information Systems Audit and Control Association (ISACA). Organizations need to choose an approach that fits their organizational culture and integrates well with the overall organizational risk management framework.

A multitiered approach[16] takes a holistic view of risk management in order to ensure that organizations conduct risk management across different levels of the organizational hierarchy. This approach also emphasizes downward and upward communication between organizational levels. By establishing two-way communication, organizations ensure that leaders communicate organizationwide risk awareness to lower organizational levels, while there is a feedback loop from lower levels to upper levels in order to facilitate continual improvement. This multilevel approach ensures that stakeholders at various organizational levels do not make decisions concerning cyber risk in isolation. The approach includes the following tiers, as shown in Figure 1.2:

Tier 1—Organization: This tier focuses on the role of governance and risk management strategy at the executive level to support the organizational mission.

Tier 2—Business process: This tier focuses on enterprise architecture and helps ensure that organizations consider cyber risk as part of process and system definitions.

Tier 3—Information systems: This tier is concerned with the selection and management of security controls to manage cyber risk as part of the system development lifecycle.

It is vital that cybersecurity professionals communicate residual risk associated with cyber threats at each of these levels. The level of residual risk directly impacts the resources that an enterprise may dedicate to cyber breach response.

Risk Assessment Process

Whereas risk management focuses on the overall continuous process of identifying, evaluating, and treating cyber risk in order to ensure that it remains at an acceptable level, *risk assessment* primarily focuses on the identification and analysis phases of risk management.

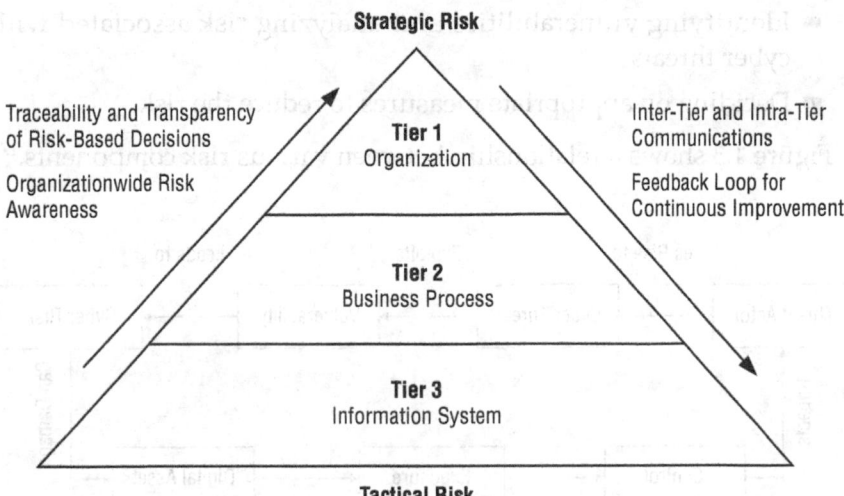

Figure 1.2: NIST multitiered organizationwide risk management

Several industry-accepted frameworks exist for performing a risk assessment, such as ISO 31000:2018 or NIST SP 800-30. Although frameworks have a varying degree of complexity and may focus on different organizational aspects, their overall goal is to help organizations identify key risks. For example, ISO 31000:2018 includes the following steps:

1. Establishment of the context
2. Risk identification
3. Risk analysis
4. Risk evaluation
5. Risk treatment

Furthermore, some approaches use qualitative methods to analyze risk as part of the assessment process, whereas other approaches lean toward quantitative techniques. Qualitative risk analysis focuses on the probability and potential impact. In contrast, quantitative risk analysis numerically evaluates the potential effect of specific risks.

Regardless of the choice, a sound risk assessment methodology typically includes the following activities:

■ Categorizing digital assets in terms of their criticality to the enterprise

- Identifying vulnerabilities and analyzing risk associated with cyber threats

- Deciding on appropriate measures to reduce the risk

Figure 1.3 shows a relationship between various risk components.[17]

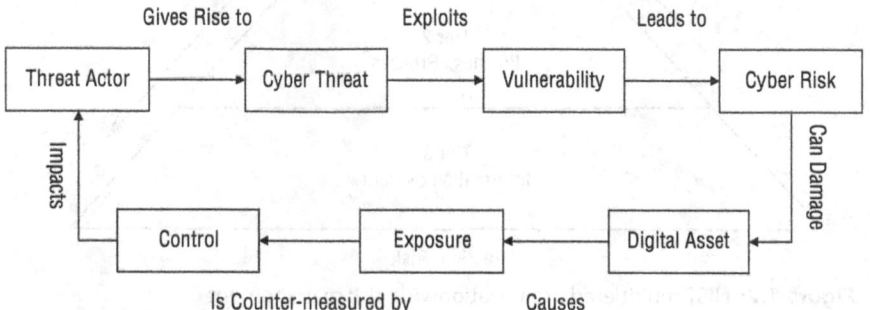

Figure 1.3: Risk components

Threat Actor   A *threat actor*, also referred to as an attack or adversary, is an individual or a group posing a threat to organizations. Threat actors often use computers to conduct malicious activities, but they can also leverage social engineering and other nontechnical means to achieve their objectives.

Cyber Threat   A *cyber threat* is an event or condition that can lead to the exploitation of a vulnerability or weakness in a computer system or software application. From a risk assessment perspective, a cyber threat is something that might occur and has the potential to cause damage to digital assets. An example of a cyber threat is ransomware, which can encrypt business-critical data and other digital information.

Vulnerability   A *vulnerability* is a weakness that a threat actor can exploit. Although cybersecurity professionals typically use this term to refer to weaknesses in computer systems and software applications, a weakness can also occur in a process or an environmental control. A vulnerability is what allows a cyberattack to succeed. For example, a vulnerable web application could allow a threat actor to exploit the vulnerability and remotely execute arbitrary code without the need to authenticate into the target system.

Cyber Risk   *Cyber risk* is an uncertain event that may lead to negative consequences, such as loss of revenue, brand reputation damage, disruption to business operations, or noncompliance with laws and regulations. For example, insufficient hardening of a file share server may lead to the risk of disruption of business operations if ransomware exploits a weakness in the underlying system and encrypts data on that server.

Digital Asset   *Digital assets* are resources that are necessary for business operations and require protection from cyberattacks. Examples of digital assets include systems, software applications, sensitive data, intellectual property, and any other information that organizations store in a digital format.

Exposure   *Exposure* is a quantifiable measure of potential loss resulting from a cyberattack. An exposure occurs when organizations do not adequately protect their digital assets. For example, if a threat actor exploits an insufficiently protected web application that processes payment card data, the exposure could include significant fines imposed by regulators, as well as the cost associated with litigation and lawsuits. A term that is closely related to exposure is impact. *Impact* is the negative outcome that results from exposure.

Control   *Control* is a safeguard or a countermeasure that helps mitigate or reduce risk associated with cyberattacks. Cybersecurity professionals typically group controls into three categories: logical, administrative, and physical. An example of a cybersecurity control is multifactor authentication that mitigates the risk associated with weaknesses in traditional access control mechanisms such as passwords.

Managing Residual Risk

Enterprises implement multiple controls as part of a defense-in-depth strategy to mitigate cyber risk. The idea behind this concept is that an attacker must penetrate multiple layers of protection before attaining their objective. However, residual risk is inevitable, even with state-of-the-art controls. For this reason, enterprises need to build cyber breach response capabilities as part of the overall risk management process and shift their focus toward *cyber resilience*.

Cyber resilience takes a more holistic and integrated approach to risk management to ensure that enterprises can continue to operate during cyber events. This approach integrates more traditional approaches to cybersecurity with business continuity and disaster recovery (BCDR). Cyber breach response is also a critical element of cyber resilience. In simple terms, enterprises can no longer assume that they can adequately protect themselves against cyber threats, so they need to prepare for eventual successful attacks.[18]

A more appropriate approach is to focus on minimizing the impact of cyberattacks and efficiently recovering business operations. This is yet another reason why enterprises should invest in building a cyber breach response program.

Cyber Threat Intelligence

Managing cyber risk without high-quality CTI is a daunting task. CTI informs enterprises about cyber threats and provides context to cyber breach response. Arguably, it is very challenging—if not impossible—for enterprises to protect themselves and effectively respond to cyberattacks without embedding high-quality CTI into the risk management process and various components of their cybersecurity programs. CTI allows organizations to answer vital questions, such as who may be behind a cyberattack, what motivates the attacker, what are their capabilities, and how to identify the attacker activity in the corporate environment.

What Is Cyber Threat Intelligence?

CTI is knowledge that organizations acquire about threat actors and their operations. Examples may include information about capabilities, modus operandi, and objectives. Gartner defines *threat intelligence* as "evidence-based knowledge, including context, mechanisms, indicators, implications, and action-oriented advice about an existing or emerging menace or hazard to assets. This intelligence can be used to inform decisions regarding the subject's response to that menace or hazard."[19] Analysts collect raw data about cyber threats that they analyze, contextualize, and structure in a rigorous way to produce CTI.

There are three primary forms in which enterprises consume CTI:[20]

Strategic Intelligence   *Strategic intelligence* is all about the big picture, and it informs executive-level personnel and boards of directors about cyber threats in support of strategic decision making. Geopolitics tends to be a significant aspect of strategic intelligence. The audience typically consumes strategic threat intelligence in the form of high-level trends, usually tailored to a specific industry or even organization.

Operational Intelligence   *Operational intelligence* focuses on higher-order TTPs and campaigns to help organizations make informed decisions about defenses and preemptively put controls in place to prevent specific types of attacks. The primary audiences for operational intelligence are security managers and technical personnel involved in designing and optimizing controls. Operational intelligence can help attribute an attack to a specific group, determine their intent and modus operandi, and provide an insight into the sophistication level of the group. Organizations can leverage this type of information to prevent specific attacks before they occur.

Tactical Intelligence   *Tactical intelligence* is low-level, granular, and often short-lived information that precisely describes how a specific threat actor deploys their capabilities. CTI analysts produce tactical intelligence nearly exclusively for technical audiences to support incident response and security operations. Examples of tactical intelligence include specific attack vectors, indicators of compromise (IOC), observables, anti-forensic techniques, tools, and other granular information that describes how a threat actor operates.

Importance of Cyber Threat Intelligence

CTI allows organizations to remain informed about cyber threats, and it is a crucial input into the risk management process. It provides enterprises with the cyber threat context that they require to make informed decisions about investments in cybersecurity, including building and expanding a cyber breach response program. For example, CTI can inform an enterprise about how specific threat groups conduct ransomware attacks. In turn, this information can help the enterprise evaluate its security posture and address key weaknesses to reduce the risk of a ransomware outbreak.

In my personal experience, CTI has been invaluable in communicating cyber risk to clients. After explaining how attackers operate and progress through the cyberattack lifecycle, some clients have made changes to their processes and invested in additional capabilities to respond to incidents more effectively.

CTI also helps alleviate challenges associated with increasing volumes of security data. Incident responders often leverage open source and proprietary CTI to contextualize security data and look for specific IOCs and patterns indicative of attacker activity. High-quality CTI is actionable; it informs and augments cyber breach response, and helps leaders make decisions about priorities during cyber breach investigations.

Laws and Regulations

Advances in technology and increasing volumes of personal data that enterprises collect and process have raised data privacy concerns in many countries. Moreover, people are increasingly becoming both aware and concerned with data privacy. In response, many governments enacted data privacy laws and regulations that require organizations to protect personal data and adequately respond to cyber breaches involving the data. Moreover, since computer crimes became prevalent, governments in many jurisdictions have enacted laws that criminalize cyberattacks.

Compliance Considerations

Nongovernmental entities, such as the Payment Card Industry (PCI) Security Standards Council, have enacted compliance standards that require organizations to protect certain types of data. Breaches of that data could lead to significant losses for both consumers and businesses, as well as fines that regulators impose on the breached organizations. In some instances, data breaches could also lead to civil litigation or even class-action lawsuits.

Inappropriate handling of personal and other protected data can result in noncompliance with laws and regulations and legal risk. As enterprises apply controls to protect regulated data, it is essential to emphasize that cyber breach response is also a control that allows organizations to manage residual risk. A cybersecurity breach does not necessarily automatically lead to a data breach and legal exposure. As previously discussed in the "Cyberattack Lifecycle" section, threat actors must often progress through a series of phases to attain their objectives, such as data theft. Breaking the attack lifecycle with cyber breach response in early phases can prevent a data breach and reduce the risk of legal exposure.

The compliance landscape is extremely complex and varies from jurisdiction to jurisdiction. Furthermore, organizations must also comply with laws and regulations specific to their industries. In the United States alone, organizations must comply, often simultaneously, with numerous laws and regulations. Examples include the Health Insurance Portability and Accountability Act (HIPAA), Sarbanes–Oxley Act (SOX), Federal Information Security Management Act of 2002 (FISMA), Gramm–Leach–Bliley Act (GLBA), Payment Card Industry Data Security Standard (PCI DSS), and Family Educational Rights and Privacy Act (FERPA) among other regulations.

Compliance Requirements for Cyber Breach Response

This section briefly discusses the *PCI DSS* and the *General Data Protection Regulation (GDPR)* as examples of standards and regulations that directly drive the need for cyber breach response.

PCI DSS is a security standard that the PCI Data Security Council designed to ensure that organizations that handle payment card data maintain a secure environment. Requirement 12.10 of the now-current version (3.2.1) of the PCI DSS necessitates that organizations implement an incident response plan and are prepared to respond immediately to a system breach. Additionally, the standard provides a list of specific elements that a plan must include to satisfy the requirement. In practical terms, it means that organizations that handle payment card data must build a cyber breach response program and demonstrate preparedness through appropriate documentation.

The GDPR is a European Union (EU) data privacy regulation that came into effect in May 2019, and it is another example of a regulation that necessitates cyber breach response. Article 33 of the GDPR compels "Notification of a personal data breach to the supervisory authority" and requires organizations that experience a data breach to notify supervisory authorities in their respective countries within 72 hours. Meeting this requirement can be challenging without an effective cyber breach response program. Noncompliance can lead to hefty fines up to €20 million ($ 21.75 at the time of writing), or 4 percent of the worldwide annual turnover of the previous financial year, whichever is higher.

To demonstrate this point, British Airways faced a record fine of $230 million for a data breach that the airline suffered in 2018. This figure represents 1.5 percent of the airline's turnover in 2017.[21]

Changing Business Objectives

Organizations continually evolve and respond to changing market conditions and regulations. With that evolution comes increased risk as well as new opportunities. Enterprises that promote a culture of innovation and flow of ideas increasingly move away from a traditional perception of cybersecurity as a cost center and start perceiving it also as a business opportunity, in addition to its function in the risk management process.

Cyberattacks ultimately impact the bottom line regardless of whether they impact business operations or customer confidence in the victim organization, or lead to legal implications. Furthermore, responding to breaches includes many hidden costs, such as loss of productivity, brand reputation damage, and hiring of external consultants and vendors to assist with response activities. Enterprises are increasingly realizing that it is more cost-effective to include cybersecurity as part of the overall system development lifecycle and rigorously test systems for vulnerabilities, as opposed to trying to fix the aftermath of a cybersecurity breach.

In the long run, good cybersecurity hygiene and prevention is more cost-effective in a world where cyberattacks grow in numbers and sophistication with each year. Cyber breach response is part of the strategy. An effective cyber breach response program helps reduce attacker dwell time on the compromised network. The cost of response and remediation is proportional to the amount of dwell time. Thus, cyber breach response also has a positive impact on the bottom line, although this is not always obvious.

Another area where cybersecurity facilitates positive organizational change is the adaptation of new technologies such as cloud computing, bring your own device (BYOD), and teleworking. Security is a crucial requirement and a vital component in implementing new technologies. For example, controls such as encryption or access control allow organizations to leverage technology to facilitate digital business, enable mobile workforces, or deliver products and services in new innovative ways. However, with the introduction of new technologies come inherent cyber threats, which leads to an increased risk of cyber breaches.

Enterprises often perceive laws and regulations as something that hinders business activities and make it more difficult for them to remain competitive in the marketplace. In some instances, new laws and regulations can also simplify business operations and lead to increased business activity. The GDPR, discussed in the previous section, introduced strict privacy requirements. However, the regulation also consolidated data privacy regulations across member states of the EU. In practical terms, this means that organizations now need to comply with a single law rather than 28 separate laws, each for an individual EU member state.

Finally, cybersecurity can lead to a competitive advantage when competing for new business in the marketplace, especially in business-to-business (B2B) settings. Organizations increasingly consider and manage third-party risk and require the enforcement of specific controls as part of contractual obligations, including industry-recognized certifications such as ISO/IEC 27001. It is also not uncommon to incorporate information about security in marketing materials, including information concerning cyber breach response. Business partners often strive to minimize the risk of a cybersecurity breach in a partner's network spreading to their network and impacting their business. Consequently, not only can a sound cyber breach response program help win additional business, but it is often a requirement when competing for new business.

Incorporating Cyber Breach Response into a Cybersecurity Program

Cyber breach response is not an isolated discipline. Enterprises need to include cyber breach response capabilities as part of a more extensive cybersecurity program.

This section briefly discusses what steps enterprises can take to create a cybersecurity program and where cyber breach response comes into play. It is important to emphasize that drivers for cybersecurity regularly change and evolve. To accommodate changing requirements, enterprises often build cybersecurity capabilities using iterative and incremental models. Figure 1.4 depicts this approach.

Strategic Planning

Strategic planning consists of two steps: assessment and strategy definition. As part of the assessment step, organizations need to identify and prioritize drivers for cyber breach response. Typical drivers include business strategy, risk appetite, legal and regulatory requirements, security culture, or contractual obligations. Another crucial element of the assessment step is a gap analysis. One way to achieve this is by mapping their current capabilities against an industry framework, such as ISO/IEC 27001, and documenting gaps.

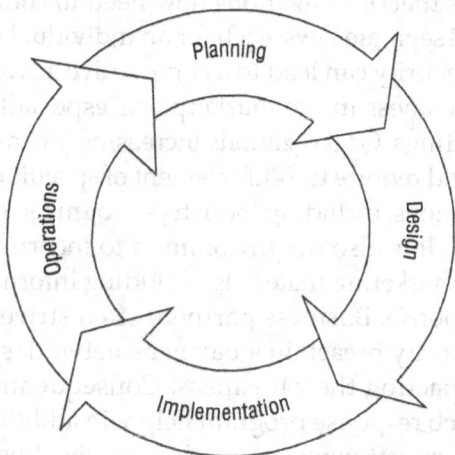

Figure 1.4: Cybersecurity program lifecycle

In contrast, during the strategy definition step, enterprises elicit requirements based on the outcome of the previous step and create a vision and mission statement, as well as define goals and objectives for future capabilities. A crucial part of strategy definition is developing a business case to obtain executive-level sponsorship and secure the necessary funding and other resources. Risk appetite is crucial in this process. For example, financial services organizations handle highly sensitive data and operate in a heavily regulated environment. Consequently, their cybersecurity strategy definition may be very different from that of a medium-sized retail organization whose risk tolerance might be significantly higher.

Designing a Program

Cybersecurity professionals and business stakeholders have different perspectives on cybersecurity and often use completely different terminology to communicate with one another. For this reason, organizations need to establish a common language between cybersecurity, technology, and busines stakeholders, and ensure that cybersecurity capabilities align with business objectives. This is where a *target operating model (TOM)* comes into play.

A sound TOM helps organizations determine an adequate design and deployment of resources to focus on risk. It enables this task by translating a strategy definition into a model that describes the structure and behavior of all the components that make up a cybersecurity program. It also helps ensure that the program's components align with risk management and the overall strategic goals of the enterprise. Furthermore, a TOM typically describes the organizational structure of each competency, the desired capabilities, sourcing of the necessary skills, continual improvement, as well as overall governance and management of the program.[22]

To enable strategy, organizations usually select a framework for implementation of outlined controls and alignment of those controls with business objectives. The choice of a control framework and organizational drivers for cybersecurity directly impacts decisions regarding where enterprises place cyber breach response within the overall cybersecurity program, its structure and level of autonomy, as well as how it integrates with other components of the program.

During the design phase, organizations also need to determine what capabilities they should retain in-house versus what parts of their program to outsource to an external vendor.

Implementing Program Components

The next natural step in building a cybersecurity program is implementation. Once an enterprise has developed a TOM and created a roadmap, it is time to transition the concepts into reality.

Implementation typically starts with planning and developing both long-term and short-term plans to transition planned cybersecurity capabilities into an operational state, including cyber breach response. Project management is vital during this step. The first project that typically takes place is to implement governance and management frameworks.

The next step is to focus on implementing and operationalizing cybersecurity capabilities. At this point, the concept of cyber breach response takes on shape and form, and enterprises implement operational capabilities defined during the strategy and design phases.

Implementation is often the biggest hurdle to tackle when operationalizing a cyber breach response program. Enterprises need to progress several activities as part of this phase. Examples include the following:

- Hiring incident response personnel and building an incident response team
- Creating an incident response plan, including an incident management process and the necessary supporting procedures
- Acquiring missing incident response technology
- Building relationships and socializing the program with crucial stakeholders

Implementation also includes integrating various program components with other organizational processes, such as IT or data privacy incident management.

Program Operations

Operations is where the "rubber meets the road." It refers to the execution of processes and activities to achieve the objectives that the previous phases defined. Cyber breach response operations consist of many components, including personnel, policies, standards, procedures, technology, and other resources necessary to respond to cyber breaches as per the objectives established in the previous phases. For example, typical cyber breach response operational activities include data acquisition and preservation, forensic examination of compromised systems, CTI enrichment, and reporting. Also, a crucial component of operations is to monitor and continuously improve the performance of cyber breach response capabilities.

ISO/IEC 27001[23] Annex 16.1 outlines essential incident management controls that organizations need to consider as part of building and operating a cyber breach response program. The Annex includes the following controls:

- A16.1.1: Responsibilities and procedures
- A16.1.2: Reporting information security events
- A16.1.3: Reporting information security weaknesses
- A16.1.4: Assessment of and decision on information security events
- A16.1.5: Response to information security incidents

- A16.1.6: Learning from information security incidents
- A16.1.7: Collection of evidence

Continual Improvement

The purpose of *continual improvement* is to monitor and evaluate the performance of a cybersecurity program, identify underperforming areas, and implement appropriate improvement initiatives in order to ensure that the program meets its objectives. Performance metrics are vital to this step. Enterprises typically define the requirement for metrics as part of creating a governance framework. The logic is quite simple: the leadership must be able to measure the performance of a cybersecurity program in order to govern it successfully.

Generally speaking, there are two categories of metrics: operational and executive-level metrics. *Operational metrics* are more technical and provide a tactical view of the program's components. Mid-level management translates operational metrics into *executive-level metrics* in order to present them at steering committee meetings or other bodies responsible for the governance of a cybersecurity program.

It is important to emphasize that organizations must achieve high process maturity to manage their cybersecurity program quantitatively. For organizations that have high-risk tolerance, this may not be a requirement. Instead, some organizations may opt for qualitative methods such as conducting regular lessons-learned sessions in order to identify underperforming areas. Chapter 4 discusses continual improvement in-depth, including metric considerations.

Strategy Development

The goal of *cybersecurity strategy* is to identify a technology, people, and process approach to allow enterprises to manage cyber risk to an acceptable level. It is a high-level, top-down approach that includes a range of objectives and priorities that an organization must achieve within a specific time frame.[24] The ITIL Strategy Management process defines three key components to developing an effective strategy:

- Strategic assessment
- Strategy definition
- Strategy execution

Strategic planning is crucial to set overall goals for a cyber breach response program, develop a high-level plan of how to achieve those goals, and ensure that the organization aligns the program with risk management objectives. Strategic planning also provides focus and direction for the program. Figure 1.5 depicts this process.

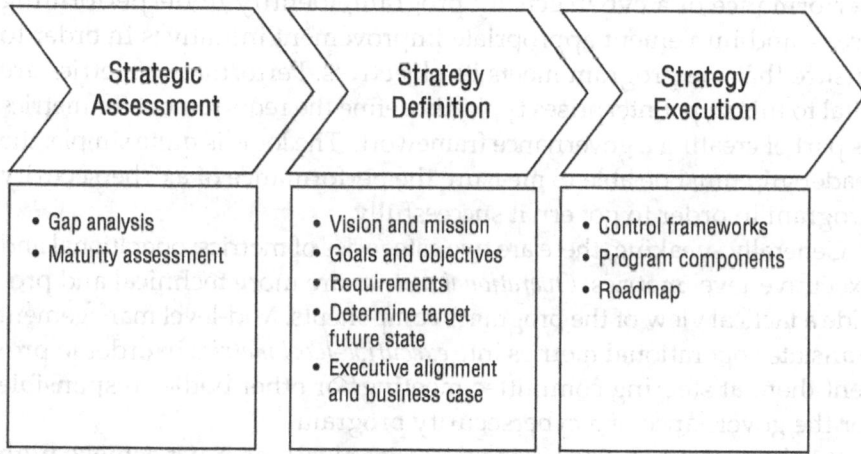

Figure 1.5: Strategy development process

Strategic Assessment

The previous section discussed vital drivers for cyber breach response. Understanding the current state is equally important for organizations that already have a cyber breach response program in place, as well as those that plan to build a program from scratch. Enterprises need to identify gaps and deficiencies in their programs clearly before formulating a vision for the desired capabilities. This section describes two common techniques that strategic analysts leverage in order to determine the current state of a cyber breach response program: gap analysis and maturity assessment.

Gap Analysis

A *gap analysis* is a method that allows organizations to examine the current cyber breach response program and identify missing components necessary to achieve the desired state. A good starting point for a gap analysis is the five-step process that follows:

- Determine the problem area
- Set realistic goals

- Determine the current state
- Determine the desired state
- Identify gaps and determine how to address them

A problem area can be an entire cyber breach response program or specific elements of the program.

In addition to helping identify gaps, a gap analysis often allows organizations to identify components of their programs that are no longer needed. For the process to be effective, organizations should consider performing a gap analysis at both operational and strategic levels.

Several tools and methods are available to strategy analysts to determine the current state of a cyber breach response program and define a desired future state. This section discusses two approaches as examples of how organizations can conduct a gap analysis:

- An assessment against an industry standard
- Strengths, weaknesses, opportunities, and threats (SWOT)

By leveraging an existing industry standard, such as ISO/IEC 27002:2013 or NIST SP 800-53, organizations can map existing capabilities against the controls that an industry standard prescribes and determine gaps. For example, ISO 27002:2013, section 16 outlines specific guidelines for managing cybersecurity incidents. Organizations can use those guidelines as a benchmark to identify gaps in their program.

SWOT is typically complementary to using an industry framework and consists of a matrix with four quadrants, each corresponding to exactly one element of the tool:

Strengths: Describes the elements of a cyber breach response program at which an organization excels

Weaknesses: Elements and inefficiencies that prevent organizations from addressing incidents optimally

Opportunities: Key improvements in the areas of people, process, and technology that allow organizations to enhance their current response capabilities

Threats: Internal and external factors that have the potential to impact the cyber breach response program negatively, such as budget constraints, staff retention, or outdated technology

After identifying crucial strengths, weaknesses, opportunities, and threats in their respective quadrants, the strategic analyst can use that information as a starting point for developing a cyber breach response strategy. Figure 1.6 shows an example of a SWOT quadrant.

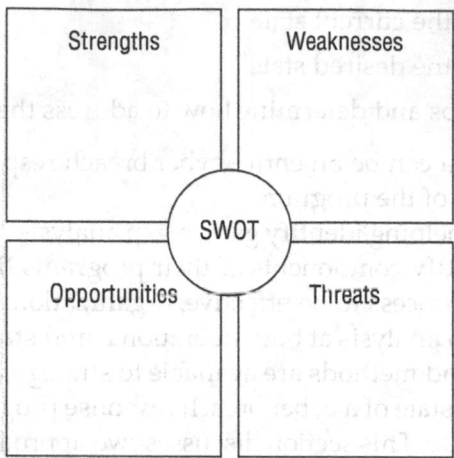

Figure 1.6: SWOT quadrant

Maturity Assessment

As part of strategy development, organizations need to understand the desired maturity level for a cyber breach response program. Ultimately, risk appetite defines the maturity target. Achieving the desired maturity level during the implementation phase is rare. Organizations usually continuously improve their process maturity by performing periodic assessments and implementing specific measures to drive maturity to the desired level. Several models are available to enterprises to facilitate process improvement. This section briefly discusses the *Capability Maturity Model Integration (CMMI®)* by the Software Engineering Institute (SEI) at the Carnegie Mellon University, which is a popular model that enterprises leverage to measure the maturity of specific capabilities. However, it is worth noting that other *maturity assessment* frameworks are available that specifically target cyber breach response assessments. The Center For Research and Evidence on Security Threats' (CREST) Cyber Security Incident Response Maturity Assessment maturity model is one example.

CMMI® is a process model that provides a set of guidelines to increase performance and process improvement of a specific practice area or capability. The model consists of process areas that include a set of related practices, such as Process and Product Quality Assurance (PPQA). It is important to emphasize that not all process areas directly apply to cyber breach response. CMMI® uses the following maturity ratings based on formal assessment methods:

Level 1: Initial—Represents a process that is reactive, ad hoc, and unpredictable

Level 2: Managed—Represents a process that is reactive and undocumented but that produces relatively consistent outcomes

Level 3: Defined—Represents a process that is proactive, documented, and well organized

Level 4: Quantitatively Managed—Represents a process with defined metrics that organizations measure using quantitative means

Level 5: Optimizing—Represents a quantitatively managed process that is under continuous improvement

Figure 1.7 provides a visual representation of the maturity levels.

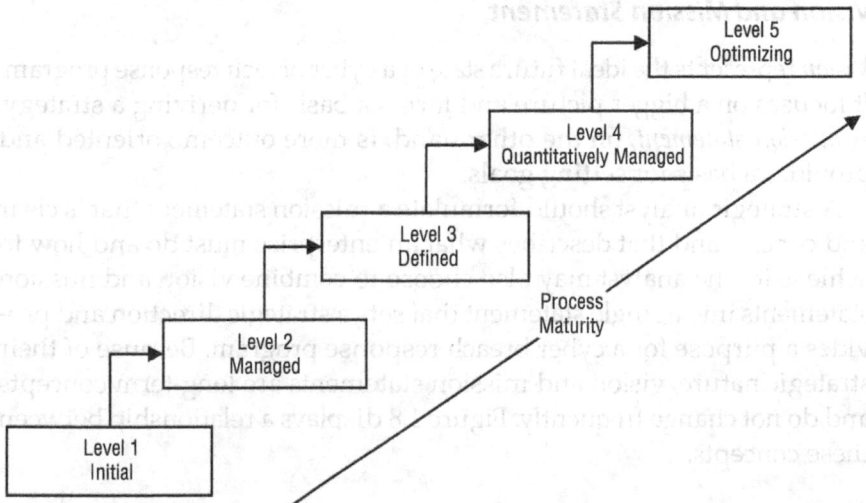

Figure 1.7: CMMI maturity levels

Organizations need to align process maturity with risk appetite and business objectives. Consequently, Level 5 may not be desired or achievable for the majority of organizations. Achieving each of these maturity levels has a cost associated with it, and the most sensible course of action for most enterprises is to achieve their desired maturity level that cost-effectively meets their risk management objectives.

An enterprise may choose to hire external consultants to assist with a maturity assessment. Reputable external firms often collect benchmarking data and may have a perspective on how the enterprise compares to similar organizations within the same industry. Furthermore, in some cases, the leadership may choose to hire external consultants, who may be more objective than internal staff.

Strategy Definition

One of the first steps in strategy definition is to create a vision and mission statement and document goals and objectives.[25] These components provide context and direction for subsequent activities and are critical to developing a sound business case. The consequent steps include establishing business requirements, defining a future target state, and developing a business case.

Vision and Mission Statement

Vision represents the ideal future state of a cyber breach response program. It focuses on a bigger picture and forms a basis for deriving a strategy. A *mission statement*, on the other hand, is more outcome oriented and provides a basis for setting goals.

A strategic analyst should formulate a mission statement that is clear and concise and that describes what an enterprise must do and how to achieve it. The analyst may also choose to combine vision and mission statements into a single statement that sets a strategic direction and provides a purpose for a cyber breach response program. Because of their strategic nature, vision and mission statements are long-term concepts and do not change frequently. Figure 1.8 displays a relationship between these concepts.

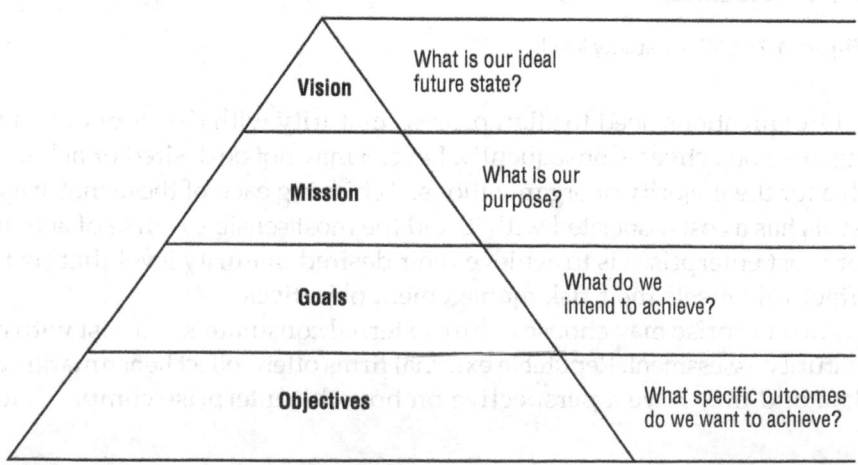

Figure 1.8: Vision, mission, goals, and objectives

Goals and Objectives

Goals align with vision and mission statements and constitute guidelines that describe the desired results. Organizations should establish long-term goals to support their vision and mission, as well as guide decisions and actions concerning cyber breach response.

Objectives, on the other hand, refer to specific and measurable outcomes. One of the more popular tools that strategic analysts leverage to create objectives is the S.M.A.R.T goals:

Specific: Clear and specific goals that allow enterprises to focus their effort on specific outcomes

Measurable: Ability to quantify and track progress against the goals

Attainable: Ensuring that the goals are realistic and achievable

Relevant: Ensuring that the goals are relevant to the cyber breach response program

Time-bound: Setting a precise target date or deadline of the implementation for meeting the goal

As opposed to vision and mission statements, goals and objectives require regular reviews to accommodate changing business requirements and threat landscape changes that necessitate modifications to a cybersecurity program, including cyber breach response. Furthermore, to continually align and support organizational vision and mission, enterprises must define goals and objectives at the operational, tactical, and strategic levels.

Establishing Requirements

Nearly every business project or initiative starts by eliciting requirements from stakeholders. Embarking on a journey without clearly articulated requirements that align with business objectives is a recipe for failure. Strategic analysts need to execute this step to identify the primary organizational drivers that necessitate the implementation of a cyber breach response program. This step also enables enterprises to ensure that their capabilities are cost-effective and align with risk management objectives. Strategic analysts typically need to complete the following activities in order to understand the requirements for a cyber breach response program:

Gathering: Collecting requirements through requirements elicitation techniques.

Documenting: Creating a statement of requirements document that clearly articulates cyber breach response requirements in a language that both technology and business stakeholders can easily understand.

Analyzing: Analyzing requirements to determine specific cyber breach response competencies and related needs.

Validating: Ensuring that the requirements established in the previous steps meet organizational needs to manage residual risk and support business objectives. Examples include checking that the requirements are realistic, complete, consistent, and written clearly and succinctly.

Several tools are available to strategic analysts to facilitate this process. The choice of tool depends on factors such as organizational culture, geographic distribution of stakeholders, availability of documentation, or historical incident information. Some popular methods that strategic analysts leverage during the process include interviewing key stakeholders, analyzing documentation and historical data, using focus groups, and conducting workshops.[26] Risk assessment results are a crucial input into this process, including compliance requirements and other mandatory factors that directly necessitate a cyber breach response program.

Strategic analysts must also identify and include stakeholders in the process who represent various organizational functions that may have a unique perspective on risk and who may help identify requirements that may not be obvious to cybersecurity personnel. For example, corporate legal counsel may bring a valuable perspective on response to breaches involving protected data. The following list presents examples of stakeholders that strategic analysts typically should include in the requirements elicitation process:

- Business unit managers
- Governance, risk, and compliance
- Security operations
- Information technology
- Legal
- Human resources
- Corporate communications
- Finance

The end product of the requirements elicitation process is a statement of requirements document containing all the requirements that leaders need to consider when building a business case.

Defining a Target Operating Model

Organizations use strategic assessment methods to determine the current state of their cybersecurity programs. As part of strategy definition, they also need to determine a TOM to describe the target future state. An TOM provides a high-level representation of a program organization to execute the vision and mission. People, process, and technology are vital components that underly a TOM.[27]

There is no single framework to build a cybersecurity TOM. However, typical components include the following:

- New capabilities and enhancements to the existing capabilities to address the gaps uncovered during the assessment phase
- People and competencies necessary to support the program objectives
- Processes to execute program activities
- Supporting technology to enable the program functions
- Interfaces between the elements mentioned earlier and other organizational processes

At this point, a security strategist may choose to engage executive leadership in order to obtain executive-level support and start formulating a high-level plan to execute the strategy.

Developing a Business Case and Executive Alignment

Obtaining executive-level sponsorship and the necessary funding is critical to building a successful cyber breach response program. The project initiator should develop a comprehensive business case that details and justifies the need for cyber breach response. The initiator must present the case to key decision makers in order to obtain the necessary approvals and secure resources to move the project along.

One way to present a business case is to describe the current state and the target state that the project strives to achieve. Figure 1.9 displays an example of a radar chart based on the NIST Cyber Security Framework (CSF).[28] The chart ranks the current capabilities for each CSF function from 1 to 5; then it uses the same ranking to show the target state after the project. By using a radar chart or another appropriate visual representation, the project initiator can easily describe the program enhancements and benefits resulting from the project.

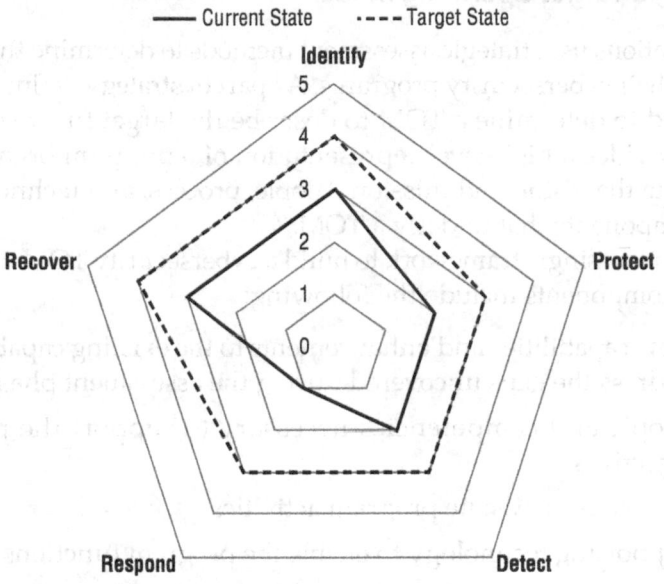

Figure 1.9: CSF radar chart

Requirements discussed in the previous section are critical to building a successful business case in order to solidify the problem and solution statements. A sound business case usually contains the following elements:

Problem description: A brief description of cyber risk and potential consequences. Examples include residual risk and losses that the organization suffers as a result of cyberattacks and how a lack of sufficient cyber breach response capabilities contribute to those costs, as well as any legal exposure that those cyberattacks cause.

Solution and benefits: A description of how an effective cyber breach reponse program can help manage residual risk, reduce legal exposure associated with cyberattacks, and support business objectives.

Cost: The cost associated with designing, implementing, and operating a cyber breach response program.

Timescale: Dates when the project achieves milestones and the expected end delivery date. It is worth mentioning that organizations may choose to build cyber breach response capabilities incrementally. Analysts need to factor this into timescales.

Risks: Any known risks that can lead to failure of the project and measures to address those risks.

Strategy Execution

To enable strategy, an enterprise must select one or more control frameworks to organize its cybersecurity program and align it to business objectives. In some instances, an organization may even choose to create a custom control framework based on unique requirements. A *cybersecurity framework* is a blueprint that allows organizations to develop, organize, and manage cybersecurity program components in a logical manner, as well as describe relationships between those components. Typical components include functions, policies, processes, procedures, and other necessary resources.

Some frameworks are generic, whereas others address the needs of specific industries. Furthermore, certain frameworks might be mandatory to support regulatory compliance. In reality, an overlap exists in terms of general concepts that those frameworks describe. Frameworks also come in varying degrees of complexity and scale. Examples of frameworks that enterprises commonly leverage include the following:

- NIST Cyber Security Framework (CSF)
- NIST 800-53 Revision 4
- ISO/IEC 27001 and 27002
- PCI DSS
- CIS Critical Security Controls

This section describes a generic set of cyber breach response requirements that I derived and abstracted from various industry frameworks. Subsequent chapters discuss the requirements in-depth.

Enacting an Incident Response Policy

An *incident response policy* governs incident response and is a foundational component of establishing a cyber breach response program within an enterprise. A sound incident response policy aligns with business objectives and includes all the necessary business, technology, and cybersecurity stakeholders who participate in response to cyber breaches. Furthermore, an incident response policy assigns authority and empowers incident response personnel to investigate cybersecurity incidents on behalf of the enterprise.

Assigning an Incident Response Team

A *cyber security incident response team (CSIRT)* is a group of individuals who are collectively responsible for responding to and remediating cybersecurity incidents, including confirmed system breaches. A CSIRT typically consists of two components: a core incident response team consisting of dedicated cybersecurity personnel, and ancillary technology and business functions that the core team calls on to provide expertise in their respective domains. I dedicate Chapter 2 entirely to this topic. Furthermore, Chapter 3 focuses on technology requirements to enable a CSIRT to fulfill its mission, whereas Chapter 5 exclusively discusses topics relating to investigating cybersecurity breaches.

Creating an Incident Response Plan

A *cyber security incident response plan (CSIRP)* is a high-level document that presents a structured methodology to respond to cybersecurity incidents. Organizations create incident response plans to effectively respond to cybersecurity incidents and minimize damage that those incidents inflict on their businesses. Enacting a plan starts with an incident response policy and leadership support for cyber breach response. At the heart of the plan is an incident management process that allows organizations to manage the lifecycle of cybersecurity incidents in an organized manner. Chapter 4 discusses this topic in detail.

Documenting Legal Requirements

Cyber breaches often lead to legal exposure. It is of vital importance that an incident response team works closely with the corporate legal counsel and considers legal and regulatory requirements at each phase of the incident response lifecycle to minimize potential legal exposure.

Documenting legal requirements also helps ensure that organizations fulfill breach notification requirements and comply with laws and regulations in their respective jurisdictions.

Roadmap Development

A *roadmap* represents a long-term and high-level view of how an organization intends to build a cyber breach response program and how it achieves it. A well-constructed roadmap visualizes strategic goals and identifies the tactical projects necessary to achieve those goals. Furthermore, a timeline view of the roadmap provides an overview of milestones and goals that the organization achieves over time. Cybersecurity strategists leverage roadmaps to illustrate the capabilities that organizations intend to build to implement a successful cyber breach response program. Figure 1.10 provides an example of a roadmap.

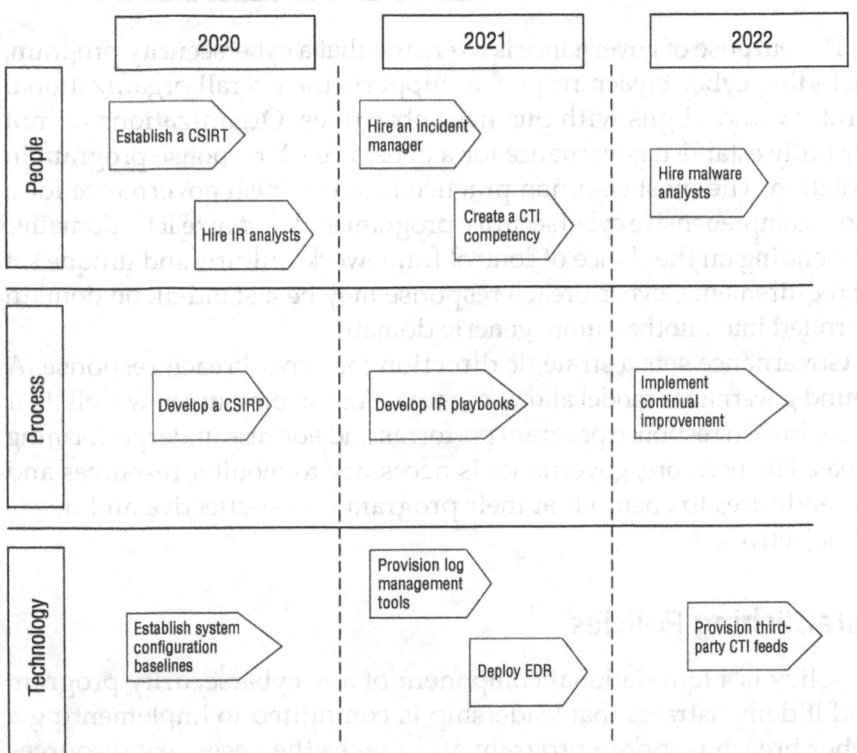

Figure 1.10: Roadmap example

Governance

The goal of cybersecurity is to support business strategy by managing cyber risk and ensuring that it remains at an acceptable level. As a result, organizations must have a means to align controls with business objectives and ensure that their cybersecurity programs are cost-effective. This is where *governance* comes into play. ISACA defines governance as follows:

> The method by which an enterprise ensures that stakeholder needs, conditions and options are evaluated to determine balanced, agreed-on enterprise objectives are achieved. It involves setting direction through prioritization and decision making; and monitoring performance and compliance against agreed-on direction and objectives.
>
> *ISACA, Glossary, Governance*

The purpose of governance is to ensure that a cybersecurity program, including cyber breach response, supports the overall organizational strategy and aligns with business objectives. Organizations do not typically establish governance for a cyber breach response program in isolation. The most common practice is to establish governance for a more comprehensive cybersecurity program and organize it by domains. Depending on the choice of control framework, culture, and unique set of requirements, cyber breach response may be a stand-alone domain or rolled into another, more generic domain.

Governance sets a strategic direction for cyber breach response. A sound governance model allows organizations to measure how well their cyber breach response program performs and address underperforming areas. Furthermore, governance is necessary to monitor resources and expenditures to ensure that their program is cost-effective and meets its objectives.

Establishing Policies

A policy is a foundational component of any cybersecurity program and it demonstrates that leadership is committed to implementing a cyber breach response program and makes the necessary resources available to enable it. More mature organizations typically establish an enterprisewide policy that defines high-level principles and actions that the organization takes to detect and respond to cybersecurity breaches, as well as issue-specific policies related to cyber breach response.

Enterprise Security Policy

An *enterprise security policy* governs cyber breach response. It establishes a CSIRT and empowers the personnel to respond to and investigate cybersecurity incidents and breaches on behalf of the enterprise. The policy also provides a high-level outline of the principles and actions that the enterprise takes throughout the incident lifecycle.

Enterprises need to enact a sound enterprise policy consisting of principles that demonstrate commitment to the cyber breach response program and defining the context in which the program operates within the organization. Organizations define principles to address various aspects of a cyber breach response program, including the following:

- Assigning ownership and overall responsibility for the program
- Establishing the scope of the program
- Applicability of the program to various stakeholders and functions within the organization
- Statement of authority empowering the CSIRT to handle cybersecurity incidents and breaches and engage other organizational functions for assistance and guidance
- Establishing a requirement to review and improve the program regularly

Issue-Specific Policies

Issue-specific policies directly support the principles that the enterprise security policy defines and constitute rules to govern decisions and actions within the program. Organizations can include issue-specific policy statements concerning cyber breach response in the enterprise security policy or create a subset of smaller policies to address specific issues and requirements in support of the overall security policy.

Issue-specific policies drive the implementation of procedures that an incident response team executes as part of the incident response lifecycle. Issue-specific policies can cover a wide range of topics related to cyber breach response. Organizations typically derive the requirements directly from the drivers that require them to implement a cyber breach response program in the first place. For example, the PCI DSS standard includes a precise requirement for data retention that has a direct impact on how long an incident response team retains forensic data. Here are examples of issue-specific policies for cyber breach response:

Confidentiality policy: Relates to communication and documentation of digital evidence throughout the lifecycle of an incident

Data privacy incident policy: Handling of incidents that have data privacy implications and the legal risks associated with them, including the involvement of corporate legal counsel and invoking legal protocols, such as the the attorney-client privilege

Escalation policy: Refers to the escalation and handling of major incidents and crises caused by significant cyber events

Employee investigation policy: Refers to the handling of employee-related incidents such as policy violations and misconduct

Data retention policy: Refers to the retention of log data and digital evidence

Identifying Key Stakeholders

As part of building a cyber breach response program, an organization must identify key stakeholders and define their roles and responsibilities in order to ensure effective governance. This section briefly discusses this topic.

Executive Leadership

In the context of cybersecurity, the executive leadership is responsible for establishing risk appetite, enacting an enterprisewide cybersecurity policy, and ensuring that the necessary resources are available to lower-level organizational functions and stakeholders who are responsible for building and operating a cyber breach response program.[29]

Project Steering Committee

At the onset of a project that seeks to establish a cyber breach response program, enterprises typically establish a steering committee. A steering committee consists of senior managers and other key stakeholders whose ultimate goal is to ensure that the project succeeds. Before commencing project activities, the steering committee often reviews and approves the project proposal to ensure that it is accurate and aligns with the business case for cyber breach response. Once the project takes off, the steering committee meets regularly to check the project status, discuss scope and risk, review expenditures, as well as review proposed changes to the scope and resolve conflicts between stakeholder groups.

Chief Information Security Officer

The *chief information security officer (CISO)* is typically the executive sponsor for a cyber breach response program and ultimately responsible for implementing it. The CISO often defines the strategy for the program and is ultimately responsible for the execution of the strategy, including long-term and short-term projects.

The CISO also sits on the steering committee, establishes a project team, and delegates the responsibility for implementing the program to the project team. Some organizations may have a chief security officer (CSO) or other senior stakeholders who fulfill this role.

Stakeholders with Interest in Cyber Breach Response

Several business and technology stakeholders may have an active interest in cyber breach response. A governance program must consider their needs and requirements. Some of those stakeholders provide expertise in their functional areas. For example, the corporate legal counsel may guide the CSIRT during investigations to minimize legal risk associated with cyber breaches. In contrast, other stakeholders may act as clients of the function. Those are typically business units that call on the CSIRT to provide cyber breach response services during internal investigations.

Organizations may choose to establish a cross-functional steering committee with representatives from various departments to discuss priorities, risks, and any required changes to the cybersecurity program, and generally build consensus on cyber breach response. Another structure available to organizations is a special interest group (SIG) that provides its members with an opportunity to discuss cyber breach response matters regularly, build trust, and socialize the importance of cyber breach response within the organization.

Chapter 2 discusses common stakeholders who have an active interest in cyber breach response.

Business Alignment

Organizations must consider each one of the previously discussed drivers and other internal and external factors to ensure that their cyber breach response program aligns with business objectives and that the program has the necessary resources available to fulfill its mission. Organizational characteristics that have a direct impact on cyber breach response include the following:[30]

Culture: An organizational culture is a combination of personnel attitudes, beliefs, and behaviors. A culture impacts the way enterprises conduct cyber breach response and how stakeholders directly involved in response activities interact with one another.

Risk management: Cyber breach response is a control that addresses residual risk when other controls fail. Some organizations may have relatively high-risk tolerance, whereas others may be more risk-averse. Risk tolerance often affects the resources that organizations dedicate to cyber breach response.

Legal, regulatory, and contractual: Noncompliance can result in significant fines and lead to legal exposure. Organizations that operate in heavily regulated industry sectors may have to establish a dedicated cyber breach response program to reduce legal risk and fulfill contractual agreements with business partners and customers.

Market conditions: Changing market conditions, expansion, mergers and acquisitions, and other market conditions influence cyber breach response. For example, an enterprise might decide to expand into a new market that may require the organization to extend support hours or build a regional incident response team.

Continual Improvement

Another critical component of effective governance that goes hand in hand with maturity assessments is continual improvement. The purpose of continual improvement is to evaluate a cyber breach response program regularly, identify underperforming areas, and implement specific improvement initiatives to provide higher-quality services to the organization. Another reason for continual improvement is to respond to changing business objectives, growing cyber risk, and changing market conditions. The following topics discuss some of the drivers for continual improvement.

Necessity to Determine if the Program Is Effective

As earlier sections articulated, organizations need to align cyber breach response capabilities to risk appetite. Measuring the performance of a cyber breach response program is vital to determining whether it is cost-effective and meets organizational needs. By identifying under-performing areas, organizations can implement specific improvement initiatives to ensure that the program performs as expected.

Changing Threat Landscape

Threat actors continuously evolve and become more sophisticated. Their motivations and intentions can also change depending on political climate and other geopolitical factors. The evolving threat landscape leads to increased risk that organizations need to manage. Continual improvement is critical to ensuring that organizations can stay up to date with the latest developments in the threat landscape and can effectively respond to cyber breaches as part of a strategy to manage residual risk.

Changing Business Objectives

Enterprises continuously evolve and respond to changing market conditions and regulations. Often, there is a risk associated with evolution. For example, an enterprise that operates in the United States might decide to expand its operations to the European market, which is governed by strict data privacy regulations. This desire for expansion would likely require changes to the cyber breach response program to accommodate European breach notification requirements.

In larger organizations, continual improvement usually takes place at three organizational levels:

Strategic   Related to long-term vision and business goals. For example, an organization may decide to implement a 24×7 monitoring model to respond to an increasing level of cyberattacks.

Tactical   Tactical improvement refers to medium-term projects geared toward achieving strategic goals. For example, an organization might decide to deploy an endpoint detect and response (EDR) tool across its enterprise to detect attacks that more traditional antivirus software might not be capable of detecting.

Operational   Operational improvements refer to day-to-day improvements that help achieve tactical goals. Examples include ongoing tuning of security tools, making necessary modifications to standard operating procedures (SOPs), or building simple software tools to automate repeatable tasks.

For continual improvement to be useful, there must be upstream and downstream communication to ensure that leadership communicates business priorities and that there is a feedback loop from the operational level to the higher levels.

One important but often forgotten aspect of continual improvement, and cybersecurity programs in general, is organizational culture. Improvement starts with leadership recognizing that a cyber breach response program is a continuous and incremental process that involves stakeholders at all levels of the organization. A positive culture empowers employees and often makes them feel responsible for the security of their organization.

Measurement is vital to continual improvement. By establishing metrics and key performance indicators (KPIs), organizations can measure how well their cyber breach response program performs, identify underperforming areas, and implement measures to address the underlying issues. I discuss continual improvement in more detail in Chapter 4.

Summary

Enterprises increasingly rely on digital information to conduct business activities. The information is often a valuable and appealing target to threat actors. To respond to cyberattacks and manage the aftermath of a cyber breach, enterprises need to build cyber breach response capabilities and align those capabilities to business objectives.

A cyber breach response program is typically a part of a more comprehensive cybersecurity program. Enterprises often leverage a lifecycle approach to building a cybersecurity program that typically includes the following phases: planning, design, implementation, and operations.

Identifying drivers for a cyber breach response program is a vital first step that allows strategy analysts to create a sound business case and map capabilities to business objectives. Typical drivers for cyber breach response include the outcome of a risk management process, CTI, laws and regulations, as well as changing business objectives.

As part of strategy development, enterprises must determine the current state of their cyber breach response capabilities, develop a business case, and create a roadmap. The final phase is to establish a sound governance framework to ensure that the program meets its objectives.

The next chapter discusses building and implementing a capable cybersecurity incident response team.

Notes

1. The Global Risks Report 2019, 14th Edition, 2019, World Economic Forum, www3.weforum.org/docs/WEF_Global_Risks_Report_2019 .pdf.

2. FireEye, Special Report, "Double Dragon: APT41, A Dual Espionage and Cyber Crime Operation," August 7, 2019, www.fireeye.com/ blog/threat-research/2019/08/apt41-dual-espionage-and- cyber-crime-operation.html.

3. Accenture Security, Ninth Annual Cost of Cybercrime Study, March 6, 2019, www.accenture.com/us-en/insights/security/ cost-cybercrime-study.

4. FBI, IC3 2018 Internet Crime Report, April 22, 2019, www.fbi.gov/ news/pressrel/press-releases/fbi-releases-the-internet- crime-complaint-center-2018-internet-crime-report.

5. Interpol, Cybercrime, "Cyberattacks know no borders and evolve at a fast pace while the Internet also facilitates a range of more traditional crimes." www.interpol.int/en/Crimes/Cybercrime.

6. Julie Mehan, *Insider Threat: A Guide to Understanding, Detecting, and Defending Against the Enemy from Within* (IT Governance Publishing, 2016).

7. TrendMicro, Security News, "Hacktivism 101: A Brief History and Timeline of Notable Incidents," August 17, 2015, www.trendmicro .com/vinfo/us/security/news/cyber-attacks/hacktivism- 101-a-brief-history-of-notable-incidents.

8. Camille Singleton, Security Intelligence, "The Decline of Hacktivism: Attacks Drop 95 Percent Since 2015," May 16, 2019, security- intelligence.com/posts/the-decline-of-hacktivism- attacks-drop-95-percent-since-2015.

9. Lockheed Martin, "Gaining the Advantage: Applying Cyber Kill Chain® Methodology to Network Defense," www.lockheedmartin .com/content/dam/lockheed-martin/rms/documents/cyber/ Gaining_the_Advantage_Cyber_Kill_Chain.pdf.

10. MITRE ATT&CK, 2019, attack.mitre.org.

11. NIST SP 800-61, Computer Security Incident Handling Guide Revision 2, August 2012, nvlpubs.nist.gov/nistpubs/ SpecialPublications/NIST.SP.800-61r2.pdf.

12. J. Michael Butler, "Observation and Response: An Intelligence Approach," SANS Institute Information Security Reading Room, August 2015, www.sans.org/reading-room/whitepapers/analyst/ observation-response-intelligent-approach-36122.

13. ENISA, Reference Incident Classification Taxonomy, January 2018, www.enisa.europa.eu/publications/reference-incident- classification-taxonomy.

14. NIST SP 800-61, Computer Security Incident Handling Guide Revision 2, August 2012, nvlpubs.nist.gov/nistpubs/ SpecialPublications/NIST.SP.800-61r2.pdf.

15. ISO Guide 73:2009, Risk Management—Vocabulary, www.iso.org/ standard/44651.html.

16. NIST SP 800-39: Managing Information Security Risk, March 2011, nvlpubs.nist.gov/nistpubs/Legacy/SP/nistspecialpublica- tion800-39.pdf.

17. Fernande Maymi and Shon Harris, *CISSP All-in-One Exam Guide*, 8th Edition (McGraw-Hill, 2019).

18. IBM A/NZ Blog, "Cyber Resilience: A State of Unreadiness," April 12, 2019, www.ibm.com/blogs/ibm-anz/cyber-resilience.

19. Gartner Research, "Definition: Threat Intelligence," May 16, 2013, www.gartner.com/en/documents/2487216/definition-threat- intelligence.

20. Scott J. Roberts and Rebekah Brown, "Intelligence-Driven Incident Response," (O'Reilly Media, Inc. 2017).

21. "What Is the British Airways Data Breach and How Does It Affect Passengers?" *Independent*, July 8, 2019, www.independent.co.uk/ travel/news-and-advice/british-airways-data-breach-privacy- details-leak-iag-cathay-pacific-information-commissioner- a8993331.html.

22. Scott Madden Management Consultants, "The Security Operating Model: A Strategic Approach for Building a More Secure Organization," www.scottmadden.com/insight/security-operating-model-strategic-approach-building-secure-organization.

23. ISO/IEC 27001-2013 Annex A16: Information Security Incident Management, www.iso.org/standard/54534.html.

24. ENISA, National Cybersecurity Strategies, www.enisa.europa.eu/topics/national-cyber-security-strategies.

25. Iowa State University, "Vision and Mission Statements—A Roadmap of Where You Want to Go and How to Get There," August 2016, www.extension.iastate.edu/agdm/wholefarm/html/c5-09.html.

26. Kupe Kupersmith, Kate McGoey, and Paul Mulvey, *Business Analysis for Dummies*, (For Dummies, 2013).

27. Deloitte Luxembourg, "Target Operating Model (TOM) at a Glance," 2014, www2.deloitte.com/lu/en/pages/strategy/solutions/target-operating-model.html.

28. NIST, Cybersecurity Framework Version 1.1, www.nist.gov/cyberframework.

29. IBM Institute for Business Value, "Securing the C-Suite: Cybersecurity Perspectives from the Boardroom and C-Suite," 2016, www.ibm.com/downloads/cas/M94RB4WR.

30. ISACA®, "Business Model for Information Security," 2009, www.isaca.org/bookstore/it-governance-and-business-management/bmis.

CHAPTER

2

Building a Cybersecurity Incident Response Team

Enterprises build defenses to protect digital assets from cyberattacks and keep cyber risk at an acceptable level. However, even with state-of-the-art controls, cybersecurity incidents are inevitable. For this reason, enterprises need a team with specialized skills to respond to incidents and coordinate activities between all of the parties that participate in the incident management process.

The structure and support model of an incident response function, and the services that it will provide to the organization, are vital considerations. Enterprises also need to decide what capabilities to build in-house versus in what areas they need to partner with outsourcing organizations.

This chapter discusses various topics that organizations need to consider when building a *cybersecurity incident response team (CSIRT)*.

Defining a CSIRT

This section discusses the characteristics of a successful team; clarifies the difference among *Computer Emergency Response Team (CERT)*, *Security Operations Center (SOC)*, and CSIRT; and provides a detailed explanation of what the term *CSIRT* really means.

CSIRT History

The history of *CSIRT* started with the "Morris Worm." On November 2, 1988, Robert Tappan Morris, a student at Cornell University, launched a self-replicating computer worm from an MIT computer via the Internet. Known as the "Morris Worm," the code crippled nearly 6,000 computers, which at that time was roughly 10 percent of all computers connected to the Internet. It took five days and an international collaborative effort to resolve the incident.[1]

In response to the incident, the Defense Advanced Research Projects Agency (DARPA) funded the *CERT* Coordination Center (CERT/CC) research project to coordinate threat intelligence sharing and disseminate information about computer vulnerabilities. DARPA selected the Software Engineering Institute (SEI) of the Carnegie Mellon University to create the center and coordinate CERT efforts. The original purpose of CERT was to disseminate information about vulnerabilities. However, over the years, CERT competencies have been extended to include incident response in addition to the collection and dissemination of cyber threat intelligence (CTI) information at the national and international levels.

The term CERT is a registered trademark owned by Carnegie Mellon University.[2] Organizations that want to use the term CERT must apply for authorization from Carnegie Mellon University. For this reason, the term CSIRT has been more prevalent in the cybersecurity industry.

The Role of a CSIRT in the Enterprise

A *CSIRT* refers to a centralized function within a cybersecurity program that enterprises assign the responsibility to respond to cybersecurity incidents and execute the incident management process. A CSIRT is a cross-functional team that includes cybersecurity, technology, and business stakeholders working together to address the aftermath of a cyberattack and manage the lifecycle of the incident. At the core of a CSIRT is an incident response team that evaluates incidents and activates the necessary technology and business functions to provide expertise in their respective domains. Unless explicitly stated otherwise, this chapter discusses the core incident response team that is at the center of a CSIRT. Figure 2.1 provides a conceptual representation of a typical CSIRT with a dedicated incident response team as the central entity.

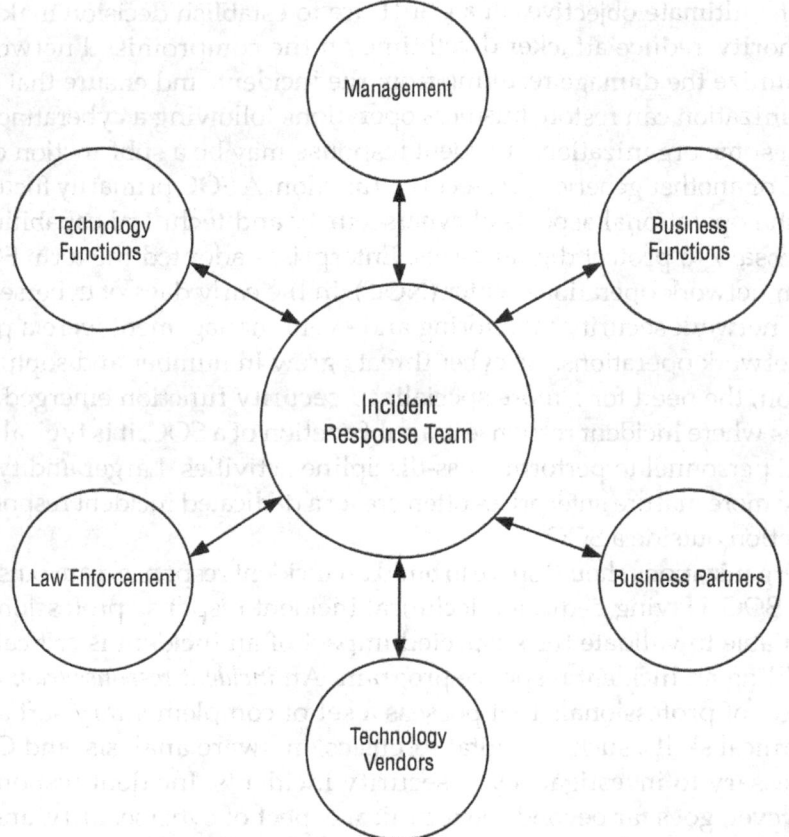

Figure 2.1: CSIRT conceptual model

Depending on the severity and the scope of an incident, an enterprise may decide to convene a CSIRT at one or more of the following organizational levels:

Operational: Handles minor incidents that typically do not result in cyber breaches or have significant impact on the enterprise.

Tactical: Handles incidents and cyber breaches that may negatively impact the enterprise and require the involvement of mid-level management.

Strategic: Requires involvement of executive-level stakeholders that set strategic priorities that drive response activities. In many organizations, convening a CSIRT at the strategic level is synonymous with activating a crisis management committee.

The ultimate objectives of a CSIRT are to establish decision making authority, reduce attacker dwell time on the compromised network, minimize the damage resulting from the incident, and ensure that the organization can restore business operations following a cyberattack.

In some organizations, incident response may be a subfunction of a *SOC* or another generic cybersecurity function. A SOC primarily focuses on the operational aspects of cybersecurity and technical capabilities necessary to protect digital assets. Enterprises adopted the term SOC from network operations center (NOC). In the early days of cybersecurity, network security monitoring and event management were a part of network operations. As cyber threats grew in number and sophistication, the need for a more specialized security function emerged. In cases where incident response is a subfunction of a SOC, it is typical for SOC personnel to perform cross-discipline activities. Larger and typically more mature enterprises often create a dedicated incident response function outside a SOC.

Organizations should strive to build an incident response team outside of a SOC. Having dedicated technical incident response professionals available to validate the suspected impact of an incident is critical to building an incident response program. An *incident response team* is a group of professionals that possess a set of complementary soft and technical skills, such as digital forensics, malware analysis, and CTI, necessary to investigate cybersecurity incidents. Incident response, however, goes far beyond the technical aspect of cybersecurity, and it involves many other parts of the enterprise. For example, when responding to an incident involving unauthorized access to highly sensitive data, an organization may convene a CSIRT that includes stakeholders representing the following functions:

- Infrastructure and application support groups
- Digital forensics and incident response
- Legal and data privacy
- Business unit leaders
- Executive leadership
- Vendors and business partners
- Other stakeholders that have an active interest in the response

Furthermore, an incident response team must operate with a degree of autonomy to be successful and focus on its core capabilities rather than being concerned with the operational aspect of cybersecurity. In my consulting experience, I observed that organizations that have a dedicated incident response team respond to cybersecurity incidents more effectively than those with incident response embedded into a SOC or a similar function concerned with the operational aspect of cybersecurity.

Defining Incident Response Competencies and Functions

According to Carnegie Mellon University, an incident response team performs several functions that enable organizations to manage the lifecycle of a cybersecurity incident.[3] An essential aspect of creating an incident response team is defining core competencies, making decisions regarding the sourcing of those competencies, and establishing what functions the team will deliver to the enterprise. For this reason, enterprises need to define a mission statement that directly drives the necessity for incident response competencies.

A *competency* refers to a combination of skills, knowledge, abilities, and capacity to fulfill specific tasks and responsibilities. Most organizations create competencies through a combination of internal hiring and outsourcing. In contrast, a service constitutes the work that an incident response team delivers to the organization to fulfill its mission and achieve a specific outcome on behalf of internal clients.

This section describes the technical and soft competencies that a core incident response team must possess to respond effectively to cybersecurity incidents and provide high-quality services to internal clients.

An incident response team performs proactive and reactive functions within the enterprise as part of higher-level services that it delivers back to the organization. Each function requires a set of specialized competencies. The topics that follow discuss each of these functions in detail.

Proactive Functions

In the context of incident response, the term *proactive functions* refers to the actions that an incident response team takes to prepare for incident response. The preparation goes beyond building and improving the technical capabilities to respond to incidents and breaches effectively. It also includes educating the enterprise and building relationships with key internal and external stakeholders. Incident response is a cross-functional discipline, and for this reason, it requires an enterprisewide effort to ensure that it will be successful. Preparation is a fundamental component of incident response. The following sections describe some common functions of an incident response team.

Developing and Maintaining Procedures

Procedures outline how to carry out specific activities within an incident management process and are a critical component of incident response. An incident response team should develop appropriate procedures to ensure that responders execute specific tasks consistently and that the process is repeatable. Examples of procedures that a typical incident response team develops include the following:

- Threat-specific response procedures to respond to similar incident types consistently
- Data acquisition and preservation through traditional forensic imaging and live response techniques
- Documenting a chain of custody to ensure that digital evidence is admissible in court if civil litigation, or even a criminal trial, is anticipated
- Communication procedure for data privacy incidents
- Vertical and horizontal escalation procedures
- Engaging external parties, such as an incident response firm, vendors, and law enforcement

Chapter 4 discusses this topic in detail.

Conducting Incident Response Exercises

Incident response exercises are simulations that allow organizations to practice incident response in a safe, controlled, and informal environment. The purpose of an incident response exercise is to evaluate responses to a particular scenario and identify opportunities for improvement.

Incident response exercises also allow an incident response team to build relationships with key business and technology stakeholders, increase collaboration, and socialize incident response within the enterprise.

Many organizations conduct incident response exercises at least once a year to meet regulatory and compliance requirements. More mature enterprises typically conduct two exercises a year or even once a quarter to improve their response capability continuously. Enterprises can conduct incident response exercises at the following levels:

Executive level: Focused on managing a crisis caused by a significant cyber event

Operational: Focused on the overall communication, coordination, and incident management process

Technical: Tests technical capabilities and competencies of the incident response personnel

Historically, enterprises conducted "tabletop" exercises that consisted of discussion-based sessions where stakeholders discussed how they would respond during a particular event in their functional areas. These tabletop exercises are still a popular and cost-effective choice, especially within organizations that have budgetary constraints. However, immersive exercises that involve audiovisual components, which more realistically simulate cyber events, are becoming popular. Furthermore, enterprises increasingly conduct *red team-blue team exercises*, also referred to as *purple team exercises*. In these exercises, a red team performs a controlled cyberattack on a corporate network and a blue team attempts to detect and mitigate the attack.

Assisting with Vulnerability Identification

Assisting with vulnerability identification is a secondary function of an incident response team. A formal risk assessment process may not always identify every possible vulnerability, especially in large, heterogeneous corporate environments. Although vulnerability identification is not the primary function of an incident response function, incident response personnel often uncover vulnerabilities during incident investigations. For this reason, the manager of an incident response team should establish a good working relationship with the vulnerability management function in order to communicate vulnerabilities effectively. For example, during a breach investigation, an analyst might determine that personnel with administrative privileges do not use *multifactor authentication (MFA)* to access high-risk environments. This vulnerability can allow an attacker to move laterally to those environments and cause severe damage to the organization. By identifying and communicating vulnerabilities to a vulnerability management function, an incident response manager can help the organization recognize and proactively address vulnerabilities before an attacker exploits them.

Deploying, Developing, and Tuning Tools

An incident response team is only as good as the data that the team is able to collect and analyze during an investigation. One of the foundational steps in building an incident response program is to ensure that the incident response team has the necessary tooling to perform its function. Each team has slightly different requirements for tooling. The following list provides a few of the most common tooling requirements for incident response teams:

- Remote collection of computer system artifacts
- Software to parse and process forensic data
- Tools to acquire and parse network telemetry and event log data
- "Go bags," or equipment that is readily shippable to remote locations
- Centralized storage for the collected evidence

An essential competency of an incident response team is to build simple software tools to automate repeatable tasks and aid data analysis. The incident response domain is continually evolving, and incident response professionals frequently come across problems during investigations for which there is no standard solution. Familiarity with modern software development and scripting languages can help incident response analysts solve problems creatively and automate certain aspects of their work.

Some scripting languages come with operating systems, such as Bash with Unix-like systems or PowerShell with Windows. Other languages, such as Python, may require installation on an operating system of choice. There is no single language that is appropriate for every task. For this reason, an incident response team should have competencies to develop simple software tools in a few modern programming languages to address a variety of issues. Examples of domains where the ability to write simple software tools comes in handy include the following:

- Automating repeatable tasks
- Incorporating sequences of commands into a single program

- Automating administrative tasks such as mounting of digital evidence
- Automating data collection and specific aspects of analysis
- Parsing new artifacts and nonstandard event logs
- Organizing unstructured data sets and event logs

Implementing Lessons Learned

An essential aspect of a successful incident response team is to capture lessons learned after cyber incidents and implement specific improvement initiatives to prevent similar incidents from reoccurring, as well as continually improving the response capability. Lessons learned can apply to one or more of the dimensions of people, process, and technology. For example, during a lessons-learned meeting, an incident response manager might identify insufficient skills in a specific technology domain, such as cloud computing. A measure to address this gap would be to provide training to employees to ensure that they can effectively respond to incidents in cloud computing environments. Capturing and implementing lessons learned is a part of continual improvement.

Reactive Functions

Reactive functions constitute a set of core competencies that an incident response function provides to the enterprise to address the aftermath of a cyberattack. Ultimately, enterprises build incident response capabilities to respond to cyber incidents and minimize their impact on their organizations. In other words, reactive services allow organizations to manage residual risk when other security controls fail.

This section focuses on core technical competencies relating to incident response. Another section in this chapter discusses business and technology competencies that augment the core incident response team as part of an enterprise CSIRT. The following topics describe some common reactive services that a typical incident response team delivers to the enterprise.

Digital Forensics and Incident Response

Digital forensics and incident response (DFIR) are two complementary disciplines that are the crux of incident response. From a technical perspective, incident response is a set of technical capabilities that allow organizations to manage the lifecycle of an incident. For example, incident response may include several complementary technical disciplines, including the following:

- Data acquisition and preservation
- Traditional forensics and live response analysis
- CTI research and enrichment
- Malware analysis

Digital forensics is a subset of incident response. It focuses on an in-depth examination of computer systems, network data, and mobile devices to gain a full understanding of how a threat actor compromised and interacted with those systems. Incident responders acquire forensic images of disk volumes and the contents of physical memory, and long-lived, historical data, such as event logs, to perform digital forensics.

In enterprise environments, incident responders typically perform a rapid triage first before targeting specific systems for more in-depth analysis to facilitate adequate and cost-effective investigations.

Cyber Threat Intelligence

Incident responders heavily rely on *CTI* during investigations. High-quality CTI enriches the data that incident responders collect during investigations and allows them to scope incidents efficiently and generally accelerate response activities.

Gathering actionable CTI allows responders to identify attacker activity in the compromised environment and provides a basis for implementing containment and eradication measures. Incident responders typically focus on gathering and analyzing tactical CTI that applies to an investigated incident. The personnel usually disseminate the intelligence to other internal and external stakeholders as required.

It is important to emphasize that incident responders typically generate and consume tactical intelligence specific to an investigated case. A SOC or other similar security operations function acquires and consumes broader intelligence information for monitoring and detection purposes.

Malware Analysis

Threat actors often leverage malware and other software utilities to progress through the cyberattack lifecycle. As part of an investigation, incident responders typically examine compromised systems for evidence of program execution to identify software programs that may be associated with attacker activity. If malware is still present on the compromised system, analysts recover and analyze the malware to determine its functionality and generate actionable CTI. This analysis may include the following:

- Examining static properties of the malware
- Performing behavioral analysis of executable files
- Interacting with the malware in a controlled environment
- Disassembling and code analysis

Incident responders often leverage static and dynamic analysis techniques to determine the functionality of the recovered binaries. Malware reverse-engineering and analysis are very specialized disciplines, and many organizations partner with external firms for this service.

Incident Management

Incident management is a structured and coordinated set of activities that an incident response team executes in response to a cybersecurity incident. The purpose of an incident management process is to manage the entire lifecycle of an incident.

Effective incident management ensures that organizations coordinate response activities across various organizational functions and that all of the involved stakeholders communicate effectively. Incident management also increases visibility across key stakeholders and leadership and helps ensure that organizations dedicate the necessary resources to address the aftermath of a cyberattack. An incident response team usually includes an incident manager, or "handler," role that is responsible for the execution of the process.

Creating an Incident Response Team

As cyber threats grow in number and sophistication, many enterprises recognize the need for a dedicated capability responsible for responding to cybersecurity incidents and coordinating the incident management process. In larger organizations, an incident response function fulfills this role. In smaller enterprises, this capability is typically incorporated into a function with broader cybersecurity capabilities, such as a SOC.

Building an incident response function starts with a mission statement that drives the competencies and services that the team will provide to the enterprise. This section discusses team models, support structures, and topics relating to hiring and training personnel.

Creating an Incident Response Mission Statement

As part of developing an incident response program, organizations create vision and mission statements, as well as define goals and objectives to provide a strategic direction of the incident response program. Creating a mission statement is also the first critical step in establishing an incident response team.

A good mission statement is clear and concise and is written in actionable language. It also aligns with the vision and mission statements that the enterprise sets for the overall incident response program. A good practice is to contain it in one, but no more than two, sentences. A mission statement, combined with competencies, ultimately determines what type of services an incident response team provides to the organization. The following is an example of a mission statement for an incident response team:

The mission of the incident response team is to respond appropriately to cybersecurity incidents, reduce attacker dwell time on the corporate network, and minimize the impact of cyberattacks on the enterprise.

Choosing a Team Model

There is no one-size-fits-all model for building an incident response team. Several internal and external factors influence what team model and support structure an enterprise may decide to implement. Examples include the following:

- Organization size and geographic distribution
- Available funding
- Culture and risk appetite
- Contractual and regulatory obligations
- The overall structure and implementation of a cybersecurity program
- Ability to source skills

Two primary models exist for organizing an incident response team in terms of geographic location: centralized and distributed. Some organizations also leverage a hybrid model with a core team residing in a central location and additional resources in remote locations.

This section discusses the different models available to enterprises and the characteristics that leaders need to consider before choosing a model that is the right fit for their organizations.

Centralized Team Model

In a *centralized team model*, an incident response team operates from a single location and employees report events and potential incidents through an established channel to a single team. This model has several advantages that make it an excellent choice for small to medium-sized organizations.

Having an incident response team in a single location with personnel located close to one another encourages horizontal and vertical communication. *Horizontal communication* occurs when peers collaborate, exchange ideas, and coordinate activities. In contrast, *vertical communication* occurs between various levels of the command chain. For example, a forensic analyst may escalate to the management investigative findings that require management-level attention.

Organizations with a centralized incident response team typically have a clear chain of command concentrated around a single leader, and personnel know who to seek out for a decision. Furthermore, a centralized team model encourages verbal communication, collaboration, and the flow of ideas.

A centralized team often requires less management overhead, which leads to an efficient implementation of decisions. Centralized teams typically communicate more effectively than distributed teams, which improves productivity and allows organizations to achieve economies-of-scale through knowledge sharing, cross-skilling, and closer collaboration. It is also easier to standardize and enforce policies, processes, and procedures within a centralized team.

A centralized team has several drawbacks as well that organizations need to consider when building an incident response capability. As an enterprise grows and expands into new markets, a centralized model may no longer be a viable option.

Organizations that need a 24x7x365 support model have to implement shift work or at least on-call support. With this necessity comes a requirement for additional resources and funding. Shift work might also lead to higher employee turnover.

There is a global shortage of cybersecurity skills, and this is especially applicable to incident response. Enterprises whose core competency is not cybersecurity often find it challenging to source skills near a centralized area, especially if they do not operate out of major cities or business hubs.

Furthermore, it is challenging to address geography-specific requirements with a centralized team. In some instances, an organization may need on-site presence during the investigation of a cybersecurity incident. With a centralized team, meeting these requirements may be challenging.

In a centralized model, there is typically single-language support. With geographic distribution across multiple countries, single-language support might be a barrier for employees and stakeholders who participate in the incident management process.

Distributed Team Model

In a traditional *distributed team model*, the members of an incident response team reside in two or more geographic locations. However, with telecommuting and outsourcing, the original meaning of the term has been diminished. These days, the term generally refers to a team whose members reside in multiple physical locations, not necessarily just corporate offices. In spite of geographic distribution, a distributed team may still appear to the enterprise as a single team. Each location usually has a regional leader who reports to the incident response director or other senior-level manager.

A distributed team model allows enterprises to overcome many of the shortcomings of a centralized team. By distributing an incident response team across multiple geographic locations, an enterprise can serve local needs and implement multilanguage support as required.

Distributed teams can balance workloads and reduce the need for shift work and on-call rotation, and in some instances eliminate it completely. Furthermore, with a distributed team model, organizations may find it easier to source the right skills. Allowing work from home and flexible working hours can significantly improve the chances of finding capable personnel.

One way to implement a distributed team is through the "follow the sun" model. This model is usually more appropriate for large organizations, and it facilitates around-the-clock coverage across various time zones without the need to implement shift work or on-call rotation. With this model, incident response team members typically work from home or office locations in their respective geographic locations.

Several considerations exist that enterprises need to take into account before implementing a distributed team model. A distributed team model has an additional level of complexity compared to a centralized team model.

Organizations incur management overhead associated with managing local resources. Each geographic region typically has a local management presence, which leads to an increased chain of command complexity. For this reason, decisions during significant incidents and breaches may take longer to reach.

Depending on the geographical distribution, some locations may need regionalized policies and procedures to cater to local needs and satisfy local regulatory requirements. Also, enterprises must create and implement handoff procedures for investigations that require around-the-clock support. Many organizations implement centralized incident management tools where personnel can enter and access incident information.

An important consideration for a distributed team is communication and collaboration. Distributed teams lean toward using written communication. For this reason, enterprises need to make sure that they provide the necessary collaboration tools and actively encourage the team members to collaborate and communicate both horizontally and vertically. Furthermore, organizing regular events where the personnel can meet face to face is a useful option for building relationships and improving collaboration between distributed teams.

Hybrid Team Model

A *hybrid team model* combines the best of both worlds by having a centralized team that drives vital decisions and provides oversight of investigations, and remote teams cater to local needs and provide coverage across different time zones. This model allows organizations to overcome the shortcomings of the centralized model and address some of the concerns associated with the distributed model.

Organizations implement the hybrid incident response team model in numerous ways. For example, an enterprise can hire local resources or contractors in various geographic locations or outsource some of the capabilities to service providers who work at the direction of the central team. The hybrid model is also popular with enterprises that employ a mobile workforce or where the incident response team members can work from home.

An Integrated Team

An *integrated team* is not a team model, strictly speaking, and it suggests the absence of a dedicated cybersecurity incident response function. Smaller organizations with a limited budget and resources may choose to incorporate an incident response function into a more general cybersecurity team, such as a SOC. This model is also typical of organizations with relatively immature cybersecurity capabilities where the leadership perceives cybersecurity as a tactical function.

An integrated incident response function is typically reactive rather than proactive, with no dedicated personnel who own the responsibility for incident response. Instead, security personnel are cross-discipline trained and perform various roles. Incident response is thus a part of their day-to-day duties. Furthermore, ad hoc response and a lack of an established incident management framework often characterize integrated teams.

Organizing an Incident Response Team

As with the choice of a team model, several factors influence the choice of a support model for incident response. Examples include organization size, risk appetite, geographic distribution, and available funding and resources.

Tiered Model

A *tiered model* is a popular approach to organizing incident response support among organizations where incident response is a subfunction of a SOC or another cybersecurity competency. Organizing support into tiers allows enterprises to address incident management and incident response strategically by swiftly resolving low-severity incidents using less experienced personnel, and escalate more complex incidents, including cyber breaches, to experienced employees.

A tiered approach, especially when combined with the hybrid team model, allows enterprises to address challenges with sourcing skills, optimize resource usage, and scale out incident response capabilities as the enterprise grows and expands into new markets.

Organizations must take some considerations into account before implementing a multitiered support model. Establishing handoff procedures, documenting roles and responsibilities, and establishing a chain of command are crucial. Also, enterprises need to consider automation to allow less experienced personnel to resolve simple incidents efficiently and ensure that the model is cost-effective.

The following section discusses a three-tier model. However, a two-tier model may also be appropriate for many organizations, particularly if cost is a concern. Figure 2.2 depicts a three-tier support model.

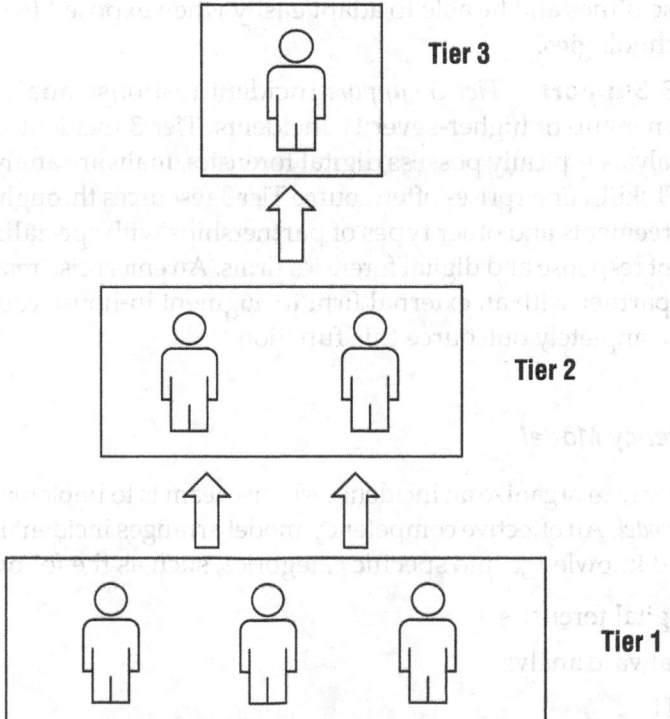

Figure 2.2: Multilevel support model

Tier 1 Support   *Tier 1 support* consists of first-level responders who take ownership of low-severity incidents that typically do not cause a significant impact on the enterprise. The personnel that comprise a Tier 1 response possess the skills necessary to triage potential incidents and take short-term containment actions, such as resetting credentials for a compromised account. However, Tier 1 personnel do not possess sufficient skills and knowledge to perform more advanced investigative activities, such as forensic analysis of compromised systems or malware analysis.

Tier 2 Support   *Tier 2 support* personnel receive escalations from Tier 1 analysts and review their work to determine the outcome of their triage. Based on their assessment, the personnel can assist Tier 1 analysts in resolving the incident or decide to take ownership if the incident reaches a specific severity threshold. Tier 2 incident response analysts typically possess basic digital forensics, malware analysis, and CTI skills. They should also demonstrate experience and knowledge of various information technology disciplines and be able to adapt easily when exposed to different technologies.

Tier 3 Support   *Tier 3 support* incident response analysts take ownership of higher-severity incidents. Tier 3 incident response analysts typically possess digital forensics, malware analysis, and CTI skills. Enterprises often source Tier 3 resources through retainer agreements and other types of partnerships with specialized incident response and digital forensics firms. An enterprise may choose to partner with an external firm to augment in-house capabilities or completely outsource this function.

Competency Model

Another way to organize an incident response team is to implement a *competency model*. An effective competency model arranges incident response skills and knowledge into specific categories, such as the following:

- Digital forensics
- Malware analysis
- CTI

A competency model consists of two types of competencies that organizations must define:

Core competencies: Baseline skills that all members of an incident response team must possess, such as adequate oral and written communication or an understanding of fundamental computer science concepts

Functional competencies: Skills specific to each job function, such as a good understanding of Windows forensic artifacts for a digital forensics competency

When implementing a competency model, organizations must determine the required competencies and define the skills and knowledge that each of those competencies should possess. The skills requirements must take into account both hard and soft skills that allow incident response personnel to succeed in their job functions.

In my personal experience, the competency model is most common in organizations where incident response is a stand-alone function within an overall cybersecurity program. A competency model has the following benefits:

- Allows organizations to arrange skills and knowledge into specific categories
- Sets a concrete direction for each competency
- Allows managers to identify strengths and deficiencies in an incident response team
- Allows team members to take ownership of specific tasks
- Allows team members to learn from one another and advance their skills

During my consulting engagements, I have observed that enterprises that implement the competency model often have more mature incident response capabilities and are more effective at handling cybersecurity incidents than those who implement the tiered model.

Hiring and Training Personnel

Finding and hiring personnel with the right skill set is arguably one of the more challenging tasks when it comes to establishing an incident response team. There is a global shortage of qualified cybersecurity professionals, which is particularly applicable to incident response. To establish a capable incident response team, an enterprise must hire personnel with the right combination of soft and technical skills, as well as critical thinking and problem-solving abilities.

The following sections discuss the typical skills and abilities that capable incident responders should possess. It is important to emphasize that incident response team members usually demonstrate complementary skills and abilities.

Technical Skills

Technical skills are the core skills that enable incident responders to accomplish tasks relating to incident response. Organizations also refer to core skills as *hard skills* to distinguish them from soft skills. Employees typically develop core incident response skills through formal training, on-the-job training, work experience, or a combination thereof.

In the field of incident response, core skills include general technical skills and skills related to the analysis and handling of incidents. Historically, enterprises sourced and adapted incident response skills from more traditional areas of information technology, such as system administration and application development. In recent years, universities have started to offer training in DFIR.

Capable incident responders typically possess a combination of skills in the following information technology domains:

- Computer networking, including an understanding of standard network protocols and services
- Common operating systems, specifically Windows and Unix-like systems, such as Linux and macOS
- Programming and scripting skills in popular languages, such as PowerShell, Python, and Bash
- Security architecture and tool deployment models

In addition to general technical skills and abilities, capable incident response personnel should demonstrate a set of core skills specific to incident response. These skills include the following:

- Understanding of *tools, tactics, and procedures (TTPs)* that threat actors leverage to advance their attacks
- Understanding of common weaknesses in technology that can lead to risk
- Knowledge of forensic artifacts and the ability to analyze operating systems for evidence of compromise
- Ability to analyze network telemetry for evidence of compromise and malicious activities
- Malware analysis and ability to apply CTI to investigations, as well as contextualize system and network data
- Proficiency in endpoint detection and response (EDR) tools
- Understanding of standard containment, eradication, and recovery techniques

The general technical and incident response skills described here are by no means comprehensive. Incident responders need to demonstrate a strong understanding of computer science concepts to adapt and continually stay abreast of new technologies.

Soft Skills

The ability to communicate effectively with a wide range of audiences and stakeholders is vital to the success of an incident response team. Demonstrating sufficient technical competencies is not enough to provide high-quality service to the enterprise. Incident responders need to possess good *soft skills* to communicate effectively and collaborate with business and technical stakeholders, as well as external entities. Soft skills include a combination of interpersonal skills and behavioral traits that allow employees to work with one another and succeed in the workplace. Examples of soft skills that incident responders need to possess and continually develop include the following:

- Technical writing skills, including report writing, developing policies and procedures, creating a summary of investigative findings, and documenting investigative information.

- Good oral communication skills necessary to communicate with technical and business stakeholders.

- Ability to translate technical jargon into a language that nontechnical audiences can easily understand.

- Presentation skills required to brief stakeholders on the status of an investigation, to present lessons learned at the closeout of an incident, or to present a business case.

- Problem-solving and critical thinking skills.

- Time management and prioritization.

- Managing stress and remaining calm during high-pressure situations. This behavioral characteristic is particularly vital in incident response. Responders often conduct investigations under pressure and are exposed to a significant amount of stress.

- Listening and being receptive to points of view presented by other team members.

As with the technical skills discussed previously, this list is by no means comprehensive. The diversity and distribution of both core and soft skills depend on the experience and seniority level of incident response personnel. A practical approach is to hire personnel with diverse and complementary skills and abilities.

Pros and Cons of Security Certifications

The value of certifications is a widely debated topic in the cybersecurity industry. Numerous vendors and certification bodies offer cybersecurity certifications for both entry-level and experienced cybersecurity professionals. This section briefly discusses the pros and cons of certifications and what role they play in hiring incident response personnel.

Certifications bring several benefits to both employers and prospective employees. Employees who hold certifications often demonstrate a commitment to self-development and growing their skills. Certifications also show employers that prospective employees can learn and demonstrate at least a basic understanding of a specific incident response discipline, such as digital forensics of Windows systems. By enrolling in a certification program, employees can keep abreast of new technologies and stay competitive in a fast-changing industry.

Certifications may also be a prerequisite for certain jobs, such as positions with government agencies or service organizations. For example, some cybersecurity service firms may require certifications to demonstrate the expertise of their personnel to prospective clients.

Certifications also have several drawbacks. Certifications do not replace work experience, critical thinking, the ability to solve problems, and other behavioral characteristics that make employees successful in their roles. One week in a classroom does not replace a few years of investigating real cyberattacks.

Furthermore, vendors and certification bodies often oversell the value of certifications due to financial incentives. For example, organizations whose core business is training and certification often inflate the value of their certification programs to create a stream of revenue.

Another drawback of certifications is the way that many certification bodies test their candidates. Answering multiple-choice questions on a computer screen does not prove that the candidate fully understands the concepts and can apply them in work situations. Also, some candidates may focus on passing a certification exam rather than truly understanding the curriculum.

In my personal experience, certifications allow entry-level incident response candidates to make a good first impression, demonstrate commitment, and prove a basic understanding of the field. Certifications are also an excellent development path for less experienced employees who want to grow their skills and take on more challenging tasks.

On the other hand, I have interviewed numerous experienced candidates for various cybersecurity roles and found very little correlation between certifications and their skills. In fact, in many cases, candidates did not demonstrate an understanding of basic concepts in the area of their certification.

Certifications are still valuable for experienced professionals and demonstrate their commitment to the field. However, judging a candidate's ability to perform a job function purely or even significantly based on their certification can be highly misleading. Good interviewers typically ask a combination of situational and behavioral questions followed by specific targeted questions to determine whether a candidate has the skills and experience needed for a specific incident response area.

Conducting Effective Interviews

Incident response is not for the fainthearted. When an enterprise experiences a significant cyber event, incident responders work under tremendous pressure and often for long and unsocial hours. Unqualified personnel and incapable management are a recipe for disaster. For this reason, as part of establishing an incident response team, organizations must hire personnel with a blend of diverse yet complementary skills and foster growth within the team.

Candidates for incident response roles typically come from different, and often diverse, employment backgrounds. They may also demonstrate varying degrees of technical proficiency and soft skills. The task of the interviewer is to determine conclusively if a candidate is the right fit for the role.

One of the most effective interviewing techniques for technical candidates is asking behavioral and situational questions. *Behavioral questions* allow the candidate to talk openly about past accomplishments and experiences, as well as to provide concrete examples that demonstrate their skills. *Situational questions,* on the other hand, focus on a hypothetical situation and test how a prospective employee would handle the situation presented.

Asking open questions about past experiences or scenario-based questions typically works well. Based on the answers that the candidate provides, the interviewer can ask targeted questions or pivot to other areas of interest. For example, I like to present a realistic incident scenario based on past incident response investigations and ask the candidate how they would approach the investigation. Based on the answers that I receive, I follow with specific, targeted questions or ask about pros and cons of the chosen approach.

Another helpful approach is to ask a prospective employee to provide an example of a challenging project or initiative that the candidate developed, what problem it solved, and what the candidate could have done better. Candidates who can critically evaluate themselves, identify failures or missteps in their approach, and articulate them constructively typically thrive in the incident response field.

In my experience, this approach to interviewing is very effective. It allows the interviewer to establish what technical and incident response skills the candidate demonstrates. Furthermore, based on the presentation style and examples, the interviewer can also determine whether the candidate possesses sufficient communication and other soft skills.

The incident response profession is still evolving. Consequently, the incident response industry still relies heavily on tribal knowledge and contributions from independent researchers and software developers. Hiring motivated personnel with critical thinking and problem-solving skills is vital.

Retaining Incident Response Talent

According to ISACA, nearly 70 percent of organizations believe their cybersecurity teams are understaffed.[4] Focusing on hiring incident response personnel without employee retention considerations is like trying to fill a bucket with a hole at the bottom. This section briefly discusses the characteristics of a high-performing team and retention strategies.

An essential characteristic of a highly competent incident response team is collaboration to solve complex problems and continually improve their capabilities. For this reason, management must encourage a non-confrontational and penalty-free culture and exchange of ideas.

For individual team members to perform well in their roles, they must feel a sense of purpose and commitment toward common goals. To achieve this, leadership must facilitate transparent and clear communication, help personnel grow, show appreciation for the team's efforts, and reward achievement.

Other important factors that contribute to high performance are motivation and opportunities for personal growth. To foster growth, leadership should encourage their incident response personnel to develop soft and domain-specific skills continuously by setting challenging yet realistic goals. Hiring personnel with a blend of complementary skills and mentoring are vital to this process. The following list contains examples of activities that may motivate and help organizations retain incident response personnel:

- Personal projects that are challenging yet realistic to achieve
- Rotation of roles to learn new areas of cybersecurity and develop new skills
- Conference attendance
- Classroom and online training courses to keep abreast of new technologies and trends in cybersecurity
- Coaching and mentoring
- Creating opportunities for career growth and progression

Establishing Authority

Authority is vital for an incident response team to fulfill its mission and provide high-quality services to the enterprise. *Authority* refers to the official responsibility and the level of control that leaders assign to an incident response team to make decisions and take specific actions.[5] Depending on organizational culture and risk appetite, the team may operate with a varying degree of authority. The most appropriate place to define incident response team authority is an enterprise security policy supported by the executive leadership. This section discusses the levels of authority that enterprises typically assign to an incident response function.

Full Authority

By assigning *full authority,* enterprises empower an incident response team to make decisions, take specific actions, and direct business and technology stakeholders during the response to an incident. Typically, only executive personnel have the necessary authority to empower an incident response team to operate with this level of autonomy.

Having full authority does not necessarily mean that incident response personnel do not consult business and technology stakeholders about their decisions. It just means that they can take specific actions to reduce risk and prevent damage where time is of vital importance. For example, an incident response manager may make a decision and instruct a network support team to isolate specific critical systems temporarily from the network during a malware outbreak incident to prevent further damage while escalating the case to senior management.

Shared Authority

In a *shared authority model*, an incident response team provides expert opinions and has the authority to influence the decision-making process. It also consults with stakeholders who have decision-making authority and advises them about risk and the impact associated with cyberattacks, especially when business stakeholders need actionable information in order to establish priorities and make decisions. For example, during an incident involving a critical system that handles data subjected to regulatory requirements, incident response personnel may provide an expert opinion to the corporate legal counsel, who may advise business stakeholders about the appropriate course of action to reduce the possibility of legal exposure.

An incident response team with shared authority can also raise specific issues and concerns with management and contribute to the risk management process.

Indirect Authority

Indirect authority refers to a situation where an incident response team can exert pressure on business and technology stakeholders in order to perform specific actions in response to an incident. Indirect authority is explicitly applicable in situations when time is of vital importance. For example, if a ransomware worm infects the corporate network and propagates within it, an incident response manager may exert pressure on technical personnel to isolate the affected network segment from the corporate network to prevent the spread of the worm and minimize further damage, especially to critical digital assets.

No Authority

An incident response team with no formal authority typically acts in an advisory capacity to business and technology stakeholders who make decisions and take specific actions in response to a cybersecurity incident. The *no authority model* is the least desirable, since business and technology functions typically focus on the availability of information technology services, and their priorities may conflict with the necessity to protect the confidentiality and integrity of digital assets.

An incident response team that has no authority or credibility within an enterprise cannot provide high-quality services and effectively respond to incidents.

Introducing an Incident Response Team to the Enterprise

A vital aspect of implementing an incident response team is to introduce it to the enterprise. Key stakeholders must be familiar with the team's mission, its role within the organization, and how to engage it for assistance.

A well-executed communication strategy is crucial to ensuring that an organization effectively introduces an incident response team. As part of the strategy, an enterprise needs to develop a communication plan that defines the target audience, messaging timelines, and communication channels.

To provide stakeholders with appropriate information, the cybersecurity strategist also needs to develop clear and concise messaging, present a compelling mission, and describe how the incident response function benefits the organization. Ideally, senior leadership should initiate the communication to maximize reach and emphasize the importance of the function to the organization.

Typically, a twofold approach works best when introducing a new incident response capability to the enterprise:

▪ Introduce the capability to business unit leaders and other senior managers. A face-to-face presentation is the most effective.

▪ Publicize the incident response function to the broader business and technical communities.

As part of the introduction, organizations need to consider making information about the team and incident reporting guidelines widely available within the enterprise. A dedicated wiki or a website on the corporate intranet is an excellent place for this information. Stakeholders also need to have access to a facility to ask questions and provide their feedback.

Finally, close collaboration with the corporate communications department is key to ensuring appropriate messaging. A corporate communications department has the necessary expertise and resources, and can help develop a communication plan, craft messaging, and disseminate information among the necessary stakeholders.

Enacting a CSIRT

A CSIRT is a cross-functional entity with an incident response team at its core, and it requires coordination to ensure that the different stakeholders involved in the incident management process work together effectively. For this reason, enterprises need to establish a *CSIRT coordination model* and determine how information flows between the stakeholders to ensure that everyone works toward the same goals.

Defining a Coordination Model

Incident response, especially to confirmed cyber breaches, requires the involvement of various internal and external entities who provide expertise in their respective domains during the incident management process.[6] Figure 2.3 displays a conceptual model that represents the relationship between the core incident response team and the various internal and external functions that form a CSIRT.

This model consists of three layers: technical, management, and executive. Activities at the *technical layer* primarily focus on the core technical capabilities required to investigate and scope incidents, such as digital forensics.

The *management layer*, on the other hand, is primarily concerned with providing overall management oversight during major incidents. Mid-level or senior management may participate in the incident response process during incidents that require the involvement from other organizational functions, such as legal. For example, legal counsel may provide direction to an incident manager regarding the acquisition and preservation of forensic data while advising senior management about potential legal exposure resulting from a cyber breach.

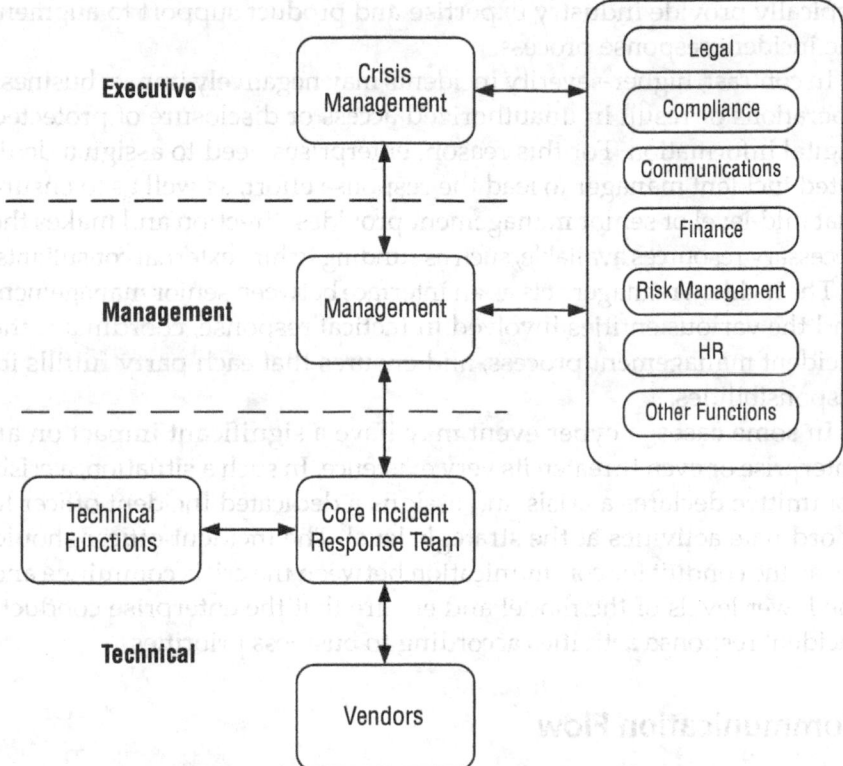

Figure 2.3: CSIRT coordination model

Executive leadership provides a strategic direction during high-severity incidents that typically lead to a crisis. For example, executive leadership may provide direction and actively participate in the response to an incident that may have a significant impact on brand reputation, leads to a serious breach of legal and regulatory compliance, or has a significant impact on the bottom line.

During less severe incidents, the core incident response team typically interacts with technical functions, as well as external entities such as vendors. Because those incidents do not impact business operations or protected data in a significant way, all response activities take place within the technical layer. Technical groups provide subject matter expertise in their respective technology areas, whereas external entities typically provide industry expertise and product support to augment the incident response process.

In contrast, higher-severity incidents may negatively impact business operations or result in unauthorized access or disclosure of protected digital information. For this reason, enterprises need to assign a dedicated incident manager to lead the response effort, as well as to ensure that mid-level or senior management provides direction and makes the necessary resources available, such as funding to hire external consultants.

The incident manager acts as an interface between senior management and the various entities involved in tactical response, coordinates the incident management process, and ensures that each party fulfills its responsibilities.

In some cases, a cyber event may have a significant impact on an enterprise or even threaten its very existence. In such a situation, a crisis committee declares a crisis and assigns a dedicated incident officer to coordinate activities at the strategic level. The incident officer should act as the conduit for communication between the crisis committee and the lower levels of the model and ensure that the enterprise conducts incident response activities according to business priorities.

Communication Flow

Incident manager and incident officer are two vital roles in the coordination model. They act as the conduit for communication between the entities that participate in the incident management process and coordinate activities at their respective layers. Figure 2.4 represents the relationship between the roles.

Incident Officer

An *incident officer*, also referred to as an *incident commander*, is a senior-level manager who provides strategic oversight and guidance to the incident manager during severe incidents and ensures that business priorities drive incident response. For example, an incident officer may decide, in consultation with other executive personnel, that minimizing risk of unauthorized data disclosure takes priority over system availability.

An incident officer also has the authority to convene a crisis committee during severe incidents that may significantly impact the enterprise. A Chief Information Security Officer (CISO) or another senior officer typically assumes this role.

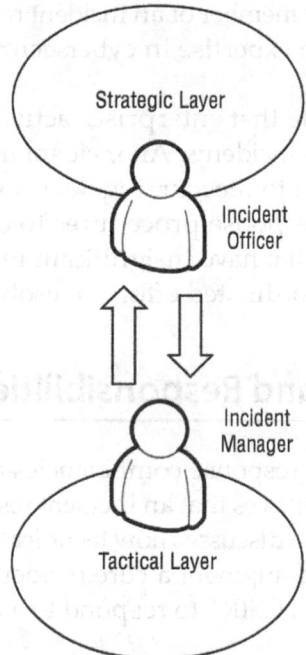

Figure 2.4: Relationship between incident manager and incident officer

An incident officer interfaces with other executive-level personnel who form the crisis management committee and provides updates to senior leadership about the status of the investigation. For example, an incident officer may hold regular status updates and receive guidance from the chief privacy officer (CPO) during breaches that may lead to unauthorized data disclosure.

Incident Manager

An *incident manager*, on the other hand, is responsible for coordinating incident management activities at the technical and management levels and ensuring that each entity fulfills its responsibilities. The role also facilitates communication between those entities and the necessary logistics. For example, an incident manager typically needs to engage technical support teams when forensic analysts require access to systems in order to acquire forensic data.

In most cases, a senior member of an incident response team or another mid-level manager with expertise in cybersecurity assumes the role of incident manager.

It is important to note that enterprises activate this role to actively manage higher-severity incidents. An incident manager is not required to manage the response to reoccurring, low-severity incidents. Many organizations define response procedures to deal with reoccurring, low-severity incidents that have insignificant impact on the enterprise and do not require a coordinated effort to resolve them.

Assigning Roles and Responsibilities

The section on incident response competencies and services discussed proactive and reactive services that an incident response team provides to an enterprise. This section discusses how technical and business functions, as well external entities, augment a core incident response team when an enterprise convenes a CSIRT to respond to a cybersecurity incident.

Business Functions

In recent years, cyberattacks have been increasingly effective and in many cases destructive; leading to a negative effect on an organization's bottom-line. For this reason, cybersecurity has become a business problem, and enterprises need to incorporate various business functions into a CSIRT to ensure an appropriate response from a business perspective.

This section briefly discusses typical business functions that enterprises need to consider as part of a CSIRT. Note that the naming conventions and responsibilities may vary from organization to organization.

Human Resources

Human Resources (HR) assists an incident response team with person-nel-related matters and guides the team during internal investigations relating to employee misconduct, policy violations, or insider threat cases. Examples of scenarios when an incident manager may consult HR personnel as part of a CSIRT include the following:

- Handling employee policy violations, misuse investigations, as well as disciplinary actions stemming from misconduct
- Assisting with interviewing employees who may have valuable information relating to an investigated incident

- Dealing with matters pertaining to labor considerations, such as compensation for work outside the contracted hours

- Creating temporary employee records for contractors and business partners who assist with an investigation

Corporate Communications

The Corporate Communications department performs two functions as part of a CSIRT: internal communications and public relations. Appropriate internal communications helps reduce rumors among employees and enhances transparency. It is the Corporate Communications department that creates and disseminates information internally and shapes employee perception about an incident.

Public relations, on the other hand, is vital to managing brand reputation during a significant cyber event. Timely and well-crafted external communication helps enterprises control the message; create the right perception among the public, customers, shareholders, and other stakeholders; and preserve brand reputation.

Examples of support that Corporate Communications provides during significant cyber events include the following:

- Creating and disseminating internal communications where it is appropriate to share incident-specific information with employees. For example, an enterprise may release internal communications during an incident that causes operational issues to prevent rumors.

- Drafting external statements during a crisis caused by a cyber event. In this case, Corporate Communications works closely with corporate legal counsel and senior management to ensure that the release does not lead to legal exposure.

- Acting as a point of contact for media and external inquiries during major cyber events.

- Monitoring social media and disseminating approved information to crucial stakeholders and the general public about impacted services

Corporate Security

Corporate Security assists the incident response team with matters of physical security. Corporate Security personnel often work closely with the HR and Legal departments to ensure that they follow the appropriate corporate protocols. Examples of support that a Corporate Security department provides during incident investigations include the following:

- Providing access to employees and contractors to physical facilities. For example, incident response personnel may need physical access to a data center to acquire and preserve digital evidence.

- Providing information such as badge access or surveillance video to support internal investigations. For example, an insider threat may claim absence from work during a particular period when an incident occurred. Badge access data and video may help to prove or disprove the claim.

- Seizing physical assets and escorting employees suspected of insider threat attacks, or identifying those who violated security policies and engaged in misconduct.

- Owning the relationship with law enforcement agencies and acting as a point of contact for those agencies. This responsibility is especially important in cases where the source of an incident notification is law enforcement.

Finance

Responding to significant cyber events often requires additional resources and funding. For example, an enterprise may need to hire external incident response consultants to assist with the investigation. Another example includes engaging professional vendor services to assist in recovering the affected systems and applications. In some instances, an enterprise may also have to purchase additional equipment and software to advance investigative activities.

Although Finance department representatives do not actively participate in incident investigations, their involvement is necessary to expedite and approve additional funding.

Furthermore, a chief financial officer (CFO) in a publicly traded company typically has an active interest in cybersecurity. The CFO may have to disclose information about cybersecurity incidents that may have a material financial impact to regulatory bodies and investors. In the United States, organizations must disclose to the Securities and Exchange Commission (SEC) information that a reasonable investor would consider important in making investment or voting decisions.[7] For example, if information about a cybersecurity incident may impact the share price of a publicly traded company, then a CFO may have to be informed about the incident and its impact on the enterprise. For this reason, in some organizations a CISO directly reports to a CFO.

Other Business Functions

Incident response is not limited to the business functions discussed thus far. Each incident is different and may require involvement from various business stakeholders. Furthermore, organizations have different corporate structures dependent on their size, the nature of their business, and other factors. For this reason, a CSIRT composition typically varies from organization to organization. The following list includes other stakeholders that may participate in the incident response process to provide expertise in their functional areas:

- Business unit leaders
- Third-party risk management
- Client relationship management
- Product leads
- Marketing
- Manufacturing
- Procurement and supply chain management
- Law enforcement agencies

Legal and Compliance

Unauthorized disclosure of sensitive data can lead to legal exposure and noncompliance with laws and regulations. Consequently, legal and compliance functions play a vital role in the incident response process. This section briefly discusses these functions. Chapter 6 discusses this topic in detail.

Legal Counsel

Engaging legal counsel and data privacy professionals early in an investigation is vital to reducing legal risk associated with cyber incidents. Legal involvement is especially applicable to breaches that result in unauthorized access to data that is subjected to legal and regulatory compliance requirements. An incident manager may also engage corporate legal counsel in cases where an incident can result in a breach of contractual obligations with third parties.

In some cases, legal counsel may take ownership of an internal investigation and enforce a legal protocol in order to reduce legal exposure and ensure the integrity of the investigation. For example, an attorney may choose to protect documents and information relating to an investigation under the umbrella of the attorney-client privilege or engage external legal counsel to lead the investigation. *Attorney-client privilege* is a legal privilege that protects the confidentiality of communications between attorneys and their clients from disclosure.

Corporate legal counsel also provides legal guidance to stakeholders, such as public relations professionals, to prevent accidental legal exposure. For example, corporate counsel may review internal and external communications before dissemination to ensure that it does not contain language that would create legal issues.

Compliance Functions

Compliance plays a vital role in incident investigations by focusing on the underlying risk associated with cyberattacks and system breaches. Incident responders forensically examine compromised systems to establish facts relating to an investigated incident. The role of *compliance* is to assess the findings in the context of legal and regulatory requirements in order to determine risk.

Chapter 1 emphasized the difference between a system breach and a data breach. A *data breach* is a legal term that refers to the unauthorized disclosure of protected information, whereas a *system breach* refers to the unauthorized access to a computer system or software application. Consequently, compliance, data privacy, and legal professionals must interpret investigative findings to determine whether a data breach occurred and to ensure adherence with breach notification requirements.

In some instances, risk management personnel may evaluate and advise about cyber insurance applicability and claim requirements resulting from cyber breaches. Compliance can also determine whether the compromised environment had a risk assessment performed and whether any known risks could have led to the breach, or whether the breach was the direct result of nonconformance with applicable policies, standards, and other requirements.

Information Technology Functions

Enterprises increasingly rely on a wide range of technologies to support business operations. Technical groups within information technology departments are responsible for managing those technologies, as well as provide expertise in their respective domains during incident investigations. The following sections provide a brief description of the role that technology stakeholders play within a CSIRT.

Technical Groups

Technical groups is a broad term that covers the operational and management aspects of information technology. Technical groups include two broad functions: technology groups and application groups.

A *technology group* includes a variety of technical skills and resources necessary to support the technologies that enterprises deploy to support business operations. Examples of technologies that technology groups support include the following:

- Networks
- Servers
- Mainframes
- Storage
- Databases
- Directory services
- End-user workstations and other user equipment
- Middleware
- Web infrastructure

Incident responders work closely with technology groups and leverage the expertise in their respective areas as part of an effort to respond to and investigate incidents. Here are examples of support that technical teams typically provide during investigations:

- Providing technology-specific subject matter expertise
- Providing technology-specific architecture and implementation context
- Sharing documentation and information about specific information technology environments

- Granting access to systems to incident response personnel for investigative purposes
- Deploying monitoring and data acquisition software tools
- Assisting with acquiring forensic data
- Applying security configuration changes as part of a containment strategy
- Testing and applying patches to close vulnerabilities exploited by a threat actor, as well as assisting with other eradication activities
- Rebuilding and recovering systems to a secure state as part of a remediation strategy

An application group, on the other hand, is a function within an information technology department that focuses on the operational and management aspects of software applications throughout their life-cycle. Application groups support incident investigations by providing technical expertise in their respective domains and supplying the necessary information to advance investigations. Examples of support that application teams typically provide during incident investigations include the following:

- Sharing documentation and providing application-specific subject matter expertise
- Applying security configuration changes as part of a containment strategy
- Developing, testing, and applying patches to close application vulnerabilities exploited by a threat actor
- Assisting with the acquisition of application event logs and other data necessary to an investigation

Disaster Recovery

Disaster recovery is a function that focuses on resuming business operations in the aftermath of a destructive event. Historically, cybersecurity and disaster recovery used to be siloed disciplines. However, in light of ransomware and other destructive cyberattacks, disaster recovery has become an integral part of cyber resilience. The premise behind this concept is to ensure that an enterprise can continue business operations during a significant cyberattack.

Enterprises typically develop a *disaster recovery plan (DRP)* to recover and resume information technology infrastructure after a significant event, including a cyberattack. Involvement of a disaster recovery function during a cybersecurity incident may include the following:

- Recovering data from backups following cyberattacks that negatively impact data availability, such as ransomware.

- Prioritizing recovery based on asset criticality when a cyberattack negatively impacts multiple systems and applications.

- Providing redundancy and switching operations to alternative sites. For example, during a distributed denial-of-service (DDoS) attack against a web application, an enterprise may decide to switch to an alternative site to continue to serve its client base.

- Providing alternative communication methods. For example, when a threat actor compromises an internal email system, the disaster recovery function may provide an alternative communication means.

Outsourcing Partners and Vendors

For the majority of enterprises, cybersecurity is not a core business function. For this reason, organizations need to develop trusted relationships with external vendors who can augment in-house capabilities by providing expertise and acting as trusted advisers. Incident response managers need to build and maintain relationships with system and software vendors, as well as professional services vendors.

System, software, and hardware vendors provide product-specific knowledge and expertise. For example, a software vendor might advise incident response personnel about specific product features, configurations, and best practices to help detect attacker activity in the compromised environment or contain an incident. In contrast, professional services vendors can assist an enterprise with incident response, forensics, and other investigative activities. Larger enterprises also need to consider establishing a relationship with hardware vendors to assist with mass hardware replacements during destructive cyberattacks.

Senior Management

Occasionally, enterprises experience cyber events that require management oversight and direction. For example, if a threat actor compromises a system that supports a core business process, an incident response manager may need to escalate the case to senior management in order to receive strategic direction. The need for an escalation is especially vital if business priorities compete with incident response priorities. Senior management needs to make decisions based on impact and risk, provide clear business guidance to the incident response team, and set priorities. Typically, a senior-level manager who assumes the role of an incident officer acts as a point of escalation for incidents that require senior management attention.

A *crisis committee* is a group of senior leaders, typically executive personnel, that makes immediate strategic decisions to address a crisis caused by a significant event. For example, if a cyberattack, such as ransomware, severely impacts business operations, a crisis committee typically decides which business functions to recover first based on a business continuity plan (BCP).

A crisis committee also focuses on brand reputation management, addressing shareholders, as well as working with key business partners and clients at the strategic level.

Working with Outsourcing Partners

Outsourcing allows organizations to overcome some of the challenges associated with sourcing skills and provides a cost-effective option for many organizations. Furthermore, enterprises may choose to outsource their cybersecurity, including incident response, to focus on their core business. There are several benefits of outsourcing incident response capabilities.

With the global shortage of cybersecurity skills, finding and retaining cybersecurity talent is a major challenge for many enterprises. Furthermore, small to medium-sized organizations may not have a business justification to hire full-time incident response personnel, such as dedicated malware reverse-engineers or CTI researchers. Retaining an external firm that specializes in DFIR allows enterprises to consume services on demand without hiring dedicated full-time personnel. This leads to a more efficient use of resources and higher quality service.

External consultants also bring in industry expertise, technology, and methods that allow organizations to scope and determine the root cause of an incident. For example, an external firm may have developed custom tools that enable it to enrich and efficiently process large amounts of data from a wide range of platforms and other technologies.

Reputable incident response firms continually research the threat landscape and track specific threat actors. Their researchers closely work with incident response consultants in order to enrich and contextualize indicators of compromise (IOC) recovered during a forensic analysis of compromised systems. This approach allows organizations to effectively scope incidents, determine their root cause, and implement specific measures to contain the incidents. Very few firms can afford and justify this capability, and leveraging external partners to source CTI is often the only option.

Outsourcing Considerations

Enterprises must consider internal and external factors when evaluating incident response vendors to ensure that they partner with an organization that is the right fit for them. Cybersecurity is a hot market, and many small and large vendors want to join the ride without having the necessary expertise, experience, and supporting infrastructure. The following sections discuss considerations that enterprises should take into account when partnering with an external firm.

Proven Track Record of Success

Many vendors rush into the incident response market without adequate investment in hiring experienced personnel, creating methodologies, or building a supporting infrastructure. It is vital to ensure that a potential partner has a proven track record of investigating a wide range of incidents and breaches across various industries. Enterprises can perform research and request client references to validate that a potential partner has the capabilities it claims to have.

Offered Services and Capabilities

External vendors may offer a variety of services. Smaller firms often focus on traditional digital forensics and investigating small cases, whereas larger firms usually offer a broader set of services and capabilities, often with more experienced personnel. However, this typically comes with a higher price tag. Examples of services that an incident response firm may offer include the following:

- Digital forensics and incident response
- CTI
- Malware reverse-engineering
- Incident management and remediation support
- Proactive services that help clients prepare for incidents and breaches

Also, reputable firms hire consultants with skills beyond incident response. For example, a well-rounded incident response consultant may help a client to communicate investigative findings to leadership in business language, considers data privacy and legal matters pertaining to incident response, or advises on the risk associated with a specific threat actor.

Global Support

Enterprises that have a global presence or operate in more than one geographic region may need to partner with a firm that has a global presence. Having capabilities in multiple geographic locations allows organizations to provide shorter response time, often around-the-clock support, and comply with local laws and regulations.

Skills and Experience

Seasoned incident response professionals possess a wide range of skills across various technical and cybersecurity domains. Not only do experienced consultants demonstrate crucial technical expertise, but they also understand their clients' needs and act as trusted advisers. For this reason, they typically have several years of experience in various technical and business domains. It does not necessarily mean that external firms should hire only experienced consultants. On the contrary, reputable incident response firms hire the right mix of junior and experienced personnel to provide cost-effective services.

Outsourcing Costs and Pricing Models

Enterprises must carefully consider costs when outsourcing their capabilities. Incident response firms provide specialized and niche skills. A hefty price tag often accompanies those skills and capabilities. With a relatively high number of incidents and breaches, the cost can add up very quickly. For this reason, in some cases it may be more cost effective to hire in-house personnel and leverage an external firm for more severe cases.

Some service organizations offer retainer services that enterprises may purchase to ensure availability of specialized and niche skills during an incident. Organizations may purchase retainer services for a variety of reasons, including:

- Augmentation of internal capabilities
- Sourcing of specialized skills, such as malware reverse-engineering
- Global coverage of incidents
- Compliance with regulations
- Cyber insurance requirements

Some service organizations offer multiple retainer tiers with different service and pricing structures to cater to various organizations.

It is crucial that enterprises fully understand the pricing, services, and retainer models before entering a retainer agreement with an external provider. For example, some service organizations require up-front payment, whereas others may agree to monthly charges. Prospective clients also need to be aware of additional potential charges, such as those for additional hours outside of a retainer agreement or travel expenses.

Establishing Successful Relationships with Vendors

A successful partnership with an external incident response firm requires building and maintaining a strong relationship. Arguably, the quality of service delivery is largely proportional to the investment that an enterprise makes into creating a strong relationship with an outsourcing partner. The following list outlines some considerations that may help enterprises build strong relationships with their incident response partners:

Set regular touchpoints.   Set regular touchpoints outside investigations to facilitate knowledge sharing and proactively address issues and concerns. Depending on the agreed-on scope of services, an external firm may share some of their observations during client engagements and the associated intelligence, advise about improving detective capabilities, or even suggest improvements to policies, processes, and procedures.

Document an engagement process. Fleshing out engagement details up front may save time and resources in the long run. For example, obtaining preapproval for travel expenses, documenting the process to engage the supplier to work under the attorney-client privilege, or establishing a process to share forensic data is vital to effective response.

Document roles and responsibilities. Document roles and responsibilities to avoid confusion and ensure that both parties fulfill their obligations during an incident.

Share knowledge. Educate the partner about the enterprise. Sharing information such as the organizational structure of the cybersecurity organization, providing information about incident response capabilities, or educating the partner about the architecture of the information technology environments is an integral component of successful incident response.

Manage communications during investigations. During investigations, establish a communication channel, communicate expectations, and establish a required frequency of updates.

Summary

A CSIRT is a cross-functional entity that enterprises task with the responsibility to respond to incidents and coordinate incident response activities. At the core of a CSIRT is an incident response team that works with business, technology, and third-party stakeholders to address the aftermath of cyberattacks and recover business operations.

An incident response team provides proactive and reactive functions to an enterprise. Proactive functions allow the team to improve its capabilities continuously, whereas reactive functions enable the enterprise to respond to and recover from incidents.

While building an incident response team, organizations need to create a mission statement, consider a team structure and a support model, hire and train personnel, and introduce the team to the enterprise.

A capable CSIRT consists of incident response personnel who work with technology and business stakeholders, vendors, and management to resolve incidents. CSIRT coordination is vital to ensuring that all of those stakeholders work well together.

Finally, a CSIRT must build positive relationships with key technology and services vendors to maximize the value that those vendors provide to the enterprise.

Notes

1. FBI News, "The Morris Worm, 30 Years Since First Major Attack on the Internet," November 2, 2018, www.fbi.gov/news/stories/morris-worm-30-years-since-first-major-attack-on-internet-110218.

2. Carnegie Mellon University, Software Engineering Institute, Authorized Users of the CERT Mark, www.sei.cmu.edu/education-outreach/computer-security-incident-response-teams/authorized-users.

3. Carnegie Mellon University, Software Engineering Institute, "Defining Incident Management Processes for CSIRTs," October 2004, resources.sei.cmu.edu/asset_files/TechnicalReport/2004_005_001_14405.pdf.

4. ISACA's State of Cybersecurity 2019 Survey: Retaining Qualified Cybersecurity Professionals Increasingly Challenging for Organizations, March 4, 2019, www.isaca.org/why-isaca/about-us/newsroom/press-releases/2019/isacas-state-of-cybersecurity-2019-survey-retaining-qualified-cybersecurity-professionals.

5. Carnegie Mellon University, Software Engineering Institute, "Organizational Models for Computer Security Incident Response Teams (CSIRTs)," December 2003, resources.sei.cmu.edu/asset_files/Handbook/2003_002_001_14099.pdf.

6. NIST SP 800-61 Revision 2 Computer Security Incident Handling Guide Revision 2, August 2012, nvlpubs.nist.gov/nistpubs/SpecialPublications/NIST.SP.800-61r2.pdf.

7. FindLaw, SEC Release on Materiality in Financial Disclosure, corporate.findlaw.com/finance/sec-release-on-materiality-in-financial-disclosure.html.

3

Technology Considerations in Cyber Breach Investigations

Technology is an essential part of every incident investigation. Depending on the nature of the investigation, incident responders may need to acquire forensic evidence in a defensible way, analyze event logs from a cloud-based service, or enumerate systems for evidence of malware execution.

In all of those cases, it is useful to understand the technologies that incident response teams leverage. Incident investigations can get complex very quickly as analysts uncover evidence of compromise and determine the attacker footprint in the compromised environment.

Given the criticality of logs and other historical artifacts to investigations, enterprises need to enact data retention policies and ensure that systems and software applications generate event logs and other data that incident responders can leverage during investigations. Furthermore, incident response teams need to build a toolkit consisting of tools that are necessary to acquire and analyze data efficiently.

This chapter discusses common technology considerations in incident response, from the perspective of both incident responders and cybersecurity managers.

Sourcing Technology

Incident response teams have numerous commercial and open source tools available at their disposal to acquire and preserve forensic data, perform analysis, and acquire cyber threat intelligence (CTI), among other tasks. It is also common for incident response teams to develop custom tools and scripts to automate repeatable tasks and solve specific problems.

This section discusses considerations that enterprises need to take into account when sourcing commercial and open source tools, as well as when developing in-house software.

Comparing Commercial vs. Open Source Tools

Incident response teams typically leverage a combination of open source software and commercial off-the-shelf (COTS) tools during investigations. Some tools focus on specific use cases, such as data acquisition, whereas other tools focus on a broader set of functionalities. However, even the most sophisticated tools cannot cater to all requirements during investigations. As part of developing an incident response program, enterprises should acquire the necessary tools and build an infrastructure to support investigations.

Commercial Tools

Commercial incident response tools are proprietary software developed for licensing and sale. Because developers of commercial incident response tools cater to a niche market, the software often comes with a hefty price tag. In spite of a relatively high up-front cost, commercial incident response tools are often an attractive choice for organizations that prefer vendors to provide maintenance and support. Vendors also have financial incentives and motivation to support new software releases, fix bugs, and regularly introduce new features to remain competitive in the marketplace. Furthermore, commercial vendors usually produce comprehensive documentation, which is sometimes an issue with open source software. Usability is another high selling point for many commercial vendors who perform usability testing as part of the software development lifecycle.

Open Source Software

Open source incident response tools are available at no cost, and enterprises do not have to pay licensing fees to developers. However, open source software can have many indirect costs associated with it that can significantly contribute to the overall *total cost of ownership (TCO)*. Users of open source software tools often rely on support from passionate developers and the wider incident response community, typically through public discussion forums. One of the significant areas of criticism for open source software is usability and documentation. In spite of the shortcomings, the incident response community heavily relies on open source tools to solve nonstandard problems, such as parsing of artifacts that commercial tools do not support. Some passionate incident response professionals contribute to the community by making their tools available on the GitHub platform[1] and other repositories.

Other Considerations

Arguably, the single most crucial factor in choosing technology to support incident response investigations is *requirements*. Enterprises acquire and develop software to support specific investigative needs, such as the parsing of system artifacts or automating some aspects of the analysis process. Additional considerations that incident response teams need to take into account as part of the technology acquisition process include the following:

- The need to support investigations at scale versus analyzing one or a small number of systems
- Integration with other software tools, such as log aggregation and case management tools
- The need to address an immediate, short-term issue versus acquiring a long-term solution
- Supported systems and artifacts
- Supporting investigations on live systems versus acquiring data for offline processing and analysis

Incident response teams can also leverage operating system native tools during investigations at no additional cost. For example, analysts can run native system commands to determine what software runs on the investigated system to find evidence of malware and other suspicious activities.

One relevant category of incident response tools that is worth mentioning is *closed source freeware*. With open source tools, developers grant the users of their software the rights to study, amend, and distribute the software. Closed source freeware, on the other hand, is available at no cost. However, its developers do not release the source code or grant permissions to study and amend the code base.

Developing In-House Software Tools

At times, an incident response team may face a nonstandard problem for which there is no off-the-shelf solution. In other cases, incident responders may want to solve a simple problem, and purchasing commercial software is not a cost-effective solution.

Furthermore, the incident response industry is still evolving, and it heavily relies on tribal knowledge and contributions from independent developers. For this reason, incident response teams often produce simple tools and scripts that allow them to parse artifacts, automate analysis, and perform other investigative activities.

Several use cases exist for which incident response teams might choose to develop in-house tools. Technologically experienced incident response teams often leverage a combination of commercial, open source, and custom tools as part of their capabilities. The following list discusses some frequent use cases for developing in-house incident response tools.

Automating Data Acquisition   Data acquisition is a common use case for developing custom tools, especially from legacy or niche platforms that other tools do not support. In some cases, incident responders may choose to collect and examine a selected set of system artifacts before acquiring a bitstream copy of a system to perform an in-depth examination. Developing a tool to automate the collection process may be an alternative when other commercial or open source software solutions are not available. Furthermore, adding support for acquisition at scale to a custom data acquisition tool can dramatically accelerate the acquisition and triage processes.

Processing Data before Analysis   Incident response teams rely on data generated in the course of system operations to find evidence of attacker activity. Before beginning analysis, analysts must convert the data into a format that they can read and interpret. Depending on the data origin and type, analysts may apply techniques such as parsing, normalization, format conversion, or removing unnecessary data points to prepare the data set for analysis. Where widely available tools do not support specific requirements, an incident response team may have to develop a custom tool to accommodate organization-specific requirements. For example, an organization may still have legacy platforms deployed within its environments with specific forensic artifacts that commercial and open source tools do not support.

Automating Analysis Tasks   With the increasing volumes of data that incident response teams acquire during investigations, automation is an invaluable tool to aid the analysis process. Several use cases exist, from intelligence enrichment, to identifying outliers in data sets, to finding evidence of malicious activity. Incident response teams may choose to develop discrete tools to automate specific tasks within the analysis process or to bundle functionality into a single tool. As with the acquisition process, custom analysis tools typically satisfy organization-specific use cases that commercial and open source tools do not cover.

Integration of Data Sources   Most incident response teams use several tools to perform various incident response tasks. The cybersecurity industry is still evolving, and integration is lacking compared to other domains. To unlock true value from security data in disparate sources, incident response teams can write integration code to meet specific use cases. Several use cases exist for integration with varying degrees of complexity. Examples include CTI enrichment, correlation of data, and automated response to specific conditions.

Procuring Hardware

In the majority of cases, incident responders use general-purpose workstations for administrative tasks, such as email or report writing, and dedicated hardware for investigative activities. The requirements that necessitate the need for dedicated hardware include the following:

Performance   Forensic processes, such as data acquisition and analysis, require high-performance hardware, such as processors, memory, and storage capacity to facilitate those processes. Furthermore, analysts often run special-purpose virtual machines within forensic workstations that require additional hardware resources.

Customization   Analysts frequently rebuild, reconfigure, or upgrade forensic workstations for specific use cases. Furthermore, forensic workstations typically require relaxed security controls to allow analysts to run their tools and perform incident response–specific tasks.

Security   Incident responders often work with malware and other malicious code that could infect computers on the corporate network if not handled carefully.

Data Isolation   Incident responders often collect sensitive data during investigations. Some of the data may be subjected to regulatory compliance requirements or litigation hold. Consequently, it is a bad idea to mix it with corporate data stored on administrative workstations.

In some cases, organizations may need to procure both desktop workstations and laptop computers to enable forensic processes, such as data acquisition, analysis, and testing of specific configurations remotely. For example, it is not uncommon for incident responders to travel to remote locations as part of an investigation.

It is of crucial importance that analysts do not connect their incident response workstations and other forensic hardware to the corporate network to avoid security risks. In cases where analysts require connectivity to the Internet or specific resources on the corporate network, organizations should create a dedicated and isolated network segment and only allow access to specific resources from that segment.

Some vendors offer purpose-built forensic workstations and other hardware. Organizations also have the choice to procure individual parts and build custom workstations to accommodate specific requirements and configurations. In addition to forensic workstations, organizations may also procure hardware, such as write blockers, external storage, or networking equipment.

Larger organizations or firms that provide incident response services to other organizations often build forensic labs to support a wide range of investigative needs.[2] Building a forensic lab requires substantial funding and a dedicated project. A detailed discussion of this topic is outside the scope of this book.

Acquiring Forensic Data

Data acquisition and preservation are vital steps in incident investigations. Several methods and tools exist to acquire and preserve forensic data. The choice of methodology primarily depends on the objectives and scope of an investigation. This section discusses the tools and methodologies that incident responders have available at their disposal to acquire and preserve data in a forensically sound manner.

Forensic Acquisition

Forensic acquisition, also referred to as *forensic imaging* or *forensic duplication*, has been historically a de facto standard for acquiring forensic data. In recent years, other approaches to data acquisition have become increasingly popular. However, forensic acquisition still remains indispensable during investigations, and it is necessary in cases where analysts need to perform an in-depth examination of a compromised system. This section focuses on traditional forensic methods. Another section exclusively discusses forensic acquisition in cloud computing environments.

Order of Volatility

One specific aspect of forensic data acquisition that incident responders need to consider is the *order of volatility*. Following the order of volatility ensures that analysts acquire the most volatile data first to preserve as much of digital evidence as possible. Some data on a live system has a much shorter life span than other data. For example, network connections associated with user applications may timeout or terminate when the corresponding application is shut down. Service processes, on the other hand, typically persist while the system is running.

Request for Comments (RFC) 3227, "Guidelines for Evidence Collection and Archiving,"[3] is an excellent source of information on digital evidence collection. The RFC lists the following order of volatility for a typical system:

- Registers, cache
- Routing table, ARP cache, process table, kernel statistics, memory
- Temporary filesystems
- Disk
- Remote logging and monitoring data that is relevant to the system in question
- Physical configuration, network topology
- Archival media

Disk Imaging

Depending on the objectives and scope of an investigation, analysts have different disk acquisition methods available at their disposal. Each method has its advantages and disadvantages. In an ideal situation, responders would acquire all data relevant to an investigated case. However, business priorities, technology constraints, and other factors may influence the choice. For this reason, it is vital that responders understand the implications of their choice and set expectations with the necessary technology and business stakeholders.

It is also important to emphasize that for many enterprises, eradicating an attacker from the compromised environment and recovering business operations is a priority, rather than gaining a full understanding of an intrusion. This priority may, in turn, influence decisions regarding data acquisition. Incident responders have the following acquisition methods available at their disposal:

Forensic Acquisition   *Forensic acquisition,* also referred to as *forensic duplication* or *forensic imaging,* refers to creating a bitstream copy of data contained on a storage device. Responders must power down the system, remove the hard drive, and connect it to another system that runs acquisition software. Often, incident responders use hardware and software write blockers to prevent the writing of data to the acquired media.

Logical Acquisition   *Logical acquisition* refers to copying files and folders using the native filesystem on which the data resides. Logical acquisition does not capture metadata or allow the recovery of deleted data. This method is commonly used in electronic discovery, and it is a good choice when forensic acquisition is not possible, or when analysts need to retrieve specific files of interest.

Targeted Acquisition   *Targeted acquisition* refers to the acquisition of specific types of forensic data or content; for example, analysts may acquire program execution artifacts to determine evidence of malware on a compromised system.

Cloning   *Cloning* refers to creating a bitstream copy of data from one storage media to another. Cloning differs from forensic acquisition. The former is just a copy, whereas the latter includes things such as handling of errors and bad sectors, applying cryptographic hashes to account for chunks of data, and producing logs as part of the acquisition.

The guiding principle of forensic data acquisition is to minimize any changes to the state of the system, including data residing on disk volumes. This principle is especially vital during investigations that may result in a legal proceeding.

One way to ensure that digital media has not been altered or modified during the acquisition process is to use a write blocker. A *write blocker* is a hardware or software tool that permits read-only access to a storage device.

In the case of hardware write blockers (see Figure 3.1), incident responders connect a storage device containing forensic data and the acquisition workstation to a portable physical write blocker device. Consequently, there is no direct connection between the acquisition workstation and the storage device containing forensic data. An acquisition workstation is a computer that analysts exclusively use to acquire and analyze forensic data.

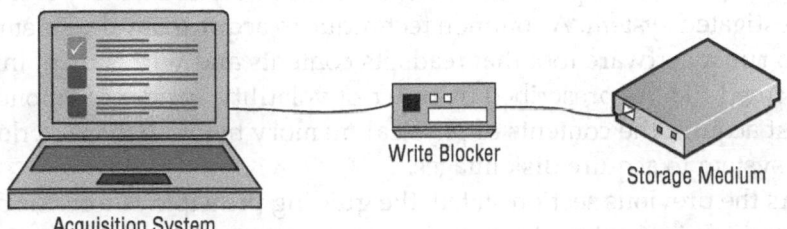

Figure 3.1: Hardware write blocker

Software write blockers (Figure 3.2), on the other hand, run on the acquisition workstation, and the storage device directly connects to it. The write blocker software monitors commands that the acquisition workstation sends to the storage device and blocks any write requests.

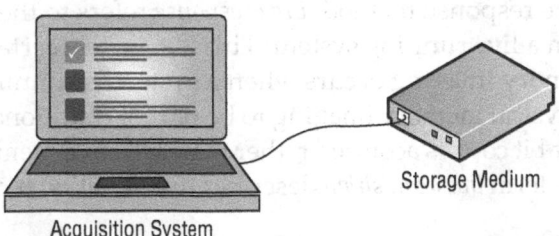

Figure 3.2: Software write blocker

System Memory Acquisition

Attackers increasingly rely on in-memory attacks, which may not leave trails on disk. Additionally, they may use the legitimate tools that they find in the compromised environment. The incident response community refers to this approach as "living off the land." Furthermore, a significant amount of data that is of vital importance to investigations resides in volatile memory only. Powering down a system inevitably destroys that data. In the breach investigations that I have led, volatile memory sometimes was the only source of digital evidence that allowed the team to determine evidence of attacker activity, such as fileless malware. For this reason, analysts should strive to acquire volatile system memory when possible.

To preserve crucial volatile data as part of forensic acquisition, incident responders acquire the contents of the physical memory from an investigated system. A common technique to acquire physical memory is to run a software tool that reads its contents and writes them into a specified file. As prescribed by order of volatility, incident responders must acquire the contents of physical memory before powering down the system to acquire disk images.

As the previous section stated, the guiding principle of forensic data acquisition is to minimize any changes to the state of the system from which incident responders can acquire data. Because the memory acquisition process takes place while the system is running, some changes are inevitable and, in some instances, can hinder the analysis process. For this reason, it is vital that incident responders keep their interaction with the system to a minimum and document all actions that they take during the imaging process to account for state changes where possible.[4]

Some incident response professionals consider physical memory acquisition as a live response method. *Live response* refers to the collection of artifacts from a live running system. This is true to a certain degree, as physical memory imaging occurs when a system is running. However, I consider physical memory imaging to be part of traditional acquisition when a bit-by-bit copy is acquired rather than selective memory contents. Arguably, the term *live acquisition* describes this situation most accurately.

Tool Considerations

Several commercial and open source tools exist that incident responders can leverage to perform forensic imaging of digital media. The choice of tool depends on the type of media and data that responders intend to acquire. Regardless of choice, a sound forensic tool should possess the following characteristics:

- Acquire an exact bit-for-bit copy of the original medium, and gracefully handle any errors that occur during the imaging process

- Prevent the writing of data and commands to the storage device
- Generate a detailed log of actions and errors that occurred during the process

Also, a crucial feature that incident responders need to consider when choosing an acquisition tool is the ability to handle encryption technologies at the device, volume, container, and file level.

Examples of popular commercial forensic acquisition tools include X-Ways Forensics,[5] EnCase Forensic Software,[6] and Magnet ACQUIRE[7] for smartphone acquisition. Incident responders also have open source alternatives available at their disposal, such as the Paladin forensic suite.[8] Forensic imaging of disk volumes is, to a certain degree, more natural with Unix-like systems that come with the dd (data duplicator) utility that duplicates data at the disk block level.

Forensic Acquisition Use Cases

Forensic acquisition is a foundational pillar of incident response. The following list presents common use cases for traditional forensic acquisition:

Comprehensive Analysis   Analysts need to conduct an in-depth examination of a compromised system to determine how an attacker compromised and interacted with the system, including reconstructing a timeline of events. This approach often follows a triage during which analysts determine that a system may contain vital digital evidence.

Legal Requirement   An organization anticipates legal action, and digital evidence is relevant to the legal case. Many courts still consider forensic acquisition as the gold standard when it comes to the admissibility of digital evidence in court. Chapter 6 discusses this topic in depth.

Data Recovery   Incident responders need to search for evidence of deleted files and, where possible, recover those files. For example, as part of an investigation, analysts often recover binary files associated with malware or data that the attacker staged for exfiltration.

Internal Investigation   An organization needs to conduct an internal investigation related to an insider threat or other employee-related case. In such a case, analysts typically acquire a forensic image of the custodian's workstation, especially if the organization anticipates a legal action against the custodian.

In addition, acquiring the contents of physical memory is often invaluable when dealing with obfuscated or encrypted malware, or malware that employs antiforensic techniques.

Live Response

The threat landscape, as well as the business environment, has significantly evolved over the last several years, and traditional forensic acquisition is no longer a viable option on its own. Incident responders increasingly rely on live response techniques to acquire and triage forensic data before acquiring forensic images of specific systems for in-depth analysis. *Live response* is the acquisition of forensic data from a system that is running. The following list presents common reasons why enterprises increasingly leverage live response during investigations:

- Powering down a system that supports a core business function to acquire an image of the hard drive can have a significant impact on business operations and may not be a viable option for many organizations.

- Traditional forensic acquisition may take hours and often requires physical presence at the system in question, and the acquired image can take up hundreds of gigabytes and, in some instances, even terabytes of storage.

- Traditional forensic acquisition does not scale out and may not be appropriate alone for investigations where an attacker gained a significant footprint in the compromised environment.

- In some instances, incident responders are interested in triaging a system to determine evidence of compromise and to qualify the threat. Acquiring a forensic image in such a case might be excessive.

Historically, the term *live response* referred to the acquisition of volatile data only. However, with the evolution of forensic tools, the term now refers to the acquisition of both volatile data that resides in the system memory and persistent data residing on disk volumes while the system is running. Many live response tools can extract and parse specific forensic artifacts without the need to extract entire files containing digital evidence or to perform live acquisition of the entire contents of the physical memory.

Live Response Considerations

In an ideal situation, incident responders can preserve the state of an investigated system during the acquisition process. Because incident responders need to run tools and utilities to acquire forensic data through live response, the acquisition process inevitably results in minor changes to the state of the system. This is a compromise between using traditional forensic acquisition and performing a rapid triage without affecting business operations. Consequently, it is vital that analysts not only understand what changes occur as a result of running utilities and software, but also document those changes alongside acquisition procedures, tools, and exact dates and times when they run those tools.

One option to perform a live response acquisition is to run utilities and acquisition software locally on the system in question. However, remote acquisition has become a common practice. Enterprises often operate in multiple geographic locations with no local incident response presence. Furthermore, enterprises typically host systems that support business functions and processes in remote data centers and cloud computing environments. For this reason, remote acquisition is a logical choice.

It is important to emphasize that live response does not replace traditional forensic acquisition and analysis. In fact, incident response teams often leverage live response methods to perform a rapid triage and determine the scope of an incident. Then, analysts acquire data from specific systems using traditional forensic methods to perform an in-depth examination of the data and determine how the attacker interacted with the compromised systems.

Live Response Tools

Live response acquisition can be as simple as running a single command on an investigated system, or as complex as deploying enterprise-grade software across an entire organization to facilitate data collection at scale. There is no single recipe for collecting forensic data through live response. Let's briefly look at three frequent approaches that incident responders leverage during investigations: manual collection, scripts, and enterprise-grade software. The choice of method depends on the specific needs of an investigation. Incident response teams typically leverage a combination of those approaches.

Manual acquisition is the simplest of the three approaches. It involves running commands and utilities to acquire specific data or a set of system artifacts. For example, an analyst might choose to run a native command to list processes and active network connections on a system of interest to determine whether there is evidence of malware on the system. This approach is suitable for a rapid assessment only. It does not scale out well, and running multiple commands and utilities on a system can inadvertently alter the state of the system and hinder the triage process.

A *script* is a simple program, or a sequence of commands written for a command interpreter available on the host system, such as Microsoft PowerShell or the Bash shell, to perform a specific task. Incident responders can bundle multiple commands into a script that they would otherwise have to run on a system manually. A script can also contain custom logic to operate on data, such as converting the returned data set into a specific output format. Another common approach is to create a script to execute a series of data collection utilities programmatically. Incident responders frequently combine native commands, custom logic, and execution of specific utilities to automate the data acquisition process. Data collection scripts are a significant enhancement compared to manual collection, and they can help incident responders acquire the necessary data efficiently. However, stand-alone scripts do not scale out well and are insufficient for large-scale investigations.

In recent years, several open source and commercial tools have emerged that allow incident responders to collect forensic data through live response at scale. Some tools can support data collection from thousands of systems simultaneously. In most cases, *enterprise-grade tools* consist of the following components: a software agent, centralized storage, and a console. To facilitate data collection, an enterprise must deploy a software agent to systems in scope. The agent runs the configured tasks and forwards the collected data to a centralized storage server. A *console* is a software application that allows responders to configure and interact with the agents, access the collected data, and perform other administrative tasks.

Many commercial products offer a cloud-configuration deployment, where the centralized console and storage resides in a public cloud. In my experience, this deployment model is typically easier to implement than an on-premises solution.

It is also important to emphasize that the primary purpose of some enterprise-grade tools is ongoing detection and response. The cybersecurity community refers to those tools as *endpoint detection and response (EDR)*. Examples of popular EDR platforms include CrowdStrike Falcon,[9]

Carbon Black,[10] and Fidelis Endpoint.[11] Figure 3.3 provides a conceptual representation of the cloud-configuration model.

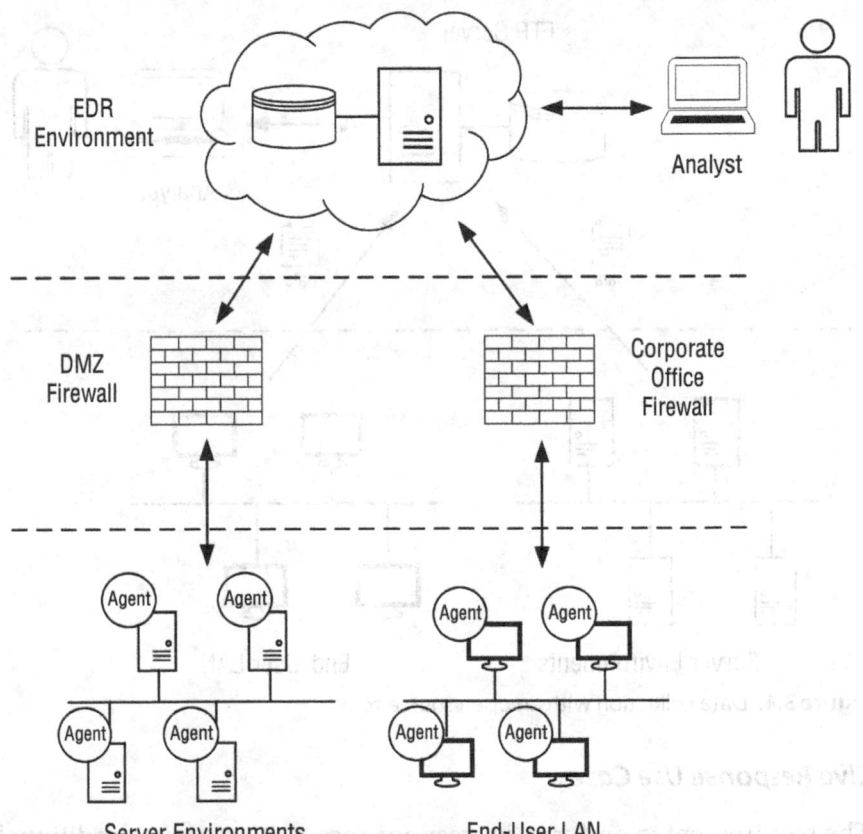

Figure 3.3: EDR deployment in cloud configuration

Several alternative open source tools, such as osquery,[12] are available that allow analysts to collect forensic data at scale. It is important to emphasize that the deployment of open source tools requires an incident response team to deploy an infrastructure to support the collection of forensic data, such as a File Transfer Protocol (FTP) server. This requirement is especially applicable during large-scale investigations where analysts must acquire data from multiple systems simultaneously. Incident response teams usually leverage a software deployment tool to deploy a data collection script at scale and configure that script to send the collected data to an FTP server, as depicted in Figure 3.4.

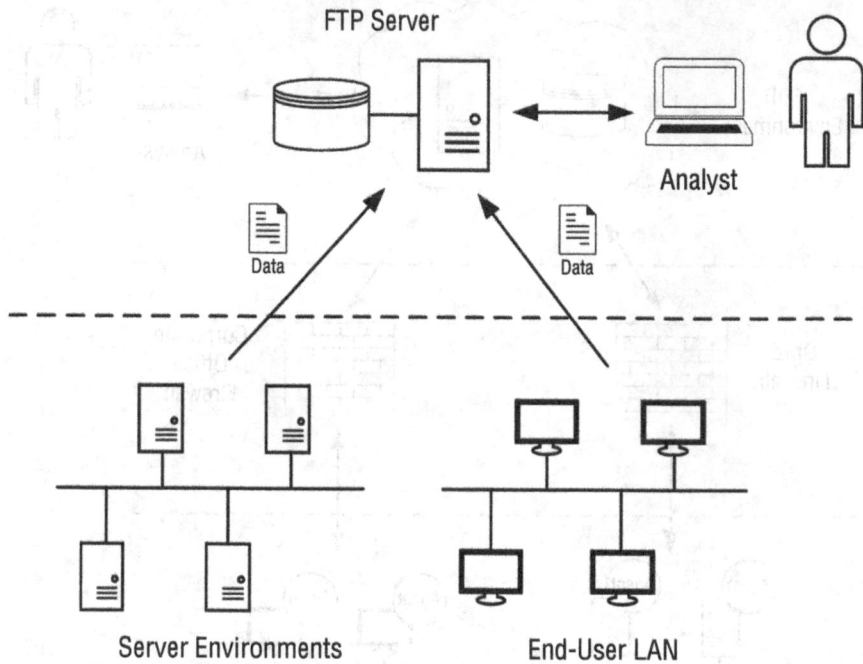

Figure 3.4: Data collection with an open source tool

Live Response Use Cases

The requirement to perform live response acquisition versus traditional forensic acquisition depends on many internal and external factors. There is no predefined guidance on when to choose one method over the other. The following list presents common use cases where incident responders typically acquire forensic data through live response:

- An investigated system is mission-critical, and the enterprise cannot afford any downtime. Acquiring forensic data through live response techniques is a sensible compromise that allows responders to conduct an investigation while taking business priorities into consideration.

- An enterprise received an alert or detected suspicious activity associated with a specific system and needs to perform a rapid triage to assess the system for evidence of compromise before deciding whether traditional forensic acquisition is required.

- A system in question resides in a remote location with no incident response personnel presence to perform forensic acquisition. With the right tool, remote acquisition through live response may be a sufficient alternative.

- Incident responders suspect that an attacker compromised multiple systems within the enterprise, and they need to perform data collection at scale. Because traditional forensic acquisition does not scale out well, this is one of the more common use cases for live response.

It is also important to mention that some cloud computing vendors that provide infrastructure-as-a-service (IaaS) offerings do not allow their customers to acquire or download virtual machines hosted in their clouds. As a result, live response may be the only option to acquire data and conduct an investigation of systems hosted in their environments.

Incident Response Investigations in Virtualized Environments

Virtualization has dramatically changed how organizations provision and utilize technology. It is also the fundamental technology that underpins cloud computing. In simple terms, *virtualization* is a technology that abstracts and emulates hardware resources and allows enterprises to run multiple virtual instances of software on the same hardware. By implementing virtualization, enterprises consolidate hardware and more efficiently use hardware resources, which leads to a higher return on investment (ROI).

Enterprises typically leverage two types of virtualization: traditional virtualized environments and cloud computing. A traditional virtualized environment consists of on-premise physical servers that run multiple virtual machines. Each physical server runs hypervisor software that emulates hardware resources for each guest virtual machine. In simple terms, an enterprise owns and maintains the physical hardware as well as the virtual machines that run on it.

In contrast, in the cloud computing model, a vendor owns physical servers and the underlying infrastructure. The services that customers provision run on shared resources and the vendor manages the underlying infrastructure. This concept is known as *multitenant architecture*.

Cloud computing vendors typically offer services that fall within the following cloud computing models, as depicted in Figure 3.5.

Infrastructure-as-a-Service   In the *Iaas* model, the vendor makes compute resources, such as virtual servers, available to its customers through self-service and manages the underlying infrastructure.

Platform-as-a-Service   In the *platform-as-a-service (PaaS)* model, the vendor provides a platform-based service, such as web servers, which allows its clients to develop and run applications without the need to provision and manage the underlying infrastructure, such as compute resources and storage.

Software-as-a-Service   In the *software-as-a-service (SaaS)* model, the vendor hosts an application and makes it available to its clients over the Internet, often leveraging a subscription-based pricing model.

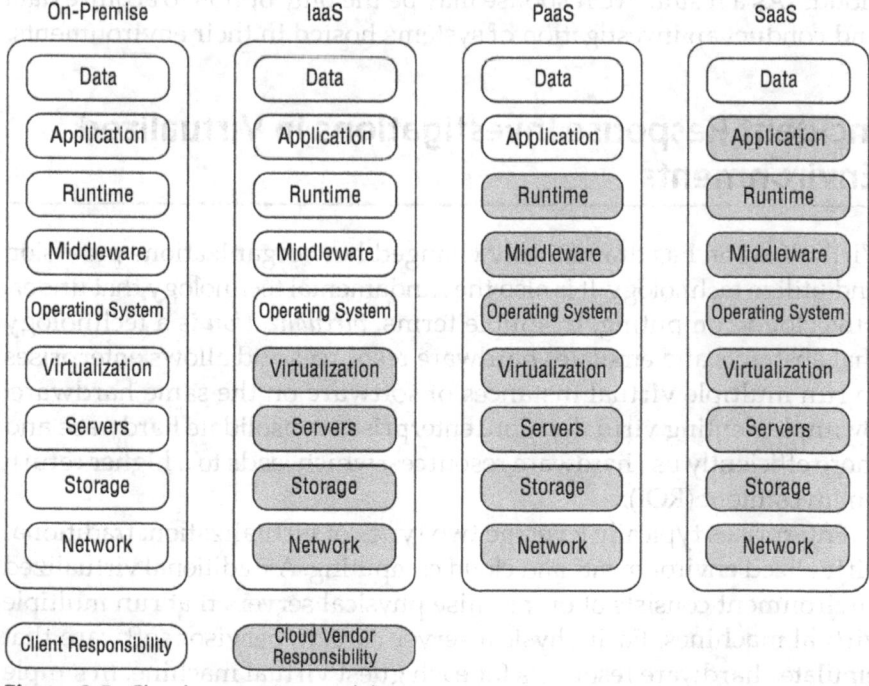

Figure 3.5: Cloud computing models

Virtualization and cloud computing have influenced how incident responders acquire digital evidence and conduct investigations. The following sections discuss considerations that incident response teams need to take into account during investigations that involve traditional virtualization and cloud computing technologies.

Traditional Virtualization

Arguably, *traditional virtualization* made the forensic acquisition of digital evidence easier to a certain degree. Instead of employing software and hardware tools to create disk and physical memory images, responders can acquire a copy of a virtual machine. Traditional virtualization has not affected live response acquisition in a significant way because the acquisition process takes place when a virtual machine is running, as in the case of a physical system.

Typically, the most effective method to acquire a virtual machine in a forensically sound manner is to create a snapshot. A *snapshot* is a point-in-time copy of a virtual machine that captures the entire state of the machine at the time of acquisition, including virtual disks and virtual memory. An added benefit of this method is that incident responders do not need physical access to the server. Instead, they remotely connect to the virtualization software, also known as a *hypervisor*, and create a snapshot. The exact process of creating a snapshot of a virtual machine depends on the underlying virtualization software. Once the snapshot is available, incident responders download it to a local machine or a forensic lab for analysis.

One consideration that incident responders need to keep in mind is the available network bandwidth. It may take a significant amount of time to download a snapshot of a large virtual machine over a network with low-bandwidth links.

Cloud Computing

Forensic acquisition of digital evidence in cloud computing environments varies from vendor to vendor. Furthermore, the type of data that incident responders can acquire depends on the provisioned services. For example, if an enterprise provisions compute resources leveraging the IaaS model, analysts may be able to acquire snapshots of virtual machines of interest if the vendor provides such functionality. With the PaaS model, responders may be able to acquire only application event logs. With SaaS services, clients typically have no access to event logs and digital evidence, and they must rely on the vendor to assist with an investigation.

Forensic Acquisition

In most cloud computing deployments, virtual servers consist of compute resources connected to virtual storage over a low-latency network link.

Consequently, forensic acquisition of virtual servers in cloud environments largely depends on the architecture of a specific cloud and the facilities that a cloud vendor makes available to its clients. The following paragraphs briefly describe the acquisition options offered by a few large cloud computing vendors as of this writing:

Microsoft Azure   Microsoft Azure allows its customers to acquire snapshots of virtual servers in numerous ways and makes them available for download in the *Virtual Hard Disk (VHD)* format.[13] Incident responders can easily download snapshots through a Graphical User Interface (GUI) as long as they have appropriate permissions.[14]

IBM Cloud   IBM took a similar approach to Microsoft by allowing its customers to create *virtual server infrastructure (VSI)* snapshots and making them accessible via remote access. The approach that both vendors took makes it easy for incident responders to acquire virtual servers of interest.

Amazon Web Services   In contrast, Amazon Web Services (AWS) does not allow full control of its *Elastic Compute Cloud (EC2)* servers and does not provide its customers with a facility to create snapshots of EC2 instances. The only option available is to create a point-in-time snapshot of the *Elastic Block Store (EBS)* volume containing the operating system files. To facilitate forensic analysis, analysts typically provision another EC2 instance in the AWS cloud, mount the system EBS volume to it, and acquire a forensic image of that volume for offline analysis using tools such as the dd utility. An alternative approach is to provision a forensic analysis system in the AWS cloud and mount the EBS volume snapshot to that system for analysis in the cloud. Because EBS volume snapshots do not preserve system memory, incident responders must rely only on disk artifacts during the analysis process.

Rackspace   Rackspace has taken a completely different approach. The vendor does not provide its clients with a facility to create snapshots of virtual servers provisioned in its cloud. Incident responders must contact Rackspace to obtain a copy of a compromised virtual server.

Unfortunately, major cloud computing providers, such as those discussed here, do not provide a facility to include virtual memory as part of snapshotting a virtual machine. The only exception to this rule is when a client provisions a bare-metal server and has root access to the hypervisor. A *hypervisor* is hardware virtualization software that creates and runs virtual machines. To acquire the memory contents of a virtual machine, analysts must use traditional approaches as described in the earlier section "System Memory Acquisition."

Log Management in Cloud Computing Environments

Incident response in cloud computing environments typically combines traditional forensic methods with methods and tools native to a specific cloud computing environment. As part of their service catalog, cloud computing vendors often offer logging and monitoring services that provide a rich set of data to incident responders. This data can be a range from events associated with programmatic access to services to alert notifications of suspicious activities. The following list provides examples of security log management solutions within the AWS and Microsoft Azure clouds:

AWS   CloudTrail and CloudWatch are two primary services that incident response teams can leverage to investigate incidents in AWS environments. CloudWatch is a service that allows organizations to collect, search, and visualize data from multiple AWS resources.[15] Administrators can configure specific resources to forward data to CloudWatch, such as security event logs for correlation, analytics, and searching. The CloudWatch Events feature also enables AWS customers to monitor for specific events and send automated notifications using one of the available notification methods. CloudTrail, on the other hand, provides detailed event logs of every activity that occurs on AWS resources, including the AWS console, AWS command-line interface, and API calls.[16] Organizations can customize the types of events that CloudTrail logs and forward those logs into CloudWatch. The service also provides an optional file integrity verification feature that analysts can use to establish if an attacker tampered with log files.

Microsoft Azure   Microsoft Azure offers the Security Center solution that continuously analyzes their cloud workloads to identify and alert on malicious activity.[17] The service leverages CTI and analytics to detect suspicious security activity. Azure's customers can create custom security alerts and integrate events from other security products into the Security Center. Analysts can use this service to create a timeline of events of interest.

It is worth mentioning that customers who provision IaaS resources often have the choice to purchase and install security tools such as EDR on provisioned virtual servers that can help them investigate intrusions through live response techniques. This topic is specific to each vendor and is outside the scope of this book.

Before concluding the discussion on incident response in cloud computing environments, it is important to note that cloud infrastructures are dynamic by nature. Administrators can configure cloud computing services to provision and manage resources dynamically to meet changing capacity requirements. Consequently, the risk of destroying forensic data is much higher than in traditional on-premises environments. For this reason, incident responders should acquire and preserve data from cloud computing resources at the earliest opportunity.

Leveraging Network Data in Investigations

Network monitoring during an incident investigation provides invaluable information on attacker activity. Incident responders leverage network data, also referred to as network telemetry, to augment forensic analysis, to gain better visibility into attacker activity, and to scope incidents more effectively.

One option to collect network data is to deploy dedicated monitoring systems and mirror the traffic that traverses a compromised network. Another option that incident response teams often leverage is to use existing systems and tools. In the case of the latter approach, incident responders can enhance the monitoring capabilities to capture data of interest. The enhancements may include ingesting indicators of compromise (IOC) discovered during forensic analysis and identified through CTI enrichment, enhancing logging, turning on additional security features, or creating custom dashboards to visualize data of interest.

This section discusses common types of network data that various tools can generate and that incident responders leverage during investigations.

Firewall Logs and Network Flows

For firewall logs to be of value to incident responders, administrators must configure appropriate logging policies. Many organizations log deny events only. Although this is a good practice, logging allow events is of high value since most threats target open network ports. It is important to emphasize that verbose logging can result in a significant amount of data that organizations need to store according to their log retention policies. In cases where logging of all traffic that a firewall allows is impractical, organizations must prioritize verbose logging for business-critical applications and services.

In contrast, network flows are aggregated connection data between a source and the destination regardless of whether or not the traffic passes through a firewall. Some network infrastructure systems, such as routers, generate network flows based on the raw network traffic that they handle. Organizations also increasingly deploy special-purpose appliances on their networks that monitor network connections and generate network flows for operational and security purposes.

Some cloud computing vendors provide a service to collect flow logs from virtual private clouds (VPCs), such as AWS VPC flow logs for AWS[18] or Network Security Group (NSG) flow logs[19] available in the Microsoft Azure cloud.

Firewall logs and network flows allow incident responders to determine key characteristics of network connections, including the following:

- Timestamp
- Source and destination of a connection
- Protocol
- Connection length
- Amount of data transferred between both ends of the connection

Analysts examine this data to determine activities such as lateral movement or connectivity to attacker command and control (C2) infrastructure, or to establish if a threat actor transported data out of the compromised environment.

Furthermore, analysts can correlate firewall logs and network flows with host-based IOC and artifacts to corroborate evidence and identify attacker activity more accurately.

In some cases, firewall logs and network flows are the only sources of evidence on which analysts can rely, such as cases where crucial digital evidence has been destroyed or overwritten in the course of system operation.

Enterprises typically send firewall logs and network flows to a centralized log aggregation solution for data retention and analysis. By storing the data in a centralized location, incident responders can easily query and correlate data from multiple sources without the need to acquire it locally from specific systems.

Proxy Servers and Web Gateways

Proxy servers and web gateways are tools that are placed between internal networks and the Internet and that allow enterprises to control connectivity to the Internet from systems hosted on the internal networks. Additional benefits that both solutions provide include the following:

- Hiding internal networks from the Internet
- Caching certain static content to improve user experience
- Enforcing security policies

Over the years, proxy servers have evolved into secure web gateways that allow organizations to enforce security policies at a granular level, including the following:

- Preventing access to certain resources such as social media
- Filtering out certain types of malicious traffic, such as connections to known attacker C2 infrastructures
- Detecting and preventing transportation of certain types of data, such as payment card numbers

Proxy servers and secure web gateways are yet another important source of evidence in incident investigations. Information that proxy servers and web gateways generate that is of value to analysts includes the following:

- IP addresses and URLs associated with resources that users accessed
- Application protocol metadata
- Connection time and length
- Amount of data transferred between the source and the destination
- Action taken by the proxy server or web gateway

Analysts can use this information to determine which users clicked on phishing links, to establish evidence of access to a malicious website, or to establish when an attacker introduced malware to the environment.

Full-Packet Capture

Full-packet capture (PCAP) is the most voluminous source of data available to incident responders. In larger environments, PCAPs could fill terabytes of storage within hours.

A PCAP records an entire network session between a source and the destination. For many organizations, this approach to collecting network telemetry is impractical. An additional hurdle that organizations must overcome is the ability to decrypt the data as it flows through their network. For this reason, many organizations choose to collect and retain PCAP in response to certain events only.

Incident responders can acquire PCAP data by leveraging existing network security systems and tools or by deploying dedicated appliances on the compromised network. Advanced enterprise-grade systems often have the capability to acquire entire session data for connections that trigger certain events. Another option is to collect partial network session data, such as a predefined message length, to capture application protocol metadata.

Incident responders may collect PCAP data to analyze network connections between malware-infected systems and an attacker C2 infrastructure, to establish whether the attacker uses exploits as part of their operations, or to identify communication patterns necessary to develop signatures for detection of the attacker activity.

A vital consideration that incident responders must take into account before collecting PCAP data is encryption. The majority of communication between client systems and web servers, especially over the Internet, uses end-to-end encryption to prevent man-in-the-middle attacks. A *man-in-the-middle attack* is one that allows a threat actor to eavesdrop on communications between two parties. Some PCAP solutions are capable of decrypting network traffic before storage. However, this capability requires organizations to implement a rigorous certificate management regime.

Collecting PCAP data is particularly useful when an adversary uses an unencrypted channel for C2 communication, such as a web shell that passes commands in clear text. I have come across cases where an attacker heavily leveraged "living off the land" techniques that left minimal forensic evidence on endpoint systems. PCAP data proved to be an invaluable source of forensic data in investigating those cases.

Incident responders have two options available at their disposal to deploy a PCAP appliance: a SPAN port and a network tap. A SPAN (Switch Port Analyzer) port is a feature available on some routers and switches that duplicates network traffic passing through those devices to the configured port that has a PCAP appliance attached. A network tap, on the other hand, is a hardware appliance placed inline between two network nodes that can mirror network traffic at the hardware level to an attached PCAP appliance.

A SPAN port is a good option for networks with relatively low throughput, because it can quickly oversubscribe and cause a negative performance impact on a switch or a router. The primary benefit of a SPAN port is that the configuration does not require network downtime. In contrast, a network tap can handle higher volumes of network traffic but requires network downtime to deploy it physically in between two network devices. Figure 3.6 provides a graphical representation of these two solutions.

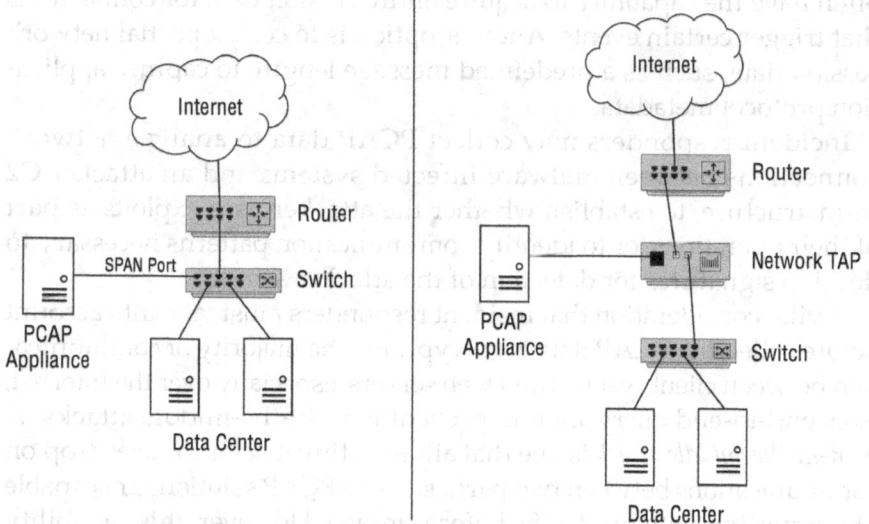

Figure 3.6: A network tap and a SPAN port

Before collecting PCAP data, organizations need to consider legal and regulatory requirements. For example, standards such as PCI DSS mandate that organizations encrypt card payment data traveling over a computer network. For this reason, a good practice is to configure filters to collect only data that is relevant to the investigated case, such as known attacker C2 IP addresses and domains.

Furthermore, if incident responders preserve PCAP data in a defensible manner, litigation attorneys can use that data as digital evidence during a legal proceeding.

Identifying Forensic Evidence in Enterprise Technology Services

Every organization needs a set of core services to provide vital information technology services to the enterprise and support core business functions. Enterprise technology services are technology resources that are typically shared across an enterprise. They include a wide range of technologies, from infrastructure technologies and applications to security tools.

The data that enterprise technologies generate is often valuable in incident investigations. In some cases, data that those technologies generate may be the only evidence of attacker activity in a compromised environment.

This section discusses some of the more common enterprise technologies that incident responders may examine to find evidence of malicious activities and to determine attacker activity.

Domain Name System

The *Domain Name System (DNS)* is central to the Internet and corporate networks. The primary function of DNS is to provide mapping between human-readable domain names and IP addresses. DNS is a registry that stores mapping between domain names and IP addresses that computers can query to retrieve IP address information in a programmatic manner. Of course, this is a simplified definition. In reality, DNS is a complex service with many low-level components whose discussion is outside the scope of this book. Figure 3.7 displays an example structure for a fictious domain name, example.com.

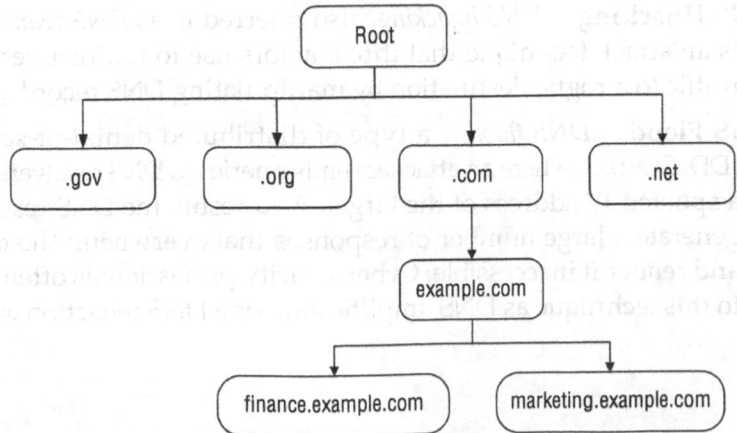

Figure 3.7: An example of DNS structure

DNS resolution data is an important source of digital evidence. Analysts can leverage DNS resolution logs to establish information such as IP addresses associated with users who clicked malicious links contained in phishing emails, or queries for attacker C2 domains associated with malware-infected systems. Historical DNS query logs can also help incident responders establish an incident timeline and, in some cases, scope the incident more accurately.

Furthermore, incident responders can enrich DNS query logs with CTI data to detect attacker C2 communication. DNS resolution logs include the following information that is of value to investigations:

- The domain for which a client system requested resolution

- The IP address of the client that requested the resolution

- The resolution result—that is, an IP address that maps to the requested domain

The following list discusses a few use cases where analyzing DNS data is invaluable.

DNS Tunneling   *DNS tunneling* is a technique that involves inserting data into DNS queries and responses. Threat actors leverage DNS tunneling for activities such as C2 or data exfiltration. Analysts can look for unusual payloads in DNS messages and perform a frequency analysis on DNS traffic to detect DNS tunneling.

Fast Flux   *Fast Flux* is a technique that involves using a single domain name that resolves to multiple IP addresses and then continually changing them at a relatively high frequency using round-robin scheduling and time-to-live (TTL) for a DNS resource record. Threats, such as botnets, often rely on this technique.

DNS Hijacking   *DNS hijacking*, also referred to as *DNS redirection*, is an attack technique that threat actors use to redirect network traffic to a rogue destination by manipulating DNS records.

DNS Flood   *DNS flood* is a type of distributed denial-of-service (DDoS) attack where an attacker sends queries to DNS resolvers with a spoofed IP address of the target. As a result, the DNS resolvers generate a large number of responses that overwhelm the target and render it inaccessible. Cybersecurity professionals often refer to this technique as DNS amplification or a DNS reflection attack.

It is crucial to emphasize that some of the techniques discussed above are challenging to detect for victim organizations without specialized tools and infrastructure. For this reason, enterprises need to work with specialized service providers, domain registrars, and vendors to detect and mitigate DNS-related attacks.

Dynamic Host Configuration Protocol

The *Dynamic Host Configuration Protocol (DHCP)* is a network protocol that enterprises use to configure end-user devices automatically with IP address information and other network parameters. The protocol assigns IP addresses to end-user devices from a pool of addresses that a network administrator configures on a DHCP server.

Incident responders can leverage DHCP logs to track down systems of interest given IP address information. For example, during a firewall log review, an analyst may establish that a particular IP address assigned to an end-user device connected to an attacker C2 infrastructure. By examining DHCP logs, the incident responder may establish what system had that particular address assigned when the event occurred and perform a forensic examination of that system.

Web Servers

A *web server* is software that runs on top of an operating system and serves web content to client systems. The content typically includes HTML documents, as well as scripts, images, and style sheets necessary to render the web content in the user's web browser.

Incident responders need to keep in mind two important considerations when investigating incidents involving web servers: virtual hosting and load balancing. *Virtual hosting* refers to cases where one web server hosts multiple websites.

Larger websites typically leverage *load balancing* to increase throughput and implement fault tolerance. This means that web clients make requests for content to a load balancer that acts as a reverse proxy and distributes those requests to a group of dedicated web servers. A *reverse proxy* is a service that retrieves requests from web servers on behalf of client computers.

If an application leverages load balancing, it is crucial that the enterprise configures its infrastructure to record the IP address of the original client that made a request. This is of vital importance to investigations.

Web server log files and web content are crucial sources of digital evidence when investigating web application incidents. The level of detail that log files contain depends on the configured logging policy. Typically, access logs contain request attributes such as the following:

- Timestamp
- Client IP address
- URL or accessed resources
- User-agent string that describes the type of client software that made the request
- Server response code

Databases

For many threat actors, the ultimate objective of their attack is stealing data that is of high value to enterprises, typically to monetize it on the dark web. Reviewing database event logs can help incident responders establish evidence of attacker access to data and data theft.

Database auditing and logging capabilities vary from technology to technology. Furthermore, transactional logging can lead to performance issues, and for this reason many organizations choose to disable it. I have come across organizations in my consulting engagements that implement dedicated logging solutions for services that generate a high volume of event logs, such as databases or firewalls, for searching and visualization of log data. System administrators then configure those services to forward security events only to security tools for correlation. The following log types are of high value to incident responders when investigating data theft cases:

Audit logs: Provide information relating to successful and failed login attempts, permission changes, and other security-related events

Error logs: Typically include error messages logged as a result of incorrectly formed queries

Transaction logs: Provide a record of transactions that occurred on a database and are invaluable in establishing how an attacker interacted with the database

Client connection logs: Include a timestamp and an IP address from which an attacker accessed the database

Security Tools

Most enterprises deploy security tools to protect their assets, even if it involves only installing anti-malware software on user workstations. Security software and security systems are a vital source of digital evidence, and the data that they generate can augment host forensics. This section briefly discusses common security tools that incident responders leverage in their investigations.

Intrusion Detection and Prevention Systems

Intrusion detection systems (IDS) and *intrusion prevention systems (IPS)* are general-purpose solutions that perform inspection of network traffic to detect known and predictable threats. These days, most enterprise-grade IDS/IPS solutions also offer one or more of the following features that are useful from an incident response perspective:

- Ingestion of threat intelligence feeds.
- Capability to buffer entire network sessions in memory.
- Decompiling of binaries.
- Execution of commands and files in a virtual environment and emulation of their effect to determine whether they are malicious. This technique is also referred to as *heuristic detection*.

Incident responders often leverage IDS/IPS products to build the custom signatures necessary to identify attacker activity, to monitor for connectivity to an attacker C2 infrastructure, or to determine whether the attacker uses exploits and other network-based tactics as part of their overall operations.

Web Application Firewalls

Web application firewalls (WAFs) work in a similar manner to IDS/IPS solutions. However, their primary use is to detect and protect web applications against Internet-borne application-level attacks. WAF solutions provide a more granular inspection of web traffic than IDS/IPS products, including protection against application logic attacks. These attacks typically exploit a flaw in the business logic of an application rather than the source code. Incident responders can leverage WAF telemetry to determine web application exploits or evidence of malware, such as web shells in the compromised environment. A *web shell* is a software script that an attacker places on a web server exposed to the Internet to maintain access to the compromised environment.

Data Loss Prevention Systems

Data loss prevention (DLP) is a technology that passively inspects the content of network communications for evidence of sensitive data that organizations try to protect. This may include information such as credit card data, certain types of personal data, documents with certain embedded marking, and any type of data that is subjected to regulatory and compliance requirements. Endpoint-based DLP technology is also becoming increasingly popular.

Vendors developed DLP technology primarily to address insider threat risks. However, events that DLP systems produce are also useful in cyber breach investigations, especially if correlated with other sources of data. In fact, many organizations detect potential cyber breaches upon reviewing DLP alerts and events.

Analysts can review DLP events to determine the type of data that a threat actor attempted to transport out of the compromised environment as well as to establish the source and timing of the activity. As with other technologies that inspect network communications, organizations need to ensure that DLP technology can decrypt those communications before inspecting the content.

Threat actors, whose primary purpose is to steal data, often collect and consolidate data from the compromised environment on a staging server. To evade network DLP, they typically create encrypted archives as part of the staging process. During breach investigations, I have observed evidence of software utilities and libraries that attackers use for encryption, such as the WinRAR utility. For this reason, organizations need to consider deploying DLP solutions close to where their highly sensitive data resides, in addition to placing a DLP appliance at the network perimeter. For example, an enterprise may install host DLP software on systems that store and process highly sensitive data or deploy a network DLP appliance on internal network segments that handle such data.

Antivirus Software

Anti-malware software logs are often a vital source of evidence during investigations, especially if the software has verbose logging. In fact, in many cases, anti-malware alerts are early signs of breaches. Incident responders can use this information to establish investigative leads, determine early evidence of a breach, develop IOCs, and correlate the data with other forensic artifacts.

Endpoint Detection and Response

One of the latest additions to the endpoint protection market are *EDR* tools. A typical EDR tool records and stores system events and other metadata associated with system behavior, including tracking changes to registries, filesystem activity, tracking processes, suspicious process relationships, and network connections. Analysts can query that data as well as create custom detection logic for specific threats.

As described in the section "Live Response," incident responders can leverage EDR tools to query system data at scale for evidence of attacker activity. For example, an incident responder can ingest IOCs recovered from a compromised system into an EDR tool and scan other systems for the presence of those indicators to determine the scope of the compromise.

Honeypots and Honeynets

Honeypots and *honeynets*, also referred to as *deception technology*, are decoy mechanisms that enterprises deploy and make appealing to threat actors to collect intelligence on attacker behavior and detect adverse events. Honeypots and honeynets typically closely resemble real systems, and often data, that appear as legitimate to the attacker. Examples of use cases for deploying honeypots and honeynets in the corporate environment include the following:

- Identifying CTI information, such as IP addresses, malware domain names, and tools, among others
- Identifying evidence of lateral movement, especially with harvested credentials
- Collecting attacker malware samples for analysis
- Identifying access attempts to protected data

For example, an incident response team may choose to deploy a honeypot server and allow an attacker to infect it with malware to recover and study the malware sample. I have led cyber breach investigations where the first indicator of adverse activity was an alert triggered by deception technology.

Incident responders must take extra care and devise strict mechanisms when implementing deception technologies to prevent an attacker from using those systems as a pivot point to access other parts of the network.

Log Management

Systems and software applications generate events in the form of log messages to provide information about state changes during the course of their operation.

Enterprises often create audit and logging policies to ensure that systems and software applications generate sufficient event logs necessary to detect and investigate cybersecurity incidents and troubleshoot issues. An enterprise may also enact log retention policies to ensure compliance with laws and regulations. System administrators interpret the policies to create logging baselines for specific technologies and enforce those policies through technical mechanisms.

This section discusses topics related to log management, and it explains its importance in incident investigations.

What Is Logging?

Logging is the process of generating and storing event logs for a specific period of time. Systems and software applications generate event logs that typically contain timestamped data that describes the events. Many of the event types, such as Windows security events or web server access logs, are invaluable in investigating cybersecurity incidents. System administrators and application developers configure logging based on policies and the need to track specific information about the behavior of systems and applications.

The types of events that systems and applications can generate vary from technology to technology. Regardless of the source, event logs that are of interest to incident responders typically fall within one of the following categories:

Application   *Application logs* are notifications specific to a software application that contain information about transactions, errors, or warnings, such as web requests that users make to a web application. For example, web server access logs provide information about client requests for web resources. Access logs often allow analysts to establish how and when an adversary compromised a web server to gain unauthorized access to a computer network.

System   *System events* contain information specific to hardware and operating system state changes, such as system reboots, installation of new services, or the addition of hardware components to the system, as well as events relating to errors and warnings. For example, service event logs allow analysts to establish evidence of malware. Threat actors often install malware to run as a service to survive system reboots and maintain persistence on the compromised system.

Security   *Security events* are messages that systems and software applications generate that contain security-related information. Security events are also known as *audit events* because systems and applications generate them according to audit policies that administrators configure, such as user authentication or changes to user permissions auditing. Security events are critical to most incident investigations. For example, analysts often leverage authentication events to establish evidence of unauthorized access to systems with harvested credentials and lateral movement within the compromised environment.

In addition to the event categories discussed here, administrators configure logging levels to set the verbosity of information that systems and software applications generate. Another way of looking at logging levels is in terms of urgency. Systems and applications are more likely to produce high volumes of informational messages as opposed to event logs that require urgent attention from administrators.

Logging capabilities vary from technology to technology. The following topics describe typical logging levels:

Debug   System administrators and software developers typically enable *debug-level logging* to troubleshoot issues and trace execution of software components. Debug messages are verbose and voluminous and can severely impact system performance. For this reason, system administrators and developers enable debugging only for a short period.

Informational   *Informational-level logging* designates log messages associated with expected changes in the state of a system or software application. Informational events do not require immediate attention, and administrators often configure them to provide context for other events. For example, an administrator may configure informational logging to track transactions that occur in a database.

Warning   *Warnings* are error conditions that systems and software applications encounter that do not immediately impact their operations in a significant way. For example, a system may generate a warning message when CPU or memory utilization exceeds a certain threshold.

Error   *Error messages* are typically associated with malfunctions of system hardware or a software application. For example, a system may generate an error message when a user attempts to access a system resource that does not exist.

Alert   An *alert* designates an event that requires immediate attention from a system administrator. For example, a system may generate an alert when a hardware component fails or a particular software subsystem stops running.

A vital consideration when configuring a logging level is the volume of event logs that a system or a software application can generate. System administrators need to provision the necessary storage capacity and ensure that the logging does not impact system performance severely. Furthermore, a higher logging level may result in significant volumes of "noise" that may obstruct relevant event logs that analysts may want to review as part of an investigation. For this reason, enterprises need to create logging baselines that allow them to capture the events that are necessary to support incident investigations while ensuring that system performance remains at the desired level.

What Is Log Management?

Logging, especially in large enterprise environments, results in significant volumes of log data that organizations must store and manage to comply with data retention policies and regulatory requirements. Retaining log data is also vital to the investigation of cybersecurity incidents. Historically, enterprises stored log messages locally on the systems that generated them. However, with increasing volumes of data and the necessity to comply with data retention policies and regulations, a requirement for a new approach emerged.

Log management is an approach to managing the lifecycle of log data that systems and applications generate in the course of their operations.

Log management is also crucial to incident response. Event logs are extremely useful in detecting and analyzing incidents. In many cases, they allow responders to establish facts about attacker activity from unauthorized access to systems to data theft.

It is not uncommon for an attacker to dwell on a compromised network for weeks or even months before an enterprise discovers the intrusion. Consequently, responders require easy access to historical event logs from compromised systems, enterprise services, security tools, network appliances, and other sources. Having all the necessary event logs in a centralized location and the ability to search and correlate those logs easily can significantly accelerate investigations.

Log Management Lifecycle

Several distinct stages occur during the log management process. When choosing a log management solution, enterprises need to evaluate product features and capabilities to ensure that a prospective solution supports the entire log management lifecycle. Scalability is a vital consideration. Enterprises that expect growth and expansion of their information technology environments need to ensure that they acquire a solution that can scale out and meet additional capacity requirements. Figure 3.8 displays a typical log management lifecycle.

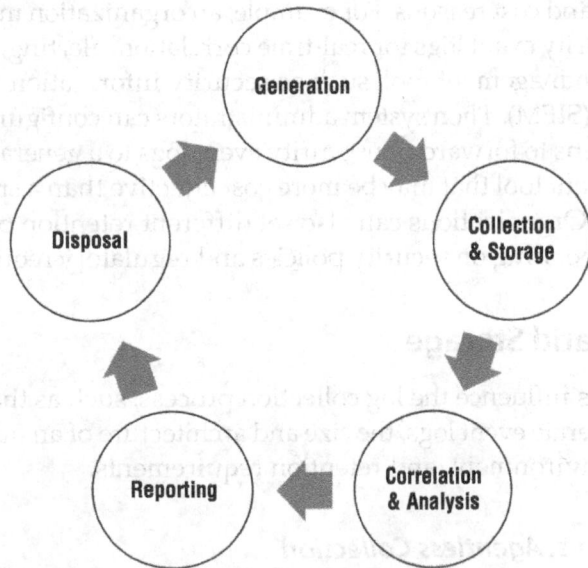

Figure 3.8: Log management lifecycle

Generation   Systems and software applications generate event logs in response to state changes, as described earlier in this chapter.

Collection and Storage   This step involves collecting and shipping event logs to a centralized log management tool. Depending on the source, organizations can collect event logs using agent or agentless technology and store the captured logs according to a data retention policy. Organizations may choose to make more recent event logs available for immediate access and archive older logs to achieve cost savings.

Correlation and Analysis   This includes looking for patterns and associations among disparate event logs, often coming from different sources, as well as a detailed examination of log data to make informed decisions.

Reporting   This involves reporting findings, as well as creating metrics and trends to facilitate decision making.

Disposal   This includes disposing of event logs when their age exceeds the data retention policy requirement. In some instances, organizations may choose to archive those logs to low-cost storage, such as tapes.

Some enterprises differentiate between security and nonsecurity event logs and take different approaches to collecting and storing those logs for performance and cost reasons. For example, an organization may choose to collect security event logs for real-time correlation, alerting, and analysis in a log management tool, such as security information and event management (SIEM). Then system administrators can configure systems and applications to forward nonsecurity event logs to a general-purpose log management tool that may be more cost effective than a specialized security tool. Organizations can also set different retention policies on those logs depending on security policies and regulatory requirements.

Collection and Storage

Several factors influence the log collection process, such as the technologies that generate event logs, the size and architecture of an information technology environment, and retention requirements.

Agent-Based vs. Agentless Collection

Enterprises leverage two primary methods to collect event logs as part of the collection process: a software agent and agentless collection.

Some platforms include native utilities that can forward log data to a remote server using de facto protocols. For example, platforms based on the Unix operating system often include a remote logging utility that can forward event logs to a centralized location using the syslog protocol. Other platforms, such as Windows, require a software agent that extracts event logs and ships them to a remote server, often using a proprietary protocol. The software agent acts as a log forwarder. In both cases, an administrator can configure what types of logs a platform sends to a remote server. It is worth noting that Windows implemented the Windows Event Collector and Windows Event Forwarder in recent years that can receive, store, and forward event logs from a local computer that leverages the subscription model.[20]

Log Management Architectures

Three primary log collection architectures exist that enterprises can leverage: centralized, distributed, and hybrid. Enterprises need to consider factors such as the volume of event logs, locations of their environments, regulatory requirements, and data retention policies when deciding on a log management architecture.

A *centralized log management architecture*, as depicted in Figure 3.9, is well suited for smaller networks where the volume of event logs that systems and applications generate is relatively low. The primary advantage of this architecture is ease of management. Furthermore, organizations can easily search for and correlate data in one centralized console. However, the major drawback is that centralized log management deployments do not scale well and can be a single point of failure. As the volume of the log events grows, this approach may become impractical.

A *distributed log management architecture*, as depicted in Figure 3.10, addresses some of the shortcomings of the centralized model. It allows enterprises to scale out their log management solution by adding extra log collectors as the volume of log data grows. An enterprise may choose to implement separate collectors for specific network segments, data centers, or even geographic locations. Flexibility is one of the primary advantages of this model. Furthermore, an enterprise may also choose to deploy a dedicated collector for event logs from systems and applications that are subject to regulatory requirements, such as PCI DSS. The primary disadvantage of this model is management overhead. Furthermore, a distributed model does not provide a single source of truth for log data, and that makes it challenging to correlate event logs across the enterprise.

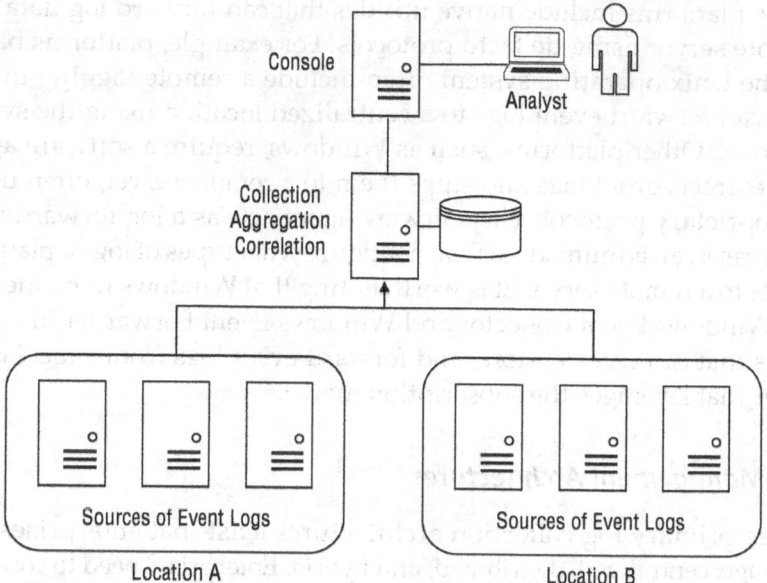

Figure 3.9: Centralized log management architecture

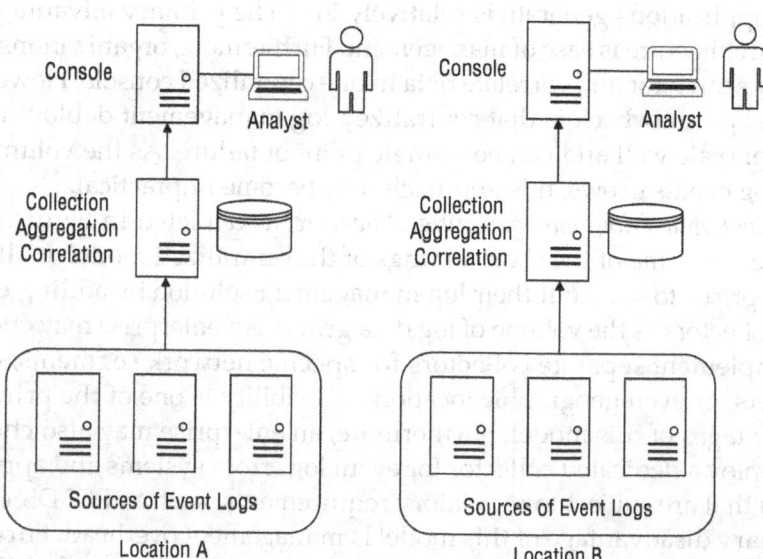

Figure 3.10: Distributed log management architecture

A *hybrid log management architecture,* as depicted in Figure 3.11, brings together the best of both worlds. With this model, enterprises deploy separate collectors to gather event logs from different locations. In turn, those collectors integrate with a centralized console that allows administrators to access and manage all of the components from a single location. This model enables enterprises to scale out their log management solution while providing administrators and analysts with the ease of management. Furthermore, a hybrid architecture allows administrators and analysts to access and correlate event logs across the enterprise without the need to access separate log management servers.

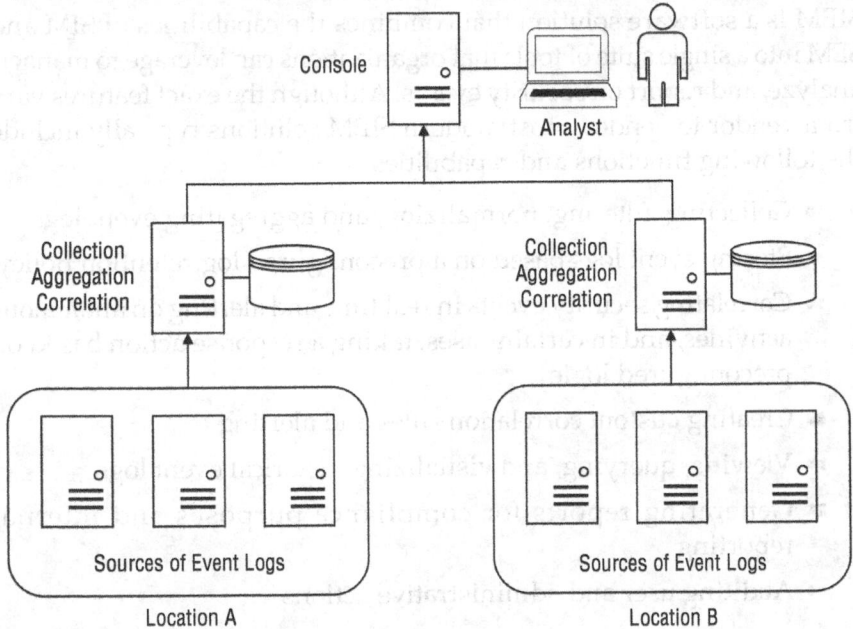

Figure 3.11: Hybrid log management architecture

One vital consideration that both system administrators and incident responders need to take into account is time. Administrators should strive to configure systems and software applications to timestamp log messages in Coordinated Universal Time (UTC). In cases where this approach is not feasible, a log management tool should have the functionality to account for time differences when correlating and visualizing log data from disparate systems.

Managing Logs with a SIEM

In response to growing volumes of log data across the enterprise and the need to manage that data effectively, different solutions have emerged on the market. Historically, organizations approached security event management (SEM) and security information management (SIM) as two separate disciplines. SEM products focused on collection, aggregation, and correlation of event logs, whereas SIM products were centered around the analysis of historical data and reporting. In the early 2000s, security vendors started to release solutions that merged the capabilities of SEM and SIM. Gartner coined the term *security information and event management (SIEM)* to describe the new approach.[21]

What Is SIEM?

SIEM is a software solution that combines the capabilities of SIM and SEM into a single suite of tools that organizations can leverage to manage, analyze, and report on security events. Although the exact features vary from vendor to vendor, most modern SIEM solutions typically include the following functions and capabilities:

- Collecting, filtering, normalizing, and aggregating event logs
- Storing event logs based on a preconfigured log retention policy
- Correlating security events in real time and alerting on anomalous activities, and in certain cases, taking a response action based on preconfigured logic
- Creating custom correlation rules and alerting
- Viewing, querying, and visualizing historical event logs
- Generating reports for compliance purposes and internal reporting
- Auditing user and administrative actions

Furthermore, some SIEM solutions can also ingest network flow data and correlate it with security events to detect anomalous activities more effectively. A sensible approach is to filter and forward to SIEM event logs from systems and applications that are necessary to satisfy specific use cases. For example, organizations may choose to send security event logs into SIEM and leverage a more cost-effective log management solution for other types of logs, as discussed earlier in this section.

The true power of SIEM lies in correlation. Security systems and software applications independently generate events that might not reveal anomalous activities by themselves. Modern SIEM solutions provide out-of-the-box correlation rules and allow administrators to build custom rules to detect anomalous activities.

Correlation rules are logical expressions that a correlation engine leverages to pair events based on predefined variables and to look for relationships, patterns, sequences, and certain values that may be indicative of attacker activity. For example, an analyst may configure a correlation rule to trigger an alert when a remote interactive logon occurs with a service account. Administrators configure service accounts to provide a security context for services running on a Windows server.[22] Consequently, remote interactive logon with service accounts should be a major concern. If the incoming event logs satisfy the logic of a particular rule, SIEM will execute a predefined action. For example, a SIEM may trigger an alert or send an email notification to an analyst. Furthermore, SIEM solutions often have the capability to augment correlations with CTI to detect threats more accurately. In recent years, vendors have also been extending SIEM capabilities with behavioral models to look for suspicious activities and big data analytics.

These days many SIEM platforms provide the capability to integrate third-party software to enhance their functionality. For example, enterprises commonly integrate Security Orchestration, Automation, and Response (SOAR) platforms with SIEM to automate response to incident types with predefined response procedures, such as phishing. Another example is user behavior analytics (UBA) software that enterprises can leverage to detect anomalies, such as behavioral patterns typical of insider threats.

SIEM Considerations

Although SIEM appears to be a silver bullet for solving many security concerns, SIEM products also have many shortcomings that organizations need to take into account before deploying them into their environments.

It is crucial to emphasize that event logs are just one of many artifacts that allow analysts to establish evidence of compromise. In many cases, event logs are not indicative of attacker activity by themselves. For example, a successful authentication with elevated credentials to a specific system may not be suspicious by itself. However, when correlated with program execution artifacts and other investigative findings, the same activity can be indicative of lateral movement. In many cases, event logs provide context and do not replace forensic analysis. Consequently, even the most sophisticated SIEM rules cannot replace human judgment and business context.

Another significant drawback of SIEM is that rule-based correlation typically produces a high number of false-positive events and organizations must dedicate significant time and resources to SIEM tuning. This characteristic is especially applicable to misconfigured environments with poor information technology management practices. Finally, many information technology environments are not mature enough for a SIEM. A lack of retention policies, configuration baselines, or standardized security audit policies can render a SIEM ineffective.

To maximize the value of SIEM, organizations must create and update correlation rules continually as the threat landscape evolves. Out-of-the-box rules are typically a good start, but they are not sufficient in the long term. Analysts need to understand the network architecture in their organizations, deployed technologies, security controls, and CTI to build meaningful rules that satisfy security use cases. This approach often requires significant effort and resources.

Summary

Technology sourcing to support incident investigations is vital to building a cyber breach response program.

Incident response teams can leverage both open source and commercial tools to acquire and analyze forensic data, as well as to automate some aspects of their work. Enterprises need to consider factors such as cost, support and maintenance, and usability when sourcing technology. Some nonstandard problems may also require incident response teams to develop custom tools.

A critical aspect of incident response is data acquisition. Incident responders have traditional forensic acquisition methods at their disposal, as well as live response. With business priorities and the need for quick answers, live response is becoming increasingly popular. However, traditional forensics still plays a vital role in investigations.

Virtualization and cloud computing brought a new dimension to incident response. Incident responders need to be familiar with common virtualization and cloud computing platforms to analyze and scope breaches effectively.

The data that network systems, enterprise technologies, and security tools generates is a valuable source of digital evidence. It can help analysts to determine attacker activity in the compromised environment, efficiently scope incidents, and generally augment host forensics.

Finally, with increasing volumes of data, enterprises need to consider implementing log management solutions to comply with data retention policies and regulations, as well as to ensure that they preserve event log data that may be vital to incident investigations.

Notes

1. github.com.

2. Interpol, "Global Guidelines for Digital Forensics Laboratories," May 2019, available at www.interpol.int/en/content/download/13501/file/INTERPOL_DFL_GlobalGuidelinesDigitalForensicsLaboratory.pdf.

3. IETF, Request for Comments: 3227, tools.ietf.org/html/rfc3227.

4. Michael Hale Ligh, Andrew Case, Jamey Levy, and AAron Walters, *The Art of Memory Forensics: Detecting Malware and Threats in Windows, Linux, and Mac Memory*, Wiley, July 2014.

5. X-Ways Forensics, www.x-ways.net/forensics.

6. OpenText, EnCase Forensic, www.guidancesoftware.com/encase-forensic.

7. Magnet Forensics, Magnet ACQUIRE, www.magnetforensics.com/resources/magnet-acquire.

8. Sumuri, Paladin Forensics Suite, sumuri.com/software/paladin.

9. CrowdStrike, Falcon Endpoint Protection, www.crowdstrike.com.

10. WMware Carbon Black, www.carbonblack.com.

11. Fidelis Cybersecurity, www.fidelissecurity.com.

12. osquery, osquery.io.

13. Microsoft Azure, Windows VMs Documentation, "Create a snapshot," docs.microsoft.com/en-us/azure/virtual-machines/windows/snapshot-copy-managed-disk.

14. Microsoft Azure, Windows VMs Documentation, "Download a Windows VHD from Azure," docs.microsoft.com/en-us/azure/virtual-machines/windows/download-vhd.

15. Amazon CloudWatch Documentation, docs.aws.amazon.com/cloudwatch/index.html.

16. Amazon CloudTrail Documentation, docs.aws.amazon.com/cloudtrail/?id=docs_gateway.

17. Azure Security Center, "Tutorial: Respond to security incidents," docs.microsoft.com/en-us/azure/security-center/tutorial-security-incident.

18. Amazon Virtual Private Cloud, "VPC Flow Logs," docs.aws.amazon.com/vpc/latest/userguide/flow-logs.html.

19. Azure, Network Watcher Documentation, Network security group flow logging, "Introduction to flow logging for network security groups," docs.microsoft.com/en-us/azure/network-watcher/network-watcher-nsg-flow-logging-overview.

20. Windows Dev Center, "Windows Event Collector," docs.microsoft.com/en-us/windows/win32/wec/windows-event-collector.

21. Gartner Glossary, "Security Information And Event Management (SIEM)," www.gartner.com/en/information-technology/glossary/security-information-and-event-management-siem.

22. Microsoft Docs, "Service Accounts," docs.microsoft.com/en-us/windows/security/identity-protection/access-control/service-accounts.

Crafting an Incident Response Plan

Having an incident response plan is a critical step in cyber breach response. The worst time for an organization to realize that they are not prepared for an incident is when a cyber breach occurs.

An effective incident response plan encompasses an incident management process, roles and responsibilities, communication flows, escalations, and postmortem activities, among other components. Each of those components is vital to respond effectively to various types of incidents and help organizations operate during significant cyberattacks.

This chapter discusses the incident response lifecycle, how to build an effective incident response plan, and how to improve incident response capabilities continuously.

Incident Response Lifecycle

An *incident response lifecycle* is a conceptual model that represents the different phases during the lifespan of a cybersecurity incident. To respond to incidents effectively, incident responders need to follow a structured and organized approach with clearly defined roles and responsibilities.

Various industry standards present slightly different lifecycle approaches. However, they draw on similar concepts, and there is usually a significant amount of overlap between them.

Figure 4.1 displays a lifecycle that the National Institute of Standards and Technology (NIST) in the United States included in its Computer Security Incident Handling Guide.[1]

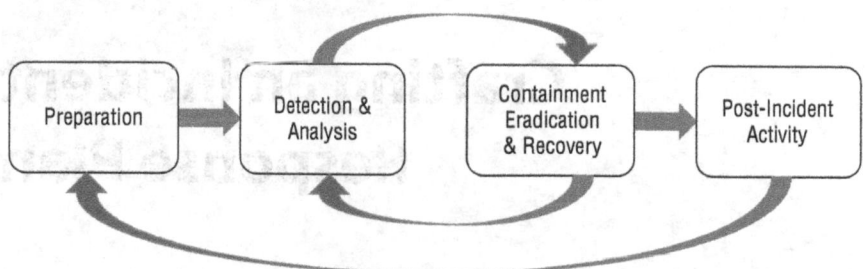

Figure 4.1: NIST Incident Response Lifecycle

In my personal experience, this lifecycle closely reflects the typical sequence of stages and functional activities during the incident response process and is a good model for organizations of all sizes to follow.

Preparing for an Incident

Preparation is a fundamental component of the incident response lifecycle that directly impacts the remaining stages. Without appropriate and continuous preparation, incident response teams cannot effectively execute activities in the remaining stages.

Preparation encompasses a wide range of activities that require an integrated and cross-functional effort, funding, and other resources, as well as executive-level support. Arguably, this book is all about preparation and ensuring that enterprises can develop capabilities to enable them to respond to and handle cybersecurity incidents effectively.

It is crucial to emphasize that preparation is not a one-off activity. Instead, it is a continuous and incremental effort that tightly integrates with a continual improvement process that I discuss later in this chapter.

The following list describes common activities that enterprises may undertake as part of the preparation phase. This list is by no means comprehensive. Strategic planning typically drives these activities.

Planning   Planning includes all the activities that enterprises must adopt before operationalizing incident response capabilities.

Depending on the current state and maturity of a cyber breach response program, enterprises may enact policies, create new or extend the existing capabilities, and dedicate additional funding and other resources to cyber breach response.

Hiring and Training Incident Response Personnel   As organizations respond to external and internal factors that drive the requirement for cyber breach response, enterprises may need to hire additional personnel or train existing employees to ensure that their skills are up to date.

Documenting Processes and Procedures   As enterprises evolve and cyber risk changes, incident response teams need to update existing documentation continuously and create new procedures to stay abreast of cyber threats and continually improve their capabilities.

Acquiring and Sourcing Technology   Innovation drives changes in the technologies that enterprises deploy to support their business operations. Incident responders need to evaluate and adjust their tools and other investigative technologies periodically to ensure that they can respond to incidents that involve a wide range of technologies deployed within the enterprise.

Building Relationships with Key Stakeholders   As discussed in Chapter 2, a Cybersecurity Incident Response Team (CSIRT) is a cross-functional team. Incident responders need to maintain and build new relationships with technology and business stakeholders to support incident investigations. This step may also include building relationships with vendors and entering into a retainer agreement with a digital forensics and incident response (DFIR) firm.

Continual Improvement   *Continual improvement* refers to the ongoing effort to identify underperforming areas of incident response and to implement specific improvements to address those areas.

Detecting and Analyzing Incidents

Incident symptoms can manifest themselves in numerous ways. Analysts must pay close attention to potential adverse events to determine whether those events are indicative of an incident, or even a breach. *Incident detection and analysis* is the process of identifying suspicious events and assessing their details to determine an appropriate response procedure.

Detection and Triage

Systems and software applications may generate a significant volume of events each day. Analysts often rely on correlation tools and alerting mechanisms to detect those events that may be indicative of potentially malicious activity.

After detecting a suspicious event, analysts must triage it to determine whether the event warrants an incident declaration. As part of the triage phase, analysts need to apply business and technology context to determine the nature of the event. For example, an analyst might review a configuration baseline of a specific application to determine whether an investigated event could have been generated in the course of normal system operations and that it represents an expected system behavior. The outcome of the detection and triage phases is a decision whether or not to proceed with incident declaration.

During the detection and triage phases, analysts typically document known event information; collect contextual data, such as asset configuration and system and network architecture; correlate the incident information with previous similar incidents; and review cyber threat intelligence (CTI) associated with the events of interest.

If an event warrants incident declaration, analysts typically determine the scope and impact, assign classification and prioritization to the incident, and log an incident ticket in a case management platform. Analysts may also escalate the incident if it reaches a specific severity threshold. It is crucial to note that as the investigation progresses and analysts establish new evidence, the scope, impact, and severity of the incident may change.

The detection and triage phases can be performed as one task or two separate activities. The latter approach is typical of organizations that have a mature incident response capability or have outsourced security monitoring to a managed security service provider (MSSP).

Analyzing Incidents

In some situations, it is clear that an event is indicative of an incident. For example, an internal server attempts to open a network connection to an infrastructure associated with a threat actor. In other cases, an analyst might escalate an event to incident response personnel to perform a more in-depth analysis to establish whether the event is indicative of a cyber incident.

Incident analysis refers to a structured process designed to examine security data and evaluate the cause of an incident. As part of the analysis phase, incident responders create indicators of compromise (IOC) that the enterprise can use to drive containment and eradication activities. To perform a sound and thorough analysis, incident responders must possess advanced skills and experience in the area of digital forensics. Chapter 2 discusses skills in detail. Depending on the nature of an incident, typical analysis activities may include the following:

- Acquiring and preserving forensic data
- Developing investigative leads
- Analyzing host and network data
- Malware analysis
- CTI enrichment
- Scoping the incident
- Creating a timeline of attacker activity
- Reporting

Containment, Eradication, and Recovery

Containment, eradication, and recovery are the final phases of the incident response lifecycle. Organizations often refer to these activities as *remediation*.

Containing a Breach

Containment encompasses specific actions that enterprises take to prevent a threat from spreading, thereby limiting the damage that a cyberattack has on their business. Depending on the nature of a cyberattack, incident responders may execute containment activities in a single step or take a two-phased approach: short-term containment and long-term containment.

Short-Term Containment   *Short-term containment* constitutes an immediate action that an enterprise may take to prevent the exacerbation or propagation of a threat. Examples include isolating systems infected with malware from the network or implementing access control mechanisms to prevent malware from connecting to an attacker's command and control (C2) infrastructure.

Long-Term Containment   *Long-term containment* refers to implementing *temporary* security measures to secure access to and prevent a threat actor from accessing crucial assets while the investigation process and remediation planning are underway. For example, as part of long-term containment, an enterprise may implement a jump host to control access to an environment that stores or processes highly confidential data. If deemed appropriate during postincident activities, these measures may become more permanent adjustments to strengthen the organization's defenses further.

Eradicating a Threat Actor

After successfully containing an incident, the next step is to take short-term and medium-term steps to eradicate the threat actor from the compromised environment. As in the case of containment, eradication strategies vary from incident to incident. For this reason, incident response teams should document containment and eradication procedures for common incident types that occur in their environments. Examples of eradication actions include the following:

- Upgrading legacy and unsupported technologies to more secure technologies
- Resetting credentials for compromised users
- Patching vulnerabilities that an attacker exploited to advance their attack strategy
- Implementing strict access control mechanisms to allow only authorized users and applications access to specific resources
- Removing malware and persistence mechanisms

Incident responders need to understand the full scope of a compromise and the associated IOCs before executing containment and eradication activities. As part of the attack strategy, attackers typically establish several footholds in the compromised environment. An insufficiently remediated environment may still allow the attacker access to the network. If there is a means for the attacker to come back to the compromised network, they will likely do so.

Containment and eradication may sometimes be at odds with forensic data acquisition. In some cases, ad hoc containment or eradication can destroy forensic evidence. For example, it is not uncommon for information technology support personnel to re-image malware-infected end-user workstations without considering the need to acquire and preserve digital evidence. Consequently, creating and documenting containment strategies for specific incident types is vital to ensure a balance between effective containment and preserving forensic evidence, especially if the evidence may be required for legal purposes.

Recovering Business Operations

The objective of the recovery phase is to restore the affected systems and software applications fully into an operational state. Also, as part of recovery, enterprises need to ensure that the restored systems and applications have appropriate controls in place to prevent similar incidents from reoccurring. For example, if a threat actor compromised domain administrative credentials, an enterprise may need to consider controls such as *multifactor authentication (MFA)* to prevent a similar compromise in the future. MFA is an authentication scheme that requires at least two independent pieces of information from separate categories of credentials, such as a password and a random number generated by an authentication token, to authenticate into a system.

During incidents and breaches that have a severe impact on business operations, enterprises may need to activate a disaster recovery (DR) plan and switch operations to alternate systems that are in a known good state during recovery. Enterprises can leverage standards, such as ISO 22301:2019, to prepare for, respond to, and recover from disruptive events.[2]

Enterprises typically recover systems and software applications in a phased approach. Depending on the nature and scope of an incident, it may take days or even weeks to recover fully. For this reason, project management and close collaboration between technology and business stakeholders, as well as vendors, is vital.

Post-Incident Activities

Post-incident activities include steps that enable organizations to capture opportunities for improvement and implement specific measures to enhance their cyber breach response program. Post-incident activities are typically part of continual improvement that enterprises implement to govern a cyber breach response program. Organizations can implement two types of measures as part of continual improvement: tactical and strategic.

Tactical measures encompass relatively simple program enhancements that do not require substantial funding or dedicated projects. Enterprises typically identify tactical measures through a *lessons-learned meeting* and a root cause analysis. To identify tactical improvement measures, organizations need to hold a lessons-learned meeting after each major incident, as well as regular meetings to review responses to minor incidents. The outcome of a lessons-learned meeting is a set of tactical measures that enterprises can implement within a relatively short time.

If an enterprise identifies major gaps and issues that cannot be resolved as part of day-to-day operations, the incident response manager must escalate those issues to senior management for risk evaluation. Based on the outcome of the risk evaluation process, an enterprise may decide to implement strategic measures that typically require funding and dedicated projects. In other words, strategic measures are long-term enhancements that require dedicated resources. For example, an organization may choose to implement an endpoint detection and response (EDR) tool as a strategic measure to reduce the risk associated with threats that evade traditional antimalware software. Another way of thinking about tactical vs. strategic measures is in terms of short-term and long-term enhancements.

Process-mature organizations typically implement strategic measures as part of a continuous improvement process. Enterprises implement this process as part of governance to evaluate the performance of a cyber breach response program continually against its objectives. A steering committee is typically a body that is responsible for implementing and enforcing governance.

Understanding Incident Management

The purpose of a cybersecurity incident management process is to minimize the operational and informational impact of a cybersecurity incident, as well as to ensure that the enterprise can continue business operations while under a cyberattack.[3] Consequently, the objectives of the incident management process include the following:

- Use standardized procedures and incident models to manage incidents and cyber breaches consistently.

- Ensure that all stakeholders who participate in the incident management process have clearly assigned roles and responsibilities.

- Increase the visibility and reinforce the need for cyber breach response among business and technology stakeholders.

- Align the response to cyberattacks with risk appetite and business priorities.
- Facilitate effective communication among tactical teams and management.

An effective incident management process helps enterprises manage residual risk and ensure that business, cybersecurity, and technology stakeholders work together toward the same goals.

The scope of an incident management process encompasses all cybersecurity incidents that negatively impact an enterprise, not only cyber breaches. If not addressed promptly, even minor incidents can progress into enterprise breaches that may negatively impact revenue, brand reputation, and business operations and lead to legal exposure. For this reason, enterprises need to create a cross-functional cybersecurity incident management process to address the aftermath of a cyberattack before real damage occurs.

An effective incident management process delivers several benefits to organizations:

- Minimizes the impact of cyberattacks on business operations
- Addresses incidents and system breaches before substantial damage occurs
- Identifies defensive weaknesses and gaps through lessons learned and continual improvement
- Reduces legal exposure resulting from cyber breaches
- Prioritizes response activities based on business priorities
- Helps to identify risks that can lead to exposure

Identifying Process Components

An *incident management process* is a structured and coordinated set of activities designed to address the aftermath of a cyberattack. A high-quality process contains several components that work in tandem to produce a desired and repeatable outcome.

Defining a Process

Enterprises should define specific events that trigger an incident management process. When an event triggers an incident management process, the process takes an input, executes a set of activities, and produces an outcome. For example, a security alert may trigger an incident management process. Incident responders take all known information about the incident and proceed through a series of activities to understand its nature and prevent its spread within the enterprise. The outcome of the process may be incident resolution and control recommendations designed to prevent similar incidents from reoccurring.

Figure 4.2 captures an incident management process as a set of components organized into three categories: controls, enablers, and the process itself. I derived this model from the Information Technology Infrastructure Library (ITIL).[4]

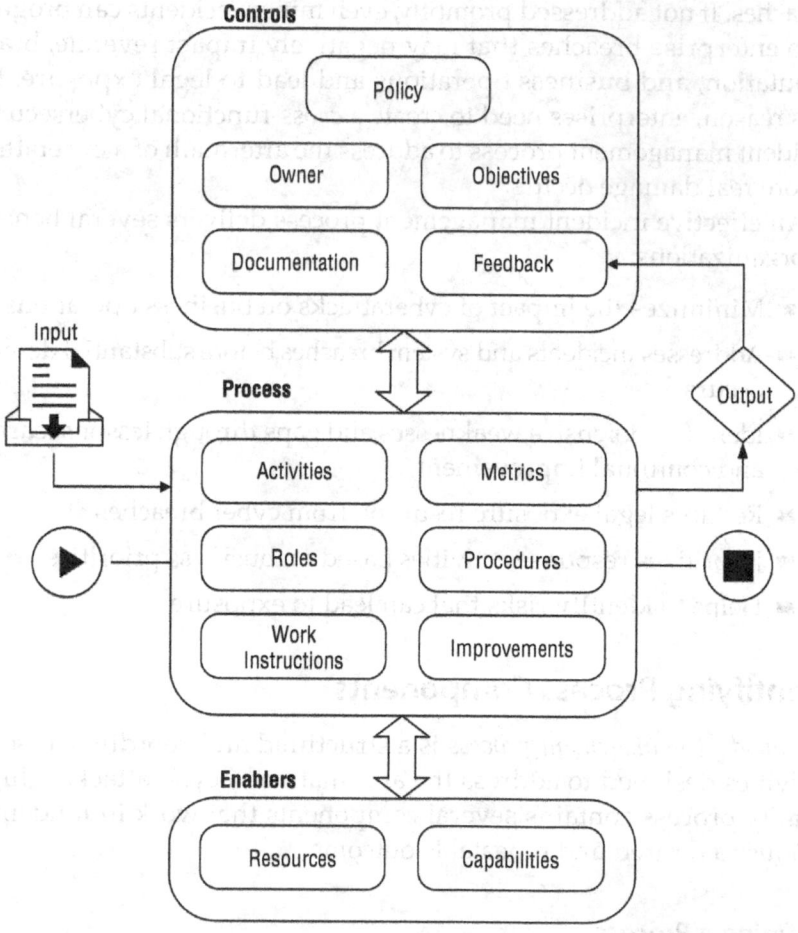

Figure 4.2: Process model

Activities   *Process activities* are a core component of an incident management process. Process activities constitute the actions that stakeholders participating in the process must execute to achieve a specific outcome, such as incident detection and classification.

Procedures   An incident management process typically has defined procedures for each activity executed as part of its workflow. An *incident management procedure* outlines how to carry out the activity.

Work Instructions   *Work instructions* provide a detailed description of how to perform a specific task referenced in a procedure; for example, a step-by-step instruction on how to acquire event logs from a specific technology.

Roles   A *role* is an entity that participates in an incident management process and is responsible for executing specific activities. A single role may be responsible for one or more activities within the incident management process.

Metrics   *Metrics* refers to standard measures that an enterprise may choose to collect and evaluate to assess how the process performs against its objectives.

Improvements   *Process improvements* are activities that an enterprise implements to address underperforming areas or proactively optimize the process and enhance its quality.

It is worth mentioning that not all organizations choose to implement metrics and process improvements. Chapter 1 discussed the Capability Maturity Model Integration (CMMI) model that defines process maturity levels.[5] Striving to quantitatively manage and optimize an incident management process may not be the end goal for all organizations. In fact, for smaller organizations that still do not grasp cybersecurity, this approach may lead to inefficient use of organizational resources.

Furthermore, the ISO 9001:2015 standard[6] established a hierarchical relationship between process, procedure, and work instruction, and helped to clarify crucial terms that apply to incident management. Figure 4.3 depicts the relationship between these concepts.

Process Controls

Controls are process components that are necessary to ensure that the process produces outcomes in accordance with the established objectives.

Process controls are also vital to continual improvement. Enterprises need to establish the following controls to ensure that their incident management process is up to managing the response to cyberattacks effectively.

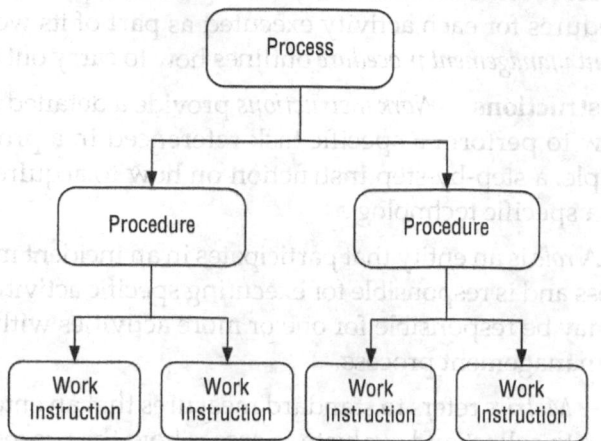

Figure 4.3: Relationship between process, procedure, and work instruction

Process Policy   A *process policy* is a set of rules and statements intended to govern the decisions and actions within an incident management process. A process policy may be composed of issue-specific policies, such as escalation policy, forensic data retention policy, or handling of incidents relating to unauthorized disclosure of protected data.

Process Objectives   A *process objective* defines the results and outcomes that the process should deliver, such as using standardized response procedures to respond to similar incidents consistently or to ensure that stakeholders are aware of their roles and responsibilities pertaining to the process.

Process Owner   A *process owner* ensures that the process is fit for its intended purpose and has the authority to make changes to the process. An owner also needs to make sure that the process integrates with other organizational processes and takes into account response aspects, such as legal and regulatory requirements. In larger enterprises, a process owner is typically a senior manager.

Process Custodian   A process owner may delegate the responsibility of managing some aspects of the process to a custodian. A *process custodian* is a stakeholder who is responsible for the implementation and day-to-day execution of the process. In smaller organizations, the roles of a process owner and a process custodian might be combined into one.

Process Documentation   *Process documentation* outlines the necessary steps and provides supporting information required to execute the process in a consistent and repeatable manner. The primary users of the documentation are stakeholders with assigned process roles who leverage the documentation to fulfill their responsibilities pertaining to the process.

Process Feedback   *Process feedback* is information that enterprises collect and analyze to determine if the process performs well against its objectives. Enterprises can use this information to identify under-performing areas and implement specific improvement initiatives.

Process Enablers

Process enablers make up the resources and capabilities required to support an incident management process and achieve specific outcomes.

Resources   *Resources* encompass all the assets that are necessary to support and execute an incident management process. Assets may include financial capital, infrastructure, applications, information, and people.

Capabilities   *Capabilities* represent the ability to achieve a specific outcome by leveraging assets. Capabilities may include management, organization, processes, and people. People can be both resources and capabilities. For example, an enterprise may hire forensic analysts and procure the necessary technology to establish a digital forensics capability.

Process Interfaces

Chapter 2 discussed a CSIRT as a cross-functional team consisting of cybersecurity, technology, and business stakeholders, as well as third parties that convene to respond to cybersecurity incidents. As part of defining an incident management process, enterprises need to establish interfaces to other organizational functions and integrate with their processes to ensure effective response.

A *process interface* determines the inputs that an incident management process receives from other processes, as well as the outputs that it produces that may trigger other, subsequent processes. In practical terms, the inputs and outputs are pieces of information that various organizational functions receive or pass into the incident management process so that it can achieve its objectives.

For example, a technology support group may investigate an operational incident, diagnose a cyberattack as its root cause, and trigger the cybersecurity incident management. The outcome from the operational investigation feeds as an input into the cybersecurity incident management process. In contrast, if the cybersecurity incident management process produces evidence of unauthorized access to data that is subjected to legal and regulatory requirements, the findings would trigger and feed into a data privacy process.

To make the transitions between various organizational processes smooth, enterprises need to create communication templates to ensure that the information they pass from one process to another is fit for its intended purpose. For example, the information should contain the necessary details, yet be succinct, written for the target audience, and actionable to facilitate decision making.

The following list briefly describes the typical processes that integrate with a cybersecurity incident management process.

IT Incident Management   In some situations, operational incidents are the first symptoms of a cyberattack. In other cases, incident responders may need to trigger the IT incident management process to receive support from technical groups. For these reasons, enterprises need to integrate those two processes. For example, a denial-of-service attack typically leads to a system or application availability issue first before it is escalated to an incident response team.

Asset and Configuration Management   *Asset management* is a process that allows enterprises to keep track of the IT assets that they deploy to support business operations. Configuration management, on the other hand, enables enterprises to track the configurations of those assets, as well as the relationships between their components. Incident responders require access to this information to analyze and scope incidents effectively. For example, an analyst may consult a configuration management database to determine whether an investigated event represents normal system behavior or is indicative of an attacker activity.

Event Management   *Event management* is a process that allows enterprises to monitor operational and security events in their environments. As part of an incident investigation, incident responders may need to implement additional monitoring to provide alerting of attacker activity and scope incidents effectively. For example, analysts may ingest IOCs, such as IP addresses, into network monitoring tools to detect malware-infected systems that connect to an attacker C2 infrastructure.

Change Management   The purpose of the *change management* process is to minimize the risk of interruptions resulting from changes in technologies that support business operations. As part of investigations, incident responders may need to make changes to systems and applications. To minimize the risk associated with those changes, inform other impacted parties, document the change details, and create a backout plan, enterprises may invoke the change management process. For example, installing a network tap in a data center requires a temporary network outage that organizations must manage through their change management process.

Vulnerability Management   *Vulnerability management* is the process of identifying, evaluating, reporting, and remediating security vulnerabilities. The output of a cybersecurity incident management process may feed into the vulnerability management process to prevent similar incidents and system breaches from reoccurring in the future. For example, if an incident response team determines that an attacker compromised administrative credentials because of deficiencies in access control policies, the information should feed into the vulnerability management process for evaluation.

Vendor Management   The purpose of the *vendor management* process is to ensure that suppliers deliver on their contractual commitments. Cybersecurity incidents involving third parties have become commonplace, and enterprises may need to engage third parties as part of the incident management process. In such cases, incident responders typically engage the vendor management function to facilitate initial communication. For example, if an attacker compromises an application component that an external vendor manages, then vendor management may initiate communication between the two parties.

Business Continuity and Disaster Recovery   *Business continuity and disaster recovery (BCDR)* is a set of processes and practices that help organizations recover from a disaster and resume business operations. With destructive cyberattacks and remediations that interrupt business activity, BCDR is an integral part of cyber resilience, and organizations need to integrate it with a cybersecurity incident management process. For example, during destructive attacks, the incident response team works closely with DR to restore impacted data from backups.

Financial Management   In some cases, responding to a cybersecurity incident may require additional funding and resources. It is the finance department that typically approves of and makes additional funding available to hire external consultants or purchase additional technology. For example, during a significant incident, an enterprise may need to obtain additional funding to hire an external DFIR firm to assist with the investigation.

Compliance and Data Privacy Management   An intrusion may lead to unauthorized access or disclosure of information that is subject to legal and regulatory requirements. Compliance and data privacy professionals need to interpret investigative findings to ensure adherence to data breach notification requirements in various jurisdictions. For this reason, incident management should integrate with compliance, data privacy, and other necessary legal processes. For example, an incident response team closely works with the compliance and data privacy functions when an organization receives a *common point of purchase (CPP)* notification by a payment brand.

Roles and Responsibilities

A cybersecurity incident management process typically includes several roles that are responsible for fulfilling various activities within the process. Chapter 2 identified typical business, technology, and third-party functions that an incident response team may call upon to assist in their respective domains. Enterprises must identify, assign, and document roles and responsibilities to those functions to ensure that they carry out and fulfill their activities within the incident management process.

An outline of roles and responsibilities should be succinct, yet contain the necessary details relating to the process. Typically, a brief description of the role and a bulleted list of responsibilities works well.

Another, often complementary, method to documenting roles and responsibilities is to create a responsibility assignment chart. A *RACI chart* allows organizations to map out roles and responsibilities to activities. The acronym is derived from four responsibilities that organizations typically designate:

Responsible   Responsible refers to the role that carries out a specific process activity.

Accountable   Accountable refers to the role that has the overall responsibility for fulfilling a specific activity but may not carry out the actual work.

Consulted   Consulted refers to the role that provides information or acts in an advisory capacity to the role that carries out an activity.

Informed   Informed refers to the role that does not actively participate in the process but is informed about its progress. Senior management is a primary example of a role that an incident manager informs about the status of an investigation.

Service Levels

Enterprises can leverage *service level agreements (SLAs)* and *operational level agreements (OLAs)* to ensure that entities that participate in the incident management process complete their tasks within the expected time frame and to the agreed-on quality. An SLA is a formal agreement between an organization and a service provider. In contrast, an OLA represents a formal commitment between internal entities.[7] For example, an enterprise may establish a response SLA with an incident response firm as part of a retainer agreement. An example of an OLA is an agreement between an incident response team and a technical group within the same organization to establish commitments, such as response time to support an investigation.

Enterprises need to establish SLAs and OLAs that are measurable to determine whether the entities that participate in the incident management process meet their targets. Chapter 1 discussed the SMART framework. Enterprises can also leverage this framework to create unambiguous targets as part of defining OLAs and SLAs.

SLAs and OLAs are excellent tools to set and measure process targets. However, a poor choice of SLAs and OLAs may lead to an incorrect perception of a cyber breach response program. For example, in the world of IT operations, incidents typically have obvious symptoms, such as the low performance of an application component. In such cases, response and resolution targets make perfect sense. In contrast, the symptoms of a cybersecurity incident may not be so obvious. In some cases, a threat actor may dwell on a compromised network for weeks or even months before detection. It may also take a complex investigation that consumes a considerable amount of time before the enterprise determines the full scope and impact of the compromise. For this reason, targets that make perfect sense in IT operations may not always be appropriate for a cyber breach response program. Organizations must very carefully define SLAs and OLEs to ensure that they convey accurate information and are useful in making decisions. For example, defining a metric focused on the time it takes to close an incident typically results in incident response teams focusing on resolving incidents to meet metric requirements at the expense of a thorough investigation. In contrast, agreeing to a support response time SLA with an incident response partner is more beneficial and sets clear expectations for how soon the partner must start providing support.

Incident Management Workflow

A *workflow* is a sequence of activities executed in a chronological order to manage the lifecycle of an incident. A typical workflow includes decision points that determine the direction of activity flow based on conditions and rules. A workflow may also contain interfaces to other processes and subprocesses. This section presents a conceptual workflow that captures the main steps in an incident management process. In practice, workflows may be more complex with many decision points. Furthermore, incident response teams often iterate over some of the steps as they scope intrusions and learn about how a threat actor operates in a compromised environment as depicted in Figure 4.4.

Sources of Incident Notifications

Enterprises can detect and identify incidents and cyber breaches through numerous sources. For this reason, it is critical that business and technology stakeholders know how to report suspicious events and incidents to the incident response team. The following list briefly discusses the typical avenues that lead to the detection or identification of an incident.

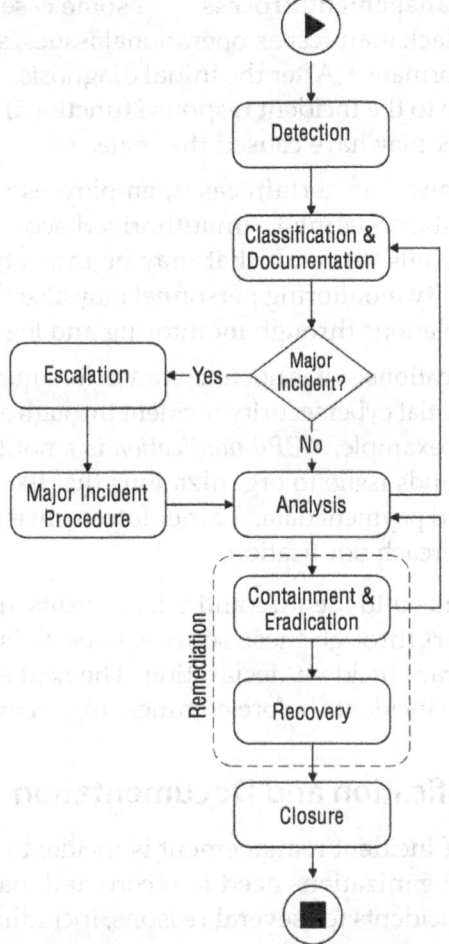

Figure 4.4: Incident management workflow

Service Desk   The majority of medium- and large-sized organizations implement a *service desk* function that acts as a single point-of-contact for employees for technology-related inquiries. Employees can report to the service desk any suspicious events and incidents. The service desk may perform a basic triage and escalate the notifications to the incident response function.

Event Management   *Event management* is a generic term that refers to the automated monitoring of events across the network to detect and report events that are outside the established baseline. Security tools, such as Security Information and Event Management (SIEM), can collect data from disparate sources and correlate that data to alert on suspicious activities.

IT Incident Management Process   In some cases, the symptoms of a cyberattack manifest as operational issues, such as degraded system performance. After the initial diagnosis, a technical group may escalate to the incident response function if they believe that a cyberattack may have caused the issue.

Policy Violations   In certain cases, employees may observe and report activities relating to unauthorized access to resources or other suspicious behavior that may be indicative of an insider threat. Security monitoring personnel may also discover evidence of policy violations through monitoring and log review.

External Notifications   It is not uncommon for organizations to learn about a potential cybersecurity incident through a third-party notification. For example, a *CPP notification* is a notification that card payment brands issue to organizations that likely experienced a breach of card payment data.[8] Law enforcement is another common source of a breach notification.

Organizations need to identify and triage events and incidents that stakeholders report through these sources to establish whether those notifications warrant incident declaration. The next step is to classify and document the incidents before commencing an in-depth analysis.

Incident Classification and Documentation

A vital element of incident management is incident classification and documentation. Organizations need to record and maintain a full historical record of incidents for several reasons, including the following:

- Regulatory compliance
- Providing groups participating in the incident management process with contextual information and the necessary details to fulfill their responsibilities
- Tracking the progress of incidents throughout their lifecycle
- Trend analysis and continual improvement
- Collecting incident data required for the vulnerability management process
- Tracking historical incident information for governance purposes

As part of incident documentation, analysts need to classify incidents by assigning an appropriate category and severity level to them. Incident classification helps communicate the nature and impact of an incident to business and technology stakeholders. It is also vital to establishing metrics and measuring a cyber breach response program.

Incident Categorization

Incident categorization involves assigning a category to an incident that reflects the nature of the incident and the resources required to address it. Organizations should establish a categorization scheme that is most appropriate for their maturity and metric requirements.

A *single-tier scheme* typically works for enterprises that are in the early phases of setting up a cyber breach response program. As the program matures and the management identifies the need to track metrics at a granular level to make precise operational adjustments, an organization may choose to implement a *two-tier scheme*.

A *single-tier scheme* typically encompasses several high-level categories, such as malware or denial of service. A *two-tier scheme*, on the other hand, defines high-level incident categories at the top tier and incident types or subcategories at the lower tier. For example, an incident of type "malware" may be further categorized as virus, ransomware, bot, or worm.

To communicate cybersecurity incidents clearly throughout the organization, enterprises must create an incident taxonomy or adopt a taxonomy established by an industry framework. For example, NIST SP 800-61 Revision 2 proposes the following taxonomy:[9]

- ▪ External/Removable Media
- ▪ Attrition
- ▪ Web
- ▪ Email
- ▪ Impersonation
- ▪ Improper Usage
- ▪ Loss of Theft of Equipment
- ▪ Other

Severity Assignment

Severity identifies the importance of an incident to the enterprise, and it is the primary driver for response actions that an organization takes to resolve it. Two primary criteria exist to determine a severity level of a cybersecurity incident: impact and urgency.

Impact is a measure of the potential damage that an incident causes before it is contained. An incident can cause an operational or informational impact.[10]

Operational Impact   *Operational impact* occurs when a cyberattack impairs an enterprise's ability to conduct business operations, such as ransomware encrypting systems that support core business functions. Enterprises can determine operational impact based on the scope of an incident or the number of business functions that the incident impacts.

Informational Impact   *Informational impact* occurs when a cyberattack negatively impacts the confidentiality, integrity, and availability of information assets. For example, if a cyberattack leads to a data privacy breach or theft of intellectual property, enterprises need to include this factor in severity calculation.

Enterprises should establish both operational and informational criteria to identify the severity of an incident accurately. Enterprises historically used impact on business operations as a criterion to calculate the severity of an IT incident. However, cybersecurity incidents may severely impact organizations while not having an operational impact. For example, unauthorized access or theft of protected data may lead to legal exposure, brand reputation damage, or a loss of competitive advantage in the marketplace in case of intellectual property theft. For this reason, cybersecurity incidents require informational impact evaluation, too. In cases when a cyberattack causes both operational and informational impact, organizations should use the higher impact score in the severity calculation.

Operational and informational impact criteria may vary among organizations, depending on factors such as risk appetite and the nature of the business. Table 4.1 and Table 4.2 provide examples of typical impact criteria that enterprises may establish.

Urgency is the time that must elapse before an incident has a significant business impact. The shorter the time, the higher the urgency. For example, a ransomware outbreak on the corporate network may need immediate action to prevent a severe business impact. Evidence of a threat actor performing reconnaissance of an Internet-exposed web application may not necessitate the same level of response.

Table 4.1: An example of operational impact criteria

IMPACT	DESCRIPTION
Extensive	An incident severely impacts multiple core business functions and significantly impairs business operations. An extensive impact may also warrant a crisis declaration.
Significant	An incident severely impacts one or two core business functions.
Moderate	An incident has little impact on business operations.
Minor	An incident has no impact on business operations and is handled as part of day-to-day operations.

Table 4.2: An example of informational impact criteria

IMPACT	DESCRIPTION
Extensive	An attacker exfiltrates trade secrets, intellectual property, or a significant amount of data that is subjected to legal and regulatory requirements.
Significant	An attacker gains unauthorized access to protected data and exfiltrates a small subset of that data. There is also a possibility that the attacker can exfiltrate additional data.
Moderate	An attacker has gained a foothold in an environment and actively enumerates systems and applications for the data of interest. However, there is no evidence of unauthorized access to or exfiltration of protected data.
Minor	An attacker has compromised a non-business-critical system or application that does not store or process protected data. Also, there is no evidence of lateral movement within the environment.

As with impact, enterprises need to establish clear urgency criteria to use in severity calculation. Table 4.3 provides an example of typical urgency criteria based on how far an attacker progressed through the cyberattack lifecycle.

By correlating impact and urgency, organizations can derive the severity level for an incident. The higher the severity, the more damage an incident may cause. The severity level drives the resources that an enterprise dedicates to resolve it.

Table 4.3: An example of urgency criteria

IMPACT	DESCRIPTION
Critical	An attacker accesses highly confidential data or actively deploys destructive malware.
High	An attacker establishes C2 communication and has moved laterally within the compromised network.
Medium	An attacker exploits a vulnerability and gains unauthorized access to a system or a software application. The attacker may also establish a foothold to maintain access to the network.
Low	An attacker performs an active attack on the organization. However, there is no evidence that the attack succeeded.

One way to establish the severity of an incident is to create a matrix of impact and urgency. Enterprises can also leverage the matrix to create a heat map by shading matrices with colors. Table 4.4 provides a matrix example based on the impact and urgency criteria discussed earlier in this section.

Table 4.4: An example of a severity matrix

| URGENCY | IMPACT | | | |
	EXTENSIVE	SIGNIFICANT	MODERATE	MINOR
Critical	1	1	2	2
High	1	2	2	3
Medium	2	2	3	3
Low	3	3	4	4

Enterprises can use a numerical or descriptive scheme to designate severity levels. Regardless of the choice of a scheme, organizations need to determine what level of response warrants each severity level. The following list contains examples of severity definitions based on the impact and urgency criteria examples discussed earlier in this section.

Severity 1   An incident has a significant impact on business operations or protected data, and the enterprise must take immediate action to minimize damage caused by the cyberattack. Senior management actively participates in the decision-making process.

Severity 2   An incident severely impacts one or two business functions or a subset of protected data, and the enterprise must respond as soon as possible to prevent further damage. Senior management provides guidance and strategic direction but does not actively participate in the incident management process.

Severity 3   An incident has a limited impact on business operations, or an attacker has compromised a non-business-critical system but has not moved laterally in the environment. The enterprise needs to respond as soon as possible to minimize the possibility of any damage. Senior management may be informed but does not actively participate in the incident management process.

Severity 4   An incident does not have any operational or informational impact. However, the enterprise needs to respond to the incident within a few days to prevent the attacker from progressing to the next stage of the attack.

Incident classification is a dynamic process, and enterprises may need to adjust the category and severity assignment throughout its lifecycle to reflect its impact and scope accurately.

Capturing Incident Information

Nowadays, most enterprises use a ticketing tool or a dedicated incident response platform to track incidents. Analysts leverage those tools to create records that contain a set of data relating to incidents. Some platforms also allow their users to associate incident records with other items, such as a known vulnerability, among other features.

Enterprises need to consider incident record requirements carefully. Specific information, such as a case number or an incident type, applies to all records. Other information may be incident-specific or not available at the time when an analyst creates an incident record, such as the incident scope. I have come across organizations that enforce strict documentation requirements in their case management systems by configuring mandatory fields. However, this approach can hinder the analyst's ability to create a ticket at the early stages of an event, especially in cases where the available information is limited or unknown. A more sensible approach is to enact a policy that requires an incident response team to document information throughout an investigation and update electronic incident records appropriately. Furthermore, management can review incident documentation regularly and implement specific controls when the documentation is lacking in detail or quality.

The following list contains typical incident attributes that enterprises may choose to track in an incident record:

- Unique incident reference number; most tools autogenerate this value
- Incident category
- Incident severity
- Date open
- Status
- Affected configuration items, service, location, or business unit
- Ownership
- Short description of the incident
- Subtasks
- Worklog
- Next expected activity

A cybersecurity incident typically progresses through several stages from the initial detection to its closure. The following list briefly explains each of those states.

Open   An analyst has raised an incident, but no one has been assigned to work on it. This situation typically happens when a service desk or a stakeholder who is external to the incident response team raises a cybersecurity incident. The incident response team receives the incident notification and then assigns an analyst to the case.

In Progress   An incident response analyst is assigned to an incident and actively investigates it. Some tools combine the Open and In Progress states into a single state.

Cancelled   An analyst may cancel an incident if a false positive event triggered it or if there is already an existing incident record for the report case.

Resolved   An analyst may place an incident into a Resolved state after containing the threat and remediating the affected assets.

Closed   Once an incident has been resolved and its symptoms do not reoccur within a specific time frame, an analyst may permanently close the incident. Some tools combine the Resolved and Closed states into a single state.

Incident Escalations

As part of their cybersecurity incident management process, enterprises need to establish escalation procedures. Incidents that typically require escalation may become major incidents, and organizations need to ensure appropriate response before they cause a significant operational or informational impact. Two types of escalations can occur: hierarchical and functional.

Hierarchical Escalations

A *hierarchical escalation* raises an incident to higher management levels. Incident response personnel may engage senior management during major incidents to set priorities and provide a strategic direction to the incident response team. For example, when containment requires the organization to isolate a system that supports a core business function from the network, senior management needs to decide whether system availability or containment takes precedence.

A hierarchical escalation may also be necessary if the incident response team requires additional resources or a higher level of support from a group that participates in the process.

Functional Escalation

Functional escalation raises an incident to a higher level of skill or expertise. Some investigations may require advanced DFIR expertise. In such cases, an analyst may escalate an incident to senior personnel to support or take over the investigation. Another example of functional escalation is hiring external consultants to assist with a specific aspect of the investigation, such as malware reverse-engineering.

Functional and hierarchical escalations are not mutually exclusive, and in some cases, they complement each other. In the previous example, an incident response team needs to escalate an incident to senior management that typically has the required level of authority to engage external consultants.

Creating and Managing Tasks

Investigating complex incidents and breaches typically requires the contribution of multiple cybersecurity, business, and technical stakeholders.

To make this effort manageable, enterprises can break down a case into tasks and assign those tasks to specific roles.

A *task* is a unit of work that a specific role must complete to advance an investigation. For example, an incident manager may assign the task of acquiring forensic images of compromised hosts to one analyst, whereas another analyst may perform log analysis. An incident manager must associate all tasks with the investigated case and track their progress. Furthermore, a single role may be responsible for one or more tasks.

Some incident response platforms allow enterprises to create templates for specific incident types. As part of a template, analysts can create predefined tasks that an incident manager can assign during an investigation. This approach saves time and helps ensure a consistent response to similar incidents. The next section discusses how organizations can leverage this approach to build playbooks for specific incident types.

Major Incidents

Major incidents are incidents that cause a significant operational or informational impact and require prompt response. Severity 1 and Severity 2 incidents, as defined in a previous section, would qualify as major incidents.

Major incidents require vertical escalation to senior management and often a dedicated management workstream in addition to the technical workstream. For this reason, enterprises need to develop a major incident response process. The process should include the necessary provisions for both tactical and management workstreams that may include the following:

- Setting up a *war room* to convene key stakeholders to respond to the incident. A war room is also known as a *command center* or a *situation room.*

- Splitting the response effort into technical and management workstreams and establishing communication between those workstreams.

- Assigning an incident manager and an incident officer to lead those workstreams, respectively.

- Establishing a communication channel for each workstream.

- Establishing alternate communications protocols. This measure may be required if an attacker compromised internal communications systems, or an incident has an informational impact and may lead to legal exposure.

Communication and collaboration are vital to managing major incidents. Both business and technical stakeholders need to be informed about the progress of the incident investigation. For this reason, enterprises need to develop a comprehensive communications plan. Chapter 2 established a CSIRT coordination model with two key roles: incident manager and incident officer. As part of the process, enterprises have to assign a dedicated incident manager to lead the tactical workstream and directly work with the incident officer to ensure that business priorities drive the investigation. These two stakeholders are crucial to managing communication at the tactical and management levels, respectively.

Furthermore, enterprises need to conduct a post-incident review after each major incident to evaluate the response and identify opportunities for improvement. The section "Continual Improvement" discusses this topic in depth.

Incident Closure

Incident closure is the final activity in the process. It follows recovery and typically includes the following steps:

- Verifying that the incident record information is complete and accurate
- Ensuring that all activities within the processes have been completed
- Verifying that the incident indicators have not reoccurred

Crafting an Incident Response Playbook

An *incident response playbook* is a predefined series of steps that an incident response team takes when responding to a particular incident type. This approach allows organizations to streamline their processes and handle similar or routine incidents efficiently and consistently. Playbooks are also known as *standard operating procedures (SOPs)*, *runbooks*, or *incident models*.

Playbook Overview

A playbook is an extension of an incident management process, and all of the steps that it contains must conform to the process. An incident management process focuses on an overarching approach to handle the lifecycle of all cybersecurity incidents. In contrast, a playbook focuses on a step-by-step procedure to respond to a specific incident type. Another way of thinking about playbooks is in terms of incident-specific response procedures. For example, a malware outbreak playbook contains concrete steps describing how to handle a malware outbreak at each phase of the incident response lifecycle.

As illustrated in Figure 4.3, organizations can also create work instructions describing how to perform specific steps within a playbook. Specific work instructions may apply across multiple playbooks and are typically valuable to new hires or junior personnel. For example, if a playbook contains a step to acquire a forensic image of a compromised system, an analyst can reference a documented work instruction on how to perform this task for a specific platform, such as Windows or Linux.

A typical playbook contains the following components:

- A workflow consisting of a series of steps arranged in sequential order, including dependencies
- Roles and responsibilities associated with each step
- Timescales for completing the steps
- Predefined severity level based on urgency and impact
- Predefined values for specific attributes, such as severity level based on impact and urgency
- Escalation procedure

A playbook may also contain interfaces to invoke other playbooks or processes. For example, an *Unauthorized Data Access* playbook could contain a step to trigger a data privacy incident process.

For playbooks to be effective, they must address specific incident types and focus on steps that are specific to those types only. For example, developing separate playbooks for ransomware and backdoor malware is more effective than creating a generic malware playbook. Also, playbooks should be concise, practical, and in the majority of cases, limited to no more than 25 steps. If a playbook requires more than 25 steps and a complex workflow with several decision points, it is likely too generic and should be broken down into more specific playbooks.

In my consulting engagements, I regularly come across organizations with a "playbook mentality," who believe that scripting response procedures is a silver bullet to incident response. This cannot be further from the truth. Enterprises should create playbooks to guide their incident response teams and provide a repeatable procedure with documented preapproved decisions. However, it is vital to understand that even incidents of the same type vary in complexity, scope, and the tools, tactics, and procedures (TTP) that an adversary employs to progress through the cyberattack lifecycle. For this reason, even the most sophisticated playbook cannot replace critical thinking and the experience of a seasoned incident response professional.

For that reason, during client engagements I emphasize to senior management that playbooks should guide rather constrain incident responders. Furthermore, depending on a specific case, analysts may need to deviate from a standard procedure based on a sound and logical judgment of a specific situation. Enterprises must be cognizant of the fact that playbooks do not replace critical thinking. Security analysts and other stakeholders that participate in the incident response process still need to apply critical thinking and demonstrate the necessary skills and experience in their respective domains.

Identifying Workflow Components

This section discusses generic content and recommendations that enterprises may choose to include in their incident response playbooks. The content is organized by the stages of the incident response lifecycle.

Detection

Arguably, an incident response team invokes a playbook after incident detection. For this reason, specific technical means of identifying incidents are typically out of scope. However, a playbook should still include specific triage steps. Triage allows incident responders to determine whether the reported event is a cybersecurity incident and collect contextual information before diving into detailed analysis. Typical steps in this phase include the following:

Triage   During the triage step, analysts must take steps to review the reported event data, establish whether the event constitutes a cybersecurity incident, and collect contextual data. This data may include technical information about the affected systems and their business context. Furthermore, analysts may want to collect additional data through live response and assess that data before declaring an incident.

Incident Classification and Documentation   As described earlier, analysts must establish impact and urgency factors to determine the severity level of an incident. In some cases, it is a good practice to establish impact and urgency factors as part of the playbook definition, especially if the playbook is for a particular scenario.

Documentation   After triaging and classifying an incident, analysts must document all the required information in an incident record. If an organization leverages an incident response platform for automation, analysts can preconfigure some attributes as part of the incident template or model, such as owner, automatic notifications of specific stakeholders, or triggering of other processes. Some platforms can also automatically calculate incident severity based on the urgency and impact factors that analysts enter or preconfigure as part of the template.

Escalation   Some incidents may be relatively straightforward to resolve and do not require advanced expertise and skills. Other incidents may require a specialized skill set or management attention. As part of a playbook definition, enterprises may choose to define the required functional and hierarchical escalations and assign specific roles as owners to the incident.

Analysis

Depending on the nature of an incident and its scope, analysts may acquire and examine different types of data. The purpose of the *analysis phase* is to determine attacker activity in the compromised environment and understand the full scope of the incident.

The analysis steps must focus on the objectives of the analysis and the type of incident that a playbook addresses. At the same time, the steps must be generic enough not to constrain the analyst. For example, when investigating a backdoor malware on a server system, an analyst may choose to focus on program execution artifacts rather than reviewing every possible forensic artifact that the system may have produced. However, including separate steps to review each program execution artifact would be excessive and impractical. Typical steps in this phase include the following:

Data Acquisition and Preservation   This step should contain information about the types of data that incident responders must acquire and preserve and the acquisition techniques. Depending on the incident type, analysts may need to collect network data, forensic images, or logs from enterprise services.

Technical Analysis   The technical analysis steps relate to the analysis objectives and methods that analysts need to leverage to achieve those objectives. The objectives and techniques that analysts employ may differ depending on an incident type. For example, to determine evidence of malware execution on a system, analysts typically examine program execution artifacts.

Scoping   The steps refer to enumerating other systems on the network for IOCs determined during the previous step. Analysts may leverage various scoping techniques and execute different scoping steps depending on the incident type and available tools. For example, analysts can leverage an EDR tool to enumerate systems on a corporate network for evidence of specific malware execution artifacts.

Creating a Timeline   For some incidents, analysts may need to conduct a timeline analysis based on the findings during previous steps. The purpose of the analysis is to reconstruct attacker activity in the compromised environment and understand the full scope of the compromise. Analysts reconstruct a timeline of attacker activity by organizing relevant time-stamped data into a timeline.

Creating Actionable Cyber Threat Intelligence   For some incidents, analysts need to create actionable CTI to inform containment and eradication activities. For example, analysts may compile a list of C2 IP addresses recovered through malware analysis and discovered through CTI enrichment. Victim organizations can then block network connections to those IP addresses to deny an attacker access to the compromised environment.

Adjust Incident Severity   Based on the findings during the previous steps, enterprises may need to adjust the urgency and impact factors to change the severity of the incident. This activity is particularly applicable in cases where incident responders discover new, significant information relating to the investigated incident.

It is crucial to emphasize that analysis is an iterative, and often incremental, process. For this reason, analysts iterate through the lifecycle until they reach diminishing returns relating to new findings, such as discovering additional compromised systems. It is essential to communicate this concept to vital stakeholders and set expectations accordingly, particularly during high-pressure incidents.

Containment and Eradication

The information that analysts compile during the analysis steps drives containment and eradication activities. These activities are specific to a threat type, and their execution heavily depends on the architecture of the compromised environment, available tools, policies, and other controls. Another crucial factor that impacts containment and eradication is business priorities. For example, isolating a critical server from a network may be a sensible containment strategy from a technical perspective, but not feasible from a business point of view.

The first activity in defining containment and eradication steps as part of a playbook definition is to create a strategy and then select tools and technology to implement that strategy. A strategy to contain an incident and eradicate a threat actor may include the following:

- Enforcing access control mechanisms
- System hardening
- Patching vulnerabilities
- Resetting credentials
- Implementing security tools
- Blocking direct attack vectors
- Adjusting system policies and locking down permissions

Furthermore, enterprises can enhance security monitoring to detect additional attacker activities or attempts to come back to the compromised network after remediation.

Recovery

Recovery is typically outside the scope of an incident response playbook. However, in some cases, organizations may want to include in an incident response playbook steps relating to invoking functions that typically participate in the recovery process, such as the DR function or technical groups. For example, an enterprise may choose to include a step in the recovery phase to re-image malware-infected workstations and assign the ownership of that step to a workplace services group.

Other Workflow Components

In addition to the steps necessary to investigate and remediate an incident, organizations need to consider these other components relating to the overall incident management process:

Communications   Different types of stakeholders may need to be informed about the progress of an investigation of specific incident types. An effective playbook should include steps to facilitate communications with key stakeholders.

Process Integration   Enterprises also must ensure to include steps that invoke other necessary organizational processes during the response to a specific threat type. For example, an analyst may need to invoke the configuration management process to determine crucial information about an investigated system or an HR process for insider threat cases.

Post-Incident Evaluation

The *post-incident phase*, also referred to as *postmortem*, includes activities that follow the recovery phase. Vulnerability management and lessons learned are two vital processes that can help organizations determine the root cause of an incident and the necessary improvements to prevent or reduce the impact of similar incidents in the future. The outcome of these processes typically feeds into the continual improvement process discussed in the next section.

Vulnerability Management

This section briefly discusses vulnerability management as it pertains to cyber breach response. The purpose of an incident management process is to address the aftermath of a cyberattack and minimize the damage it causes to the enterprise. However, if the enterprise does not address the underlying security weaknesses that allow attackers to compromise systems in the first place, similar incident types are likely to recur. This reactive approach often leads to inefficient use of resources and reduced security posture. Vulnerability management is a process that allows enterprises to address the issue.[11]

Purpose and Objectives

As stated previously, vulnerability management is the process of identifying, evaluating, reporting, and remediating security vulnerabilities. A vulnerability is a weakness in a computer system, software application, design, implementation, or control that a threat actor can exploit to gain unauthorized access to a computer network and progress through the cyberattack lifecycle. The purpose of vulnerability management is to identify and mitigate vulnerabilities and minimize the attack surface of computer systems and software applications.

Vulnerability management is often an independent function within the overall cybersecurity program. Investigative findings and security posture weaknesses discovered during incident response must feed into the vulnerability management process to prevent similar incident types from reoccurring. In simple terms, incident management is a reactive process, whereas vulnerability management attempts to address issues proactively.

Vulnerability Management Lifecycle

The *vulnerability management lifecycle*, as it pertains to incident response, consists of five steps necessary to identify and address vulnerabilities that lead to cybersecurity incidents. The lifecycle approach applies to vulnerabilities that incident responders identify during incident investigations. A comprehensive vulnerability management program contains additional stages, such as asset discovery and prioritization, that the approach does not include. Figure 4.5 depicts the lifecycle.

Identify   The first step in the process is to identify and recognize that there is a security weakness that gives rise to cybersecurity incidents. An organization may identify a vulnerability by performing an incident root cause analysis. Furthermore, in organizations with mature governance practices, the leadership may identify a pattern of reoccurring incidents and request a root cause analysis to identify the underlying weakness.

Evaluate   Most enterprises do not have unlimited resources and must address more severe vulnerabilities first. For this reason, organizations need to assess and prioritize the identified vulnerabilities that can lead to the most significant impact on their business first. Addressing vulnerabilities in system design and implementation often requires dedicated projects and funding.

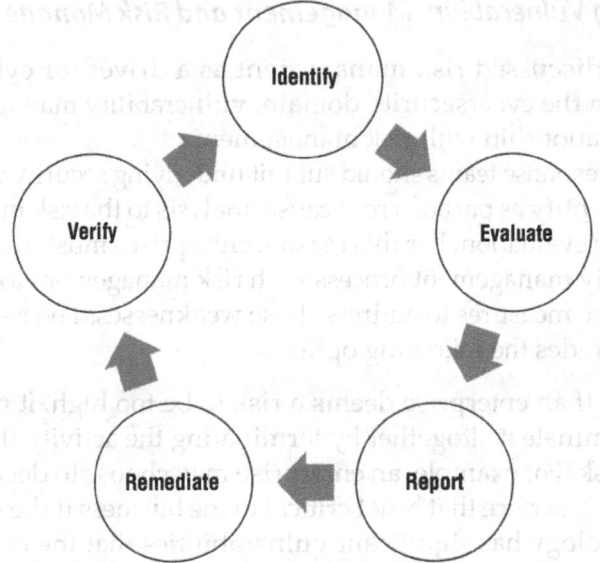

Figure 4.5: Vulnerability management lifecycle

Report Incident responders must document and report to management any identified weaknesses during an investigation. Reporting less severe weaknesses, such as missing patches for noncritical vulnerabilities, to mid-level management is typically sufficient. However, high-severity weaknesses, such as poor network segmentation, typically require the attention of senior management.

Remediate Some security weaknesses may be relatively easy to address, whereas others may require cross-functional coordination and management support. In some cases, organizations may also be able to implement a compensating control if addressing a security weakness may require significant effort and resources. Enterprises must evaluate each vulnerability from a risk perspective and apply cost-effective risk mitigation measures.

Verify After remediating a vulnerability, enterprises must verify that the vulnerability no longer exists in the environment. This approach may include verifying installed patches and configuration settings, performing vulnerability scanning, or attempting to exploit the vulnerability.

Integrating Vulnerability Management and Risk Management

Chapter 1 discussed risk management as a driver for cyber breach response. In the cybersecurity domain, vulnerability management has a strong relationship with risk management.

Incident response teams should submit underlying security weaknesses that they identify as part of a root cause analysis to the risk management function for evaluation. For this reason, enterprises must integrate their vulnerability management process with risk management to determine cost-effective measures to address those weaknesses. The risk response process includes the following options:

Avoid   If an enterprise deems a risk to be too high, it may decide to eliminate it altogether by terminating the activity that leads to the risk. For example, an enterprise may choose to decommission a legacy service that is not critical to the business if the underlying technology has significant vulnerabilities that the organization cannot address in a cost-effective manner.

Transfer   An enterprise may choose to transfer a risk to a third party. Outsourcing a certain business function or process is one option. Another popular option is to purchase a cyber insurance policy.

Reduce   To reduce a risk, enterprises implement specific administrative, physical, or logical controls that make it more challenging for a threat actor to compromise a system. For example, an enterprise may choose to upgrade unsupported platforms or migrate a service to newer technology.

Accept   Organizations may choose to accept a risk if the cost of the consequences is lower than mitigating the risk.

Lessons Learned

Lessons learned is the learning that enterprises gain from responding to cybersecurity incidents. The purpose of lessons learned is to identify and document information about positive aspects of incident response, as well as to identify any roadblocks and issues. The outcome of a lessons-learned session is a set of specific action items designed to improve future response.

Action items may fall within one of the following categories: operational, tactical, or strategic. Organizations can implement operational items as part of day-to-day operations. However, tactical and strategic action items typically require funding and other resources. For this reason, they must feed into the continual improvement process. I discuss this topic in more detail in the "Continual Improvement" section.

Organizations should conduct a lessons-learned meeting after every major incident. It is also a good practice to hold regular lessons-learned meetings to evaluate the response to less severe incidents to identify actionable improvements.

Lessons-Learned Process Components

Lessons learned is an iterative process consisting of several steps necessary to evaluate and improve response to cyberattacks continuously, as depicted in Figure 4.6.

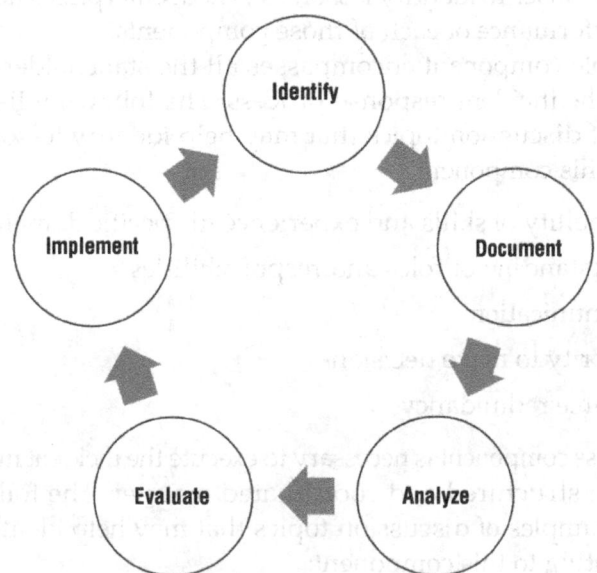

Figure 4.6: Lessons-learned process

Identify   Identify what worked well and any gaps or problematic areas that the enterprise should address to improve response to future incidents.

Document   Document and share the findings identified during the previous step with key stakeholders. One way to organize the findings is to assign each finding to one of the following categories: people, process, or technology.

Analyze   Analyze each gap and problematic area identified in the first step and determine possible solutions. Enterprises need to raise issues with senior management that may lead to significant risk.

Evaluate   Evaluate the feasibility of each solution determined during the previous step and obtain approval from key stakeholders to implement feasible solutions.

Implement   Implement solutions to address gaps and problematic areas identified in the first step. Tactical and strategic solution proposals must feed into the continual improvement process as an input and may require a business case to secure funding and other necessary resources for implementation.

People, process, and technology are critical components of effective incident response. To identify lessons learned, enterprises need to evaluate the performance of each of those components.

The people component encompasses all the stakeholders who participate in the incident response process. The following list provides examples of discussion topics that may help identify lessons learned relating to this component:

- Availability of skills and experience in specific domains
- Understanding of roles and responsibilities
- Communication
- Authority to make decisions
- Resource redundancy

The process component is necessary to execute the incident management process in a structured and coordinated manner. The following list provides examples of discussion topics that may help identify lessons learned relating to this component:

- Coordination of activities between roles participating in the incident management process
- Availability of specific incident response playbooks
- Vertical and horizontal escalations
- Specific process elements, with emphasis on gaps and problematic areas
- Fulfillment of each activity within the process
- Availability of information necessary to execute the process

- Information tracking
- Interfacing with other processes and organizational functions

The technology component refers to the tools and technologies necessary to respond to incidents effectively, as well as other technology considerations during incident investigations. The following list provides examples of discussion topics that may help identify lessons learned for this component:

- Availability of tools and other technologies necessary to support investigations
- Availability of forensic data
- Any challenges with acquiring forensic data
- Ability to detect attacker activity on the compromised network

Conducting a Lessons-Learned Meeting

This section contains general recommendations for conducting fruitful lessons-learned sessions.

General Rules   Plan a meeting structure, send out the agenda in advance, and encourage all participants to document their observations before the meeting. Also, develop a standard template for documenting lessons learned and other observations.

During the Meeting   Stick to the meeting structure and agenda, and keep the discussion focused. Ensure that there is one person who leads the discussion and another person responsible for taking notes. It is easy for a discussion to sidetrack, and having a clear plan helps keep the meeting focused. An excellent way to start a meeting is to discuss what went well first.

After the Meeting   Document, analyze, and evaluate action items identified during the meeting and disseminate this information to the participants. Be sure to assign an owner to each action. Also, make sure to follow up on the action items to ensure that stakeholders advance them.

It is critical that the person who leads the discussion makes the attendees comfortable and facilitates the discussion in a nonconfrontational way. During review meetings, stakeholders tend bring up negative experiences, so keeping the discussion balanced is vital to ensuring that stakeholders identify lessons learned as opposed to assigning blame.

Some participants may be introverted or lack the confidence to speak. Encourage them to participate. In my personal experience, some of the most valuable contributions come from those who quietly evaluate their observations before bringing them up in front of others.

Lastly, an excellent technique to facilitate a meeting is to ask open-ended questions and then follow up with specific targeted questions to extrapolate further details. Starting with open-ended questions allows the facilitator to collect general feedback before drilling into specific areas of interest.

Continual Improvement

Chapter 1 briefly discussed the need for continual improvement as a vehicle to evaluate and improve a cyber breach response program continuously. The chapter also discussed the drivers for continual improvement, as well as the organizational levels at which it can take place. This section discusses this topic in depth and provides a methodology that can help organizations successfully implement a continual improvement process.

Continual Improvement Principles

This section presents two conceptual models that form the foundation of continual improvement: the Deming cycle and the *Data, Information, Knowledge, Wisdom (DIKW)* hierarchy. The former model describes quality management principles, whereas the latter model explains the principles of knowledge management.

The Deming Cycle

The *Deming cycle* is a continuous quality improvement model that consists of a sequence of four steps: Plan, Do, Check, and Act (PDCA), as depicted in Figure 4.7. The PDCA cycle is a fundamental tenet of many quality management standards, such as ISO/IEC 27001.[12]

Plan   Review and evaluate a cyber breach response program regularly. The purpose of the review is to identify any underperforming areas, as well as to determine any required changes to the program in response to increased cyber risk, legal and regulatory requirements, or changing business objectives. As part of this step, organizations also need to establish the current state and a future desired state, as well as the metrics necessary to measure progress against improvement objectives.

Do   Conduct a trial of specific improvement initiatives through a small pilot project. As part of the trial, collect the quantitative data necessary to establish whether the initiatives achieve the desired outcome.

Check   After conducting a trial, process, organize, and analyze the collected data. The purpose of this phase is to produce and analyze metrics to determine whether the initiatives achieved the desired outcome. If the initiatives failed to produce the desired results, go back to planning.

Act   If the piloted improvement initiatives produced the desired outcome, make them permanent and update processes and the necessary documentation. The improved state becomes the baseline for the next iteration of the PDCA cycle.

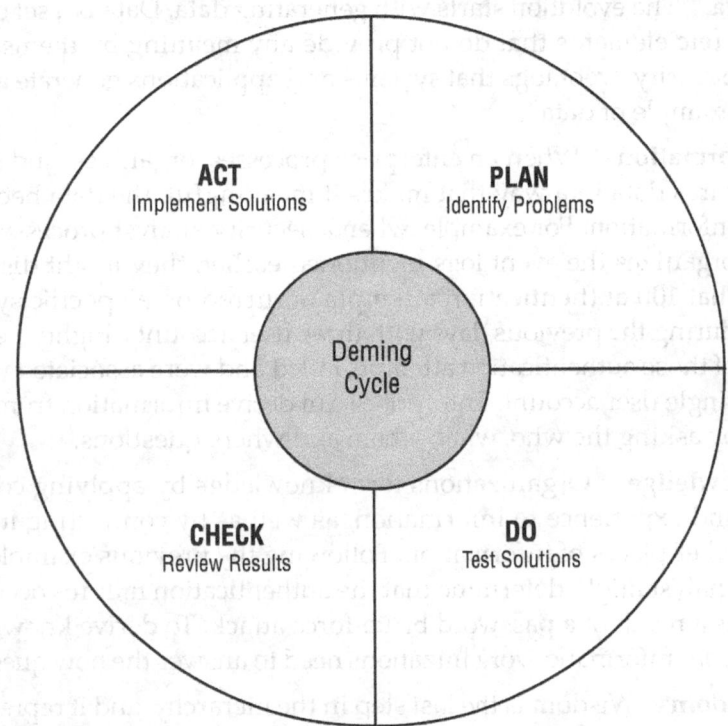

Figure 4.7: Deming cycle

DIKW Hierarchy

The *DIKW* hierarchy is a knowledge management model that describes how data evolves into information, knowledge, and wisdom, respectively, as represented in Figure 4.8.[13]

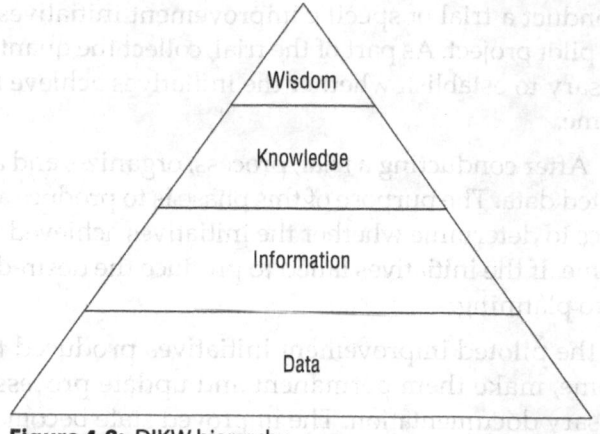

Figure 4.8: DIKW hierarchy

Data   The evolution starts with generating data. Data is a set of discrete elements that do not provide any meaning by themselves. Security event logs that systems and applications generate are an example of data.

Information   When an enterprise processes, organizes, and structures data in a way that makes it meaningful, the data becomes information. For example, when a security analyst processes and organizes the event logs mentioned earlier, they might discover that 100 authentication attempts occurred on a specific system during the previous days with three user accounts. Eighty percent of those authentication attempts failed and were associated with a single user account. Enterprises can derive information from data by asking the who, what, when, and where questions.

Knowledge   Organizations form knowledge by applying context and experience to information, as well as by connecting it with other pieces of information. Following the previous example, the analyst might determine that the authentication failures occurred as a result of a password brute-force attack. To derive knowledge from information, organizations need to answer the how question.

Wisdom   Wisdom is the last step in the hierarchy, and it represents knowledge applied in action. Considering the previous example, the analyst may determine that a threat actor gained access to the network and performed a password brute-force attack in an attempt to elevate their privileges.

The Seven-Step Improvement Process

The ITIL *seven-step improvement process* builds on the improvement principles discussed in the previous section. It presents a sequence of actionable steps that can help organizations implement a continual improvement process as part of their governance.[14]

Step 1: Define a vision for improvement including goals and objectives.

Step 2: Define metrics.

Step 3: Collect the data necessary to produce the metrics.

Step 4: Process and organize the data to derive information.

Step 5: Analyze the information, identify trends, and determine whether the improvement initiatives produce the desired outcome. In this step, information becomes knowledge.

Step 6: Assess the findings and create an appropriate improvement plan.

Step 7: Implement the plan.

Figure 4.9 provides a visual representation of this process. The next section provides practical guidance on how to implement each step.

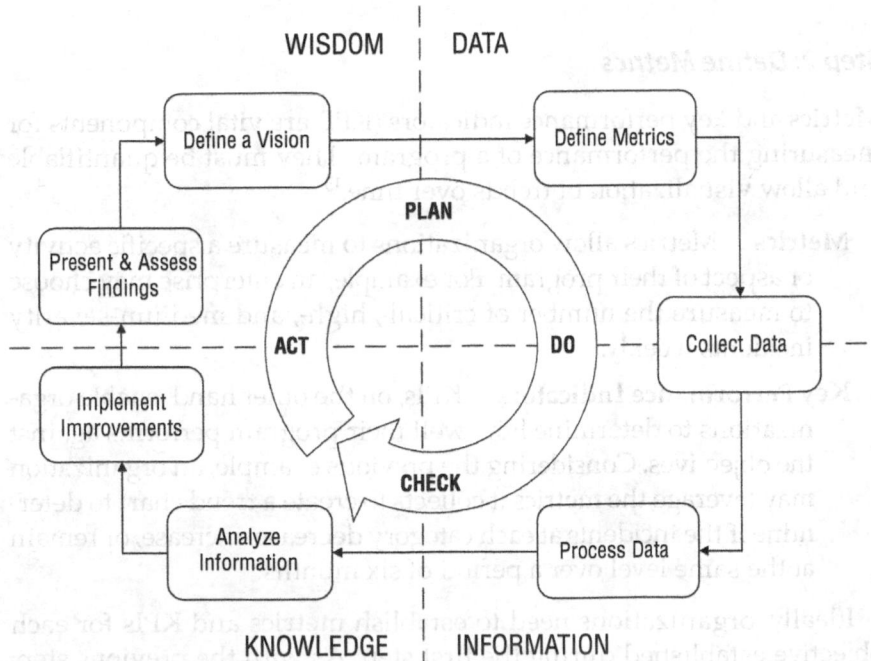

Figure 4.9: The seven-step improvement process

Step 1: Define a Vision for Improvement

Chapter 1 discussed how to create a vision as part of the overall cyber breach response program. The same strategies apply to defining a vision for improvement.

As part of this step, enterprises need to make sure that their strategy is realistic and aligned to their risk appetite. Answering the following questions is a good start for developing a continual improvement strategy:

- Is there any new business development under way that may require changes to the cyber breach response program?
- Are there any new developments in the threat landscape that lead to increased cyber risk?
- Are there any legislative changes that may impact how the organization currently responds to incidents?
- Does the organization contain most incidents before they cause a negative impact?

After identifying specific improvement initiatives, organizations must document them in a continual improvement register, assign an owner to each initiative, and review them regularly.

Step 2: Define Metrics

Metrics and key performance indicators (KPI) are vital components for measuring the performance of a program. They must be quantifiable and allow visualization of trends over time.[15]

Metrics   Metrics allow organizations to measure a specific activity or aspect of their program. For example, an enterprise may choose to measure the number of critical-, high-, and medium-severity incidents weekly.

Key Performance Indicators   KPIs, on the other hand, enable organizations to determine how well their program performs against the objectives. Considering the previous example, an organization may leverage the metrics it collects to create a trend chart to determine if the incidents at each category decrease, increase, or remain at the same level over a period of six months.

Ideally, organizations need to establish metrics and KPIs for each objective established during the first step. As with the previous step, enterprises must document the metrics and KPIs that they decide to measure. The following list contains practical tips for getting started with metrics and KPIs:

- Keep it simple and focus on fewer but vital metrics that can facilitate decision making. Creating a complex metric system often leads to confusion and unnecessary overhead.

- Ensure that the metrics are quantifiable and that the organization can collect the necessary data to support those metrics.

- Leverage automation tools that allow you to preconfigure metrics, visualize trends, and provide point-in-time information.

A common mistake is to create a metric system that is not suitable for the target audience. For example, presenting data relating to SQL injection attacks against a web application to a board of directors is not the most effective way to communicate risk. Instead, focus on metrics that can support KPIs and communicate the intended message. For example, measuring the occurrence of specific incident types and presenting trends over a period of time helps senior management communicate risk more effectively and secure the necessary resources to keep that risk at an acceptable level.

Enterprises may also choose to create a metric database or some other index to provide metadata on metrics. The metadata can include the following elements for each metric:

- A unique identifier
- What question the metric answers
- Target audience
- Update frequency
- Sources of data
- An example for presentation purposes

This approach can help organizations understand their metric system and keep it organized.

Step 3: Collect Data

The quality of metrics that an enterprise produces heavily depends on the data that the organization uses to produce those metrics. The characteristics that define data quality include the following:

Availability   Ensure that all data needed to support the necessary metrics is available. In some cases, organizations may need to audit and adjust their logging baselines to ensure that systems and applications generate the necessary log data to support metrics.

Accuracy   The collected data must be accurate. For example, including false-positive events in metrics that demonstrate adverse activities against the corporate network can lead to poor decisions and inefficient use of organizational resources.

Completeness   Make sure that the collected data is comprehensive. When certain types of data cannot be collected from certain segments, this must be clearly communicated to management when presenting metrics.

Reliability   Reliability means that data from one source does not contradict data from another source. If various pieces of data contradict each other, the enterprise cannot rely on the data to produce accurate metrics.

Relevance   Ensure that the collected data is relevant for the metrics that the organization produces.

Timeliness   Timeliness means that the required data to produce metrics must be up to date and available when needed.

The following list contains practical tips for ensuring data quality in support of metrics:

- Define data collection requirements for metrics.
- Establish whether the necessary data is available in the enterprise.
- Determine the means to collect the data.
- Determine collection frequency based on reporting requirements.
- Assign an owner and a custodian to the data collection task to ensure accountability and fulfillment, respectively.

Step 4: Process Data

After the collection phase, organizations must convert raw data into information. Data processing usually consists of the following steps:

Validation   Ensure that the data is correct and relevant. Checking a sample of values after each collection for anomalies, such as empty or missing data fields, is a good start.

Determine Formatting   Establish a presentation format that is appropriate for the target audience. Senior leadership may be interested in high-level trends, whereas mid-level management typically needs more detailed information to make decisions.

Choose Tools   Determine and choose the tools suited to transform the data into the required format. In simple cases, an Excel worksheet might be sufficient. Large and complex data typically require specialized tools.

Convert Data   Convert data into the required format. This may require techniques such as sorting, aggregations, frequency analysis, or other statistical methods to convert the raw data into information.

Step 5: Analyze Information

In this step, organizations extract actionable intelligence by applying business context to the information and metrics established during the previous step. Stakeholders typically review the presented information for trends and patterns to guide decision making. They may also ask specific questions relating to the program, such as these:

- Does the analysis show any undesired trends?
- Is there an identifiable cause for a trend?
- Is there a specific cause for anomalies?
- Do we have the necessary capabilities to keep risk at an acceptable level?
- Is our program performing as per the established objectives?

Step 6: Assess Findings and Create Plan

In this step, management assesses the analysis results and makes decisions regarding specific improvement plans. The presentation style and level of detail must be appropriate for management to enable them to make decisions. The following list contains practical tips for ensuring effective presentation:

- Know your target audience and tailor the presentation to their requirements. For example, executive personnel are typically interested in understanding the bigger picture rather than low-level details.

- Choose the correct format for the audience, such as a slide deck or a report.
- Be clear and concise, and remain focused. Present only the relevant information.
- Present information impartially and remain objective.
- Use visual formats where appropriate, such as trend charts.
- Attempt to garner the audience's interest by giving examples, telling a story, or personalizing the presented information.

Step 7: Implement the plan

In this step, an enterprise implements the improvement plans agreed to during the previous step. This step may include the following:

- Evaluating a proposed plan to determine whether it is cost-effective
- Building and submitting a business case
- Securing funding and other resources
- Planning and executing projects

Summary

An incident response plan contains several components that must work in tandem to allow organizations to respond to cybersecurity incidents effectively.

Most incidents have a predictable lifecycle. An effective incident management process helps organizations manage incident response activities in a structured and coordinated manner and ensure that they can continue business operations during cyberattacks. It consists of several components and activities that integrate the people, process, and technology dimensions.

For specific incident types, organizations may choose to create playbooks. Playbooks allow organizations to create repeatable procedures and accelerate response activities. However, organizations need to remember that even a state-of-the-art playbook cannot replace skills, experience, and critical thinking.

Finally, to improve their cyber breach response capabilities continually, enterprises need to conduct lessons learned, identify vulnerabilities, and implement measures to prevent reoccurring incidents or reduce their impact on their business. Continual improvement is vital to successful governance, and it helps organizations mature and improve their programs incrementally.

Notes

1. NIST SP 800-61, "Computer Security Incident Handling Guide Revision 2," August 2012, nvlpubs.nist.gov/nistpubs/ SpecialPublications/NIST.SP.800-61r2.pdf.

2. ISO 22301:2019, "Security and resilience—Business continuity management systems — Requirements," www.iso.org/ standard/75106.html.

3. Carnegie Mellon University, "CRR Supplemental Resource Guide: Volume 5, Incident Management," Version 1.1, www.us-cert.gov/ sites/default/files/c3vp/crr_resources_guides/ CRR_Resource_Guide-IM.pdf.

4. "ITIL Maturity Model and Self-assessment Service: User Guide," October 2013, www.tsoshop.co.uk/gempdf/ITIL_Maturity_Model_ SA_User_Guide_v1_2W.pdf.

5. CMMI Institute, cmmiinstitute.com.

6. ISO 9001:2015, " Quality management systems — Requirements," www.iso.org/standard/62085.html.

7. Helen Morris and Liz Gallacher, *ITIL Intermediate Certification Companion Study Guide*, Sybex, September 2017.

8. VISA, "What to Do If Compromised: Visa Supplemental Requirements, Version 6," usa.visa.com/dam/VCOM/download/ merchants/cisp-what-to-do-if-compromised.pdf.

9. NIST SP 800-61, "Computer Security Incident Handling Guide Revision 2," August 2012, nvlpubs.nist.gov/nistpubs/ SpecialPublications/NIST.SP.800-61r2.pdf.

10. "CISA Cyber Incident Scoring System," www.us-cert.gov/ CISA-Cyber-Incident-Scoring-System.

11. Morey J. Haber and Brad Hibbert, *Asset Attack Vectors: Building Effective Vulnerability Management Strategies to Protect Organizations*, Apress, June 2018.

12. ISO/IEC 27001:2013, " Information technology — Security techniques — Information security management systems — Requirements," www.iso.org/standard/54534.html.

13. Waseem Afzal, *Management of Information Organizations*, Chandos Publishing, June 2012.

14. Helen Morris and Liz Gallacher, *ITIL Intermediate Certification Companion Study Guide*, Sybex, September 2017.

15. Douglas W. Hubbard, Richard Seiersen, Daniel E. Geer Jr., and Stuart McClure, *How to Measure Anything in Cybersecurity Risk*, Wiley, July 2016.

Investigating and Remediating Cyber Breaches

Investigating a cyber breach can be a complex and often long process. The level of sophistication of the attacker, dwell time on the compromised network, and how far the attacker progressed through the cyberattack lifecycle directly contribute to the complexity of the investigation.

Incident responders follow a lifecycle-based process to investigate cyber breaches. The process typically includes multiple iterations of data collection and analysis in order to identify evidence of attacker activity. In some cases, the evidence is indisputable. In other cases, analysts must correlate and corroborate data from multiple sources to draw conclusions about attacker activity.

An investigation consists of many components that must work in tandem in order to determine the scope and extent of a breach. Investigating a large-scale breach requires a team of professionals with complementary skill sets, such as digital forensics, malware analysis, and cyber threat intelligence (CTI). Moreover, the order in which analysts discover evidence of attacker activity may not correspond to the order of the attack progression. For this reason, it is helpful to map digital evidence to a cyberattack framework in order to identify additional sources of potential evidence and reconstruct the "full picture" of an attack.

The evidence that analysts identify is crucial for containment and eradication. A remediation team uses information relating to the attacker operation to secure crucial assets and eradicate the attacker from the compromised environment.

This chapter draws on the information discussed thus far in this book, and it provides an in-depth discussion about investigating and remediating cyber breaches. The primary focus of this chapter is on large-scale network compromises. However, the reader can easily use the information presented to investigate smaller incidents as well.

Investigating Incidents

Historically, enterprises leveraged traditional computer forensics to determine attacker activity on a compromised system. However, scalability was a significant challenge associated with this approach. Furthermore, the methodologies that underpinned traditional computer forensics focused on investigating computer crimes and were not flexible enough to support large-scale investigations in enterprise environments.

With the evolution of live response tools, *enterprise incident response* emerged. This approach combines digital forensics, live response technology, and CTI to allow organizations to respond to large-scale incidents efficiently. To facilitate enterprise incident response, victim organizations deploy incident response technology into their environments in order to collect and analyze forensic data at scale. Traditional computer forensic techniques still play a vital role in this process. However, incident responders acquire forensic images of specific systems of interest for more targeted analysis driven by investigative objectives.

With the introduction of endpoint detection and response (EDR) tools into the security market, organizations now have the ability to collect system events and other system metadata in the course of system operations to detect and investigate threats.

Regardless of the approach, effective incident response investigations follow a well-established process to gain a full understanding of an incident and remediate it successfully, as depicted in Figure 5.1.

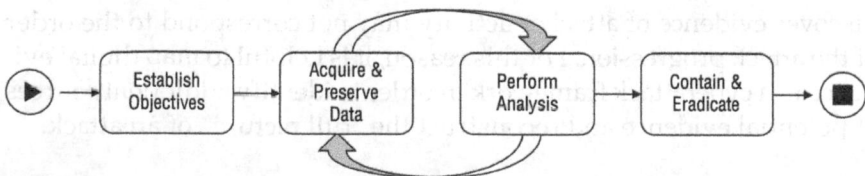

Figure 5.1: Incident investigation process

Determine Objectives

The first step in the incident investigation process is to gather initial information about a reported incident and establish objectives for the investigation. Not all incidents require the same level of response. Furthermore, depending on the nature and scope of an incident, an organization may have different priorities and objectives for the investigation. For example, if analysts identify evidence of data theft, the discovery may lead to legal exposure if the data is subjected to regulatory compliance. Consequently, the objectives of the investigation may be different from those of a ransomware attack.

Incident responders must establish objectives for an investigation and use the information to drive investigative activities. Incident response is about managing residual risk, and the response effort must be proportional to the level of risk and impact associated with an incident. The following list briefly discusses typical activities in this step.

Review initial incident data.   The first step in the investigation process is to review incident information. Depending on the nature of the incident, this data may include readily available indicators of compromise (IOC), observables, alerts generated by security tools, and evidence of connectivity to an IP address with a poor reputation, among others. This information is necessary to establish the investigative leads discussed later in this section.

Interview personnel.   Interviewing personnel is another critical step necessary to gather contextual information about an incident. The interview process should include technical personnel who detected and reported the incident, as well as business stakeholders who set priorities for the investigation, such as a business unit leader or legal counsel. Interviewing personnel who may have business context and who understand the architecture and configuration of the impacted technology is also essential.

Establish objectives.   Based on the information gathered during the previous two steps, establish objectives for the investigation. Objectives serve as a reference point and allow stakeholders to determine whether an investigation progresses in the right direction. Ensure that crucial stakeholders are in agreement about the objectives and priorities. A good practice is to document the objectives and get written approval from the key stakeholders. Establishing objectives for an investigation is also a crucial step in planning.

Establish a hypothesis. This is a critical, and often missed, step in incident investigations. It is rare that a malware alert or evidence of command and control (C2) communication is an isolated event. In many cases, attackers progress through earlier phases of the cyber-attack lifecycle, such as privilege escalation or lateral movement, before their activity tirggers an alert. For this reason, establishing a hypothesis and investigative leads is critical to ensuring that an investigation does not miss critical findings. Mapping evidence of attacker activity to a cyberattack framework throughout an investigation can help establish and refine a hypothesis. For example, if analysts discover evidence of data staging in a compromised environment, then it is likely that evidence of lateral movement exists too.

Create a plan. Based on the information established during the previous steps, create an investigation plan. A short plan listing crucial activities, their respective owners, and target dates is sufficient to start an investigation on the right foot. A plan may contain activities, such as technology deployment for live response, data collection through traditional forensics, cadence of communication with key stakeholders, roles and responsibilities, and data preservation. The plan must be aligned with the objectives and agreed on with key stakeholders. Some of the stakeholders may be vendors or even regulators, which adds another layer of complexity to planning and execution.

Acquire and Preserve Data

Chapter 3 discussed data acquisition methods in detail. Furthermore, Chapter 6 discusses this topic from a legal perspective with a particular emphasis on data preservation. The following list focuses on general data acquisition and preservation considerations and best practices for small- and large-scale incidents.

Identify data of interest. The first step in the acquisition process is to decide what data to acquire. This step is necessary to answer crucial questions about the incident and to accomplish the objectives of the investigation. In some cases, an analyst may want to examine data from multiple systems to determine the root cause of an incident. For example, if a system triggered a malware alert, the analyst may also want to acquire firewall or Internet proxy logs to establish evidence of communication to an attacker C2 infrastructure.

Decide on an acquisition method.   Depending on the nature of the incident, affected systems, and their locations, as well as business priorities, analysts may leverage various acquisition methods, such as forensic imaging, live response, memory acquisition, and log acquisition from enterprise services, or a combination thereof. Incident responders need to choose a method that captures the data necessary to answer crucial investigative questions. The temporal aspect of data is a vital consideration during data acquisition. Volatile data, such as network connections, typically has a short lifespan. Other types of data, such as artifacts in Windows registry files, persist on disk even if a system is powered down. Furthermore, the attacker dwell time may also drive decisions during this step.

Create a plan to preserve data.   At first, data preservation seems to be a straightforward task. However, in practice, data preservation can quickly become complex to manage as the scope of an investigation grows and analysts acquire data from multiple sources. This consideration is particularly applicable in cases where an incident response investigation might result in a legal proceeding, such as civil litigation. In some cases, an organization may even hire an external firm to preserve forensic data. An essential aspect of data preservation is ensuring data integrity, chain of custody, and a data retention policy. Chapter 6 discusses this topic in detail.

Acquire data.   A vital consideration in data acquisition, especially in the case of live response and memory acquisition, is to limit changes to the state of the acquired system. Small changes are inevitable, since most acquisition methods must interact with the system to collect forensic data. For this reason, analysts must produce detailed documentation of the acquisition process. Another consideration is to use sound, industry-accepted data acquisition protocols. The premise behind a sound and defensible technical protocol is that another analyst can repeat the protocol and arrive at the same results.

Document actions and decisions.   I cannot stress enough the importance of this step. Analysts must document the decisions that they make and the actions that they take in order to ensure that the acquisition and preservation protocol is defensible and accounts for deviations from standard practices. This step is of vital importance in cases that may result in a legal proceeding or are subject to scrutiny from regulators and auditors. Furthermore, adequate and complete documentation survives employee turnover, and it can provide information about an investigation years after its completion.

It is important to emphasize that the data that analysts require to answer crucial investigative questions may not exist. This scenario frequently happens during investigations of cyber breaches. For example, it is not uncommon for IT personnel to destroy forensic data by reimaging or rebuilding systems to contain an incident. In other cases, systems may not comply with security configuration baselines or retain log data as per the data retention policy. The result is that often vital forensic data is missing. Incident responders must document any missing data and communicate it with crucial stakeholders. Missing data is another reason why adequate and complete documentation is vital to the acquisition and preservation process.

The final point is that organizations must establish data acquisition and retention protocols as part of their incident response plan. Attempting to determine a protocol during an incident typically leads to confusion, conflicts of priorities, and inappropriate handling of digital evidence.

Perform Analysis

Arguably, analysis is the crux of incident response. The purpose of this step is to analyze available artifacts and other data to determine the root cause and full extent of an incident.

It is vital to emphasize that analysis is an iterative process. Analysts iterate through the lifecycle until they reach diminishing returns relating to new findings, such as discovering additional compromised systems or identifying additional attacker tools, tactics, and procedures (TTP) relevant to the investigated case. In simple terms, if consecutive iterations of the lifecycle no longer produce relevant findings, that is when the process typically terminates.

Analysis is a complex discipline, and it requires skills in multiple incident response domains, such as digital forensics, CTI, or malware reverse-engineering. During large-scale investigations, organizations typically assemble a team of analysts with complementary skills to progress analysis.

During enterprise incident response, organizations typically employ a lifecycle approach, as depicted in Figure 5.2, to analyze incidents.

Analyze data.   Analyzing data entails examining the data acquired during the acquisition and preservation step to answer crucial investigative questions. This step is typically the more labor-intensive process that involves digital forensics, malware analysis, and CTI. During significant incidents, enterprises often choose to hire an external firm with specialized skills and capabilities in this area.

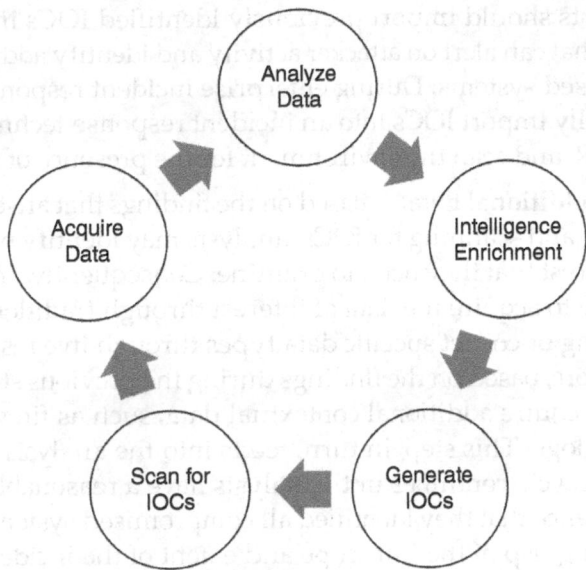

Figure 5.2: Analysis lifecycle

Perform intelligence enrichment.   CTI augments the analysis step by providing contextual information to help drive further investigative activities. Malware analysis and contextual CTI research are vital parts of this process. CTI analysts often leverage incident information that forensic analysts determine based on the analysis of compromised systems. Malware analysis is another rich source of information for CTI analysts. For example, a CTI analyst may use the data initially gathered to make a preliminary attribution assessment of the responsible threat actor. With this knowledge, the analyst can provide relevant IOCs and observables to incident responders to identify other compromised systems and rapidly scope the incident. IOCs are forensic artifacts indicative of attacker activity.

Generate IOCs.   Based on the outcome of the analysis and CTI augmentation, the next step is to generate IOCs to continue scoping the compromise. IOCs can take many forms, including IP addresses, hashes of malicious files, signatures of exploits, or compromised accounts, among others. As analysts continue to investigate and scope the incident, the list of indicators typically grows.

Scan for IOCs.   During enterprisewide intrusions, attackers typically compromise multiple systems and establish persistence in the compromised environment. To scope the compromise effectively, analysts should import previously identified IOCs into security tools that can alert on attacker activity and identify additional compromised systems. During enterprise incident response, analysts typically import IOCs into an incident response technology, such as EDR, and scan the environment for the presence of those IOCs.

Acquire additional data.   Based on the findings that arise from monitoring and scanning for IOCs, analysts may identify new systems of interest that they need to examine. Consequently, analysts may choose to acquire the data of interest through traditional forensic imaging or collect specific data types through live response. Furthermore, based on the findings during the previous step, analysts often acquire additional contextual data, such as firewall or web proxy logs. This step, in turn, feeds into the analysis phase, and the lifecycle continues until analysts have a reasonable degree of confidence that they identified all compromised systems and have a good grasp of the full scope and extent of the incident.

Analysis is an iterative process. As analysts investigate an incident, they may decide to acquire and analyze additional data in order to understand the attacker's operations. This approach is particularly applicable to large-scale investigations. For example, during a forensic examination of a compromised system, an analyst may recover new IOCs. A logical step is to scan the environment for the indicators to determine if there were previously unknown compromised systems. If there are matches, the analyst may acquire data from the new systems for further analysis.

Contain and Eradicate

Once incident responders have a reasonable degree of confidence that they have understood the scope of an incident and have answers to the investigative questions, it is time to contain the incident and eradicate the threat actor from the compromised environment. Chapter 4 briefly discusses remediation as part of the incident response lifecycle. This topic is so important to cyber breach response that I dedicate an entire section to incident containment and eradication later in this chapter.

Conducting Analysis

As previously mentioned, incident analysis is a complex process that requires skills in domains, such as digital forensics, CTI, and malware analysis. Each of these domains in turn is a complex discipline and requires specialized skills. During large-scale incidents, victim organizations typically convene a team with complementary skills across these domains. The personnel work together to answer crucial investigative questions and understand the scope of the incident. This section discusses each of the domains mentioned earlier and how they contribute to the overall investigative process.

Digital Forensics

Digital forensics is a specialized discipline that focuses on the analysis and recovery of digital data from compromised systems. Forensic analysts use specialized tools and techniques to reconstruct events on an examined system to determine how an attacker interacted with the system and to develop IOCs. Digital forensics can also help organizations recover deleted data to prove or refute a hypothesis. For example, in some cases, analysts may recover files deleted by an attacker that provide evidence of data staging.

Digital forensics is a broad discipline that requires skills and experience across various technologies. Three primary areas of digital forensics are computer, network, and mobile forensics. However, with cloud computing and other trends in technology, traditional forensics skills by themselves are no longer enough. Incident responders must be well versed in numerous technologies and be able to adapt to investigate incidents effectively. Arguably, specific knowledge and skills in traditional computer forensics are no longer enough in today's evolving digital work. Incident response professionals must understand the underlying methodologies that underpin the digital forensics and incident response (DFIR) domain to respond to different types of incidents and effectively work with business and technology stakeholders.

Digital Forensics Disciplines

The following list discusses various aspects of digital forensics that organizations need to consider when building incident response capabilities.

Computer Forensics   Historically, traditional computer forensics has been associated with law enforcement and electronic discovery cases. *Computer forensics* focuses on analyzing persistent and volatile system artifacts in order to answer investigative questions. For example, a forensic analyst may review program execution artifacts to determine when an attacker has installed malware on the examined system. Analysts may leverage traditional disk forensics, also referred to as "dead box" forensics, live response, memory forensics, or a combination thereof. Chapter 3 discusses this topic in detail from a technology perspective.

It is important to emphasize that during large-scale investigations, analysts typically leverage a combination of the methods mentioned earlier. One frequent use case is to leverage live response techniques for rapid triage and acquire disk and physical memory images for an in-depth analysis. This approach makes the incident response process scalable.

Network Forensics   *Network forensics* is a branch of digital forensics that focuses on analyzing network data for intrusion detection. Gathering network telemetry has two primary uses: reconstructing network events associated with past attacker activity and monitoring for additional activities to scope an incident. Some network data is volatile and dynamic, whereas other data is persistent. For example, data that flows through the network is volatile and requires in-transit capture. Firewall traffic logs, on the other hand, are more persistent.

Network forensics can be a stand-alone discipline and is sometimes the only source of evidence of attacker activity. However, in the majority of enterprise incident response cases, network forensics complements traditional host forensics and live response, and it provides corroborating evidence of attacker activity.

There are many challenges associated with network forensics. Organizations often encrypt communications, and decrypting the data can be a challenge, as well as violate regulatory requirements in some cases. Furthermore, network address translation (NAT) and the dynamic nature of IP address assignment on client systems, most of which use Dynamic Host Configuration Protocol (DHCP) to obtain ephemeral IP addresses, makes it challenging to track the sources of network connections. Finally, due to a significant amount of telemetry, network data is often stored for a short period of time unless specifically retained in a long-term storage solution.

Mobile Device Forensics   Historically, mobile forensics has played an important role in law enforcement cases and electronic discovery. However, attackers have been increasingly targeting mobile enterprise users by exploiting vulnerabilities in apps, installing malware on mobile devices, and using other techniques to harvest sensitive data, such as credentials.

Although *mobile device forensics* is not a mainstream discipline in enterprise incident response, it plays an increasingly important role in internal investigations, such as employee-related cases or electronic discovery for civil litigation. Analysts may recover and analyze a variety of artifacts from mobile devices, such as historical geolocation data, Internet browsing history, call history, documents, and data from installed apps, and they may even recover deleted data, among other artifacts. As of this writing, I have not come across cases where a threat actor used a compromised mobile device to pivot to an enterprise network.

Cloud Computing Forensics   *Cloud computing forensics* is a relatively new addition to the digital forensics field. Cloud computing forensics combines traditional forensic techniques with cloud-native tools. The steps that incident responders take to investigate breaches of cloud systems depend on the level of access to those systems. With the infrastructure as a service (IaaS) model, incident responders may acquire virtual machines, cloud service logs, and other data. However, with platform as a service (PaaS) and software as a service (SaaS), incident responders may be limited to log analysis, such as event logs associated with programmatic access to cloud service resources. Chapter 3 discusses data acquisition from cloud platforms in detail.

As a field, digital forensics continually evolves, and there is ongoing research into various technologies to uncover system artifacts that may be of value to forensic analysts. Another important consideration is that forensic artifacts and techniques may vary from system to system. For these reasons, incident responders must continually strive to acquire new skills and stay abreast of new developments in this field.

Timeline Analysis

Operating systems create many artifacts that have temporal characteristics, including filesystem, event logs, application logs, network connection logs, and registry entries, among others. *Timeline analysis* is a forensic technique that allows analysts to reconstruct events on the examined systems by arranging relevant events in a timeline. Timeline analysis is a powerful technique that allows analysts to answer questions relating to which events occurred before and after a given event, such as malware infection, and to gain valuable insights into attacker activity.

Timeline analysis is a particularly powerful tool during large-scale investigations. To arrive at a timeline of attacker activity during an incident, incident responders typically create timelines for individual compromised systems and combine them into a single master timeline consisting of significant events. This information is invaluable for reporting and reconstruing the picture of an attack. In my personal experience, a timeline with a narrative in business security language is particularly useful for reporting and communicating investigative findings to senior-level management.

One crucial consideration in building a timeline is to ensure that all timestamps are expressed in Coordinated Universal Time (UTC). UTC is the de facto standard for timestamping event logs. However, some organizations choose to use a time that is local to their geographic region instead. As a result, analysts must translate non-UTC time to UTC time before timelining events.

Other Considerations in Digital Forensics

Digital forensics often relies on artifacts produced in the course of system operation, such as program execution artifacts, to answer vital investigative questions. In some cases, the data necessary to answer those questions may not be available. For example, a system has overwritten specific artifacts in the course of its operations or the necessary logging policies were not configured to capture the data of interest.

Even if specific artifacts are available, analysts may have to correlate and corroborate them with other sources of data, such as network telemetry to determine attacker activity. For example, during data theft cases, analysts typically correlate system artifacts with data relating to network connections in order to prove or refute a data theft hypothesis.

It is essential to keep in mind that digital forensics may not always provide all the answers to questions that business stakeholders ask. Another crucial consideration is that sophisticated threat actors often leverage anti-forensic techniques to make the discovery and investigation of their attacks challenging. For example, an attacker may manipulate the timestamps of a malware binary file to minimize the possibility of detection. Incident response professionals refer to this technique as *timestomping*.

To maximize the chances of answering vital investigative questions, enterprises need to configure logging and log retention policies to support incident response investigations. The enforcement of those policies across the enterprise is vital.

Cyber Threat Intelligence

Chapter 1 briefly described CTI as a driver for cyber breach response. This section discusses intelligence-driven incident response, with a particular focus on tactical intelligence to support investigations.

Intelligence-driven response is an approach to incident response that leverages intelligence processes and concepts as an integral part of the overall investigation process.[1] CTI augments digital forensic processes by researching and applying contextual threat information in order to identify attacker activity and scope an incident effectively. Not only is CTI necessary to understand the root cause and scope of a compromise, but it is also essential in containing an incident and eradicating the threat actor from the compromised environment.

CTI analysts leverage various techniques to gather information necessary to support incident investigations, such as attacker-centric and asset-centric approaches.[2] This book discusses the attacker-centric approach only. Analysts also rely on structured analytical techniques, such as analysis of competing hypotheses (ACH),[3] in order to reduce or eliminate analytical bias in the process. All too often, even the most veteran analysts have at some point made an attribution assessment based on past experiences instead of applying the appropriate rigor to their assessment.

CTI research typically starts with known information about an incident. For example, an organization has detected malware, a network connection to a known C2 domain, or evidence of a suspicious tool, such as credential harvesting software. The initial information acts as a starting point for the research. Analysts start with the initial indicators and perform research that may provide an insight into the TTP that an attacker leverages, uncover additional IOC, or even attribute the attack. CTI professionals often refer to this approach as *intelligence enrichment*. CTI research is like unraveling a thread. For example, I worked on cases where CTI enrichment of a single IOC opened up an entire investigation and allowed the analysts to uncover additional evidence of attacker activity in the compromised environment.

Attributing a cyberattack to a specific threat actor is often a part of the CTI process. Chapter 6 discusses attribution in depth. For the purposes of this chapter, it is worth noting that cyber attribution is becoming increasingly difficult as threat actors move away from using custom malware and leverage tools that they find in compromised environments to progress through the cyberattack lifecycle.

Cyber Threat Intelligence Lifecycle

CTI analysts gather threat information and analyze the information to answer specific questions relating to an investigation. This section discusses the CTI lifecycle, with a particular emphasis on tactical intelligence to support incident response investigations.

CTI enrichment is an iterative process consisting of five phases. The last phase provides a feedback loop to the first phase to continue the process until the analysts have enough information to achieve the investigation's objectives or they reach diminishing returns relating to new findings This process is tightly coupled with forensic analysis and monitoring for attacker activity, as depicted in Figure 5.3.

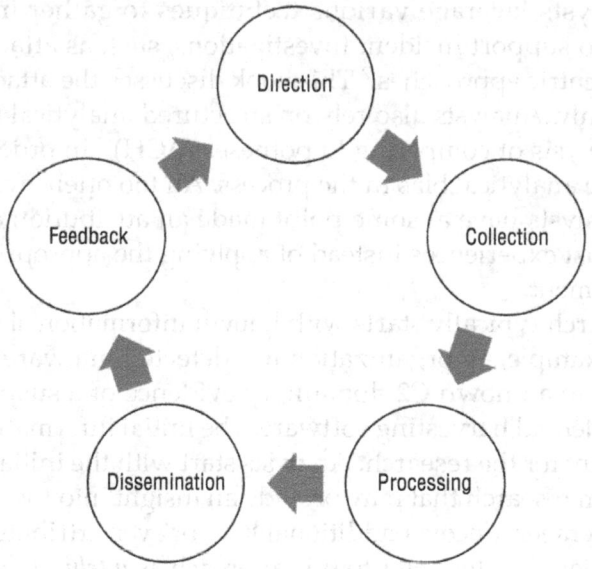

Figure 5.3: The CTI lifecycle

Direction   Initial findings and leads that incident responders establish early on during an investigation provide a preliminary direction for CTI gathering. These leads can come from security monitoring, network traffic analysis, malware analysis, forensic findings, or third-party notifications, such as law enforcement. Analysts must establish objectives for the CTI research. The overall investigation objectives typically drive this activity.

Collection   In this step, analysts typically pivot on the initial findings and investigative leads and collect information about past potentially related incidents and reports from researchers, vendors, and law enforcement agencies in order to perform an attacker-centric research and gather contextual information about the incident. As part of this step, analysts also verify if the collected information is relevant to the investigated case.

Processing   After collecting data, analysts must process the data into an appropriate format for the target audience, such as a listing of IP addresses and domain names for importing into security tools or a dossier on a particular, identified group for consumption by the incident response team.

Dissemination   As the next step, analysts disseminate the produced intelligence to the appropriate stakeholders, such as incident responders for scoping or managers to make decisions about investigative priorities. For example, management may be interested in attacker goals, whereas a forensic analyst typically is more interested in stand-alone IOCs, such as malware hashes or C2 domains.

Feedback   Feedback occurs at the incident management and technical levels. From a technical perspective, forensic analysts can notify CTI analysts if they identify any systems with the indicators discovered through CTI enrichment. In contrast, from an incident management perspective, an incident manager or a senior stakeholder may leverage CTI findings to drive investigative priorities. For example, if CTI analysts determine that the goal of the threat actor behind an attack is to steal intellectual property, the enterprise may choose to focus on securing the environments that host that type of data while the investigation continues to minimize the possibility of data theft.

It is crucial to emphasize that the intelligence-driven approach involves all the components mentioned here to support an investigation.

Identifying Attacker Activity with Cyber Threat Intelligence

The following list briefly describes common components of the attacker-centric approach that analysts often leverage in investigations.

Attack Vector   An *attack vector* is a means by which an attacker gains unauthorized access to a system or network. There are numerous attack vectors that attackers can leverage to gain initial access to a system or computer network before progressing through the remaining phases of the cyberattack lifecycle. For example, phishing is a popular attack vector that attackers use to entice their victims to open an attachment or click on a link that takes the victim to a rogue website. This technique allows attackers to deliver a malicious payload that executes on the victim's system and leads to unauthorized access. In the case of phishing, a malicious attachment contains embedded code that constitutes the payload.

Indicators of Compromise   In simple terms, an IOC is a forensic artifact indicative of attacker activity. Analysts often derive IOCs through forensic analysis of compromised systems and CTI enrichment. Examples of IOCs are hash values, IP addresses, domain names, filesystem and program execution artifacts, or signatures of attack patterns, among others. I discuss IOC categorization later in this chapter.

It is important not to confuse IOCs with indicators of attack (IOA). The latter represents the actions that an attacker takes before compromising a system or network, such as reconnaissance.

Behavioral Characteristics   Behavioral characteristics refer to the TTPs that represent the way that an attacker operates to progress through the cyberattack lifecycle. Behavioral characteristics are useful in developing contextual information associated with specific threat groups. For example, a specific threat group may exploit vulnerable web servers and place a web shell on those web servers for remote access. A web shell is a script that allows an attacker to use a web server as an entry point into a system or network.

Goals   Goals require specific effort and represent the desired outcome that an attacker tries to achieve. Threat actors compromise systems and networks to achieve specific goals, such as financial data theft, theft of intellectual property, encryption of systems and data for ransom, or espionage. Attacker goals are arguably the most abstract type of information that CTI analysts can gather. Also, some attackers may adjust the way that they operate in response to detection, but goals typically do not change.

Not all CTI is equal. Attackers may easily change some indicators, whereas others are more difficult to change without significantly adjusting the way that a particular attacker operates. To demonstrate this concept, David Bianco created the Pyramid of Pain,[4] as represented in Figure 5.4. The pyramid orders IOCs in an increasing level of difficulty for attackers to change. At the bottom, the pyramid lists more volatile indicators that are trivial to change, such as hashes and IP addresses. Toward the top, the pyramid lists indicators that are harder for attackers to change and that have more extended longevity.

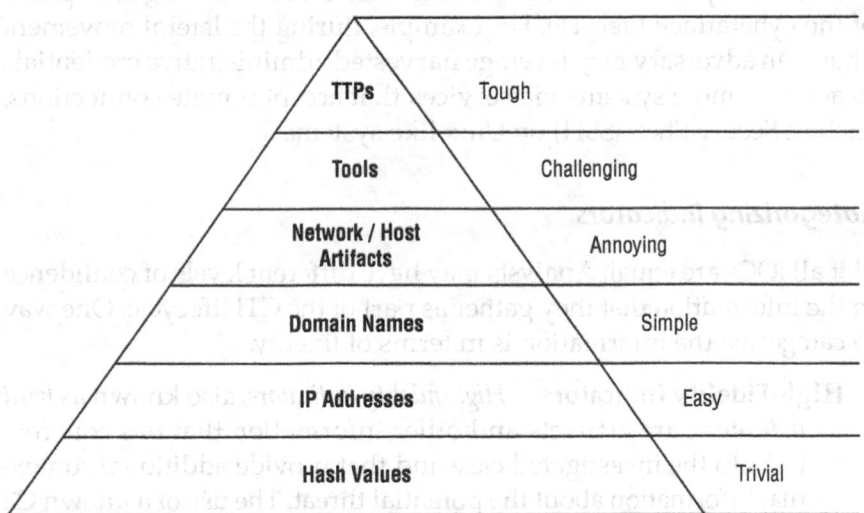

Figure 5.4: The Pyramid of Pain

According to David Bianco, the entire point of indicators is to use them in response and remediation. For this reason, incident responders need to keep in mind that some indicators are temporal. In contrast, other indicators, such as a particular way of executing an attack, are more reliable in the long term. For example, during client incident investigations, I have observed that indicators, such as C2 IP addresses or malware hash values, change. However, I have not come across a case where an attacker would suddenly change their behavioral characteristics in response to an investigation.

The CTI community uses the same acronym "TTP" to refer to two different but related terms that describe how threat actors operate: 1) tactics, techniques, and procedures and 2) tools, tactics, and procedures. In this book, I use the latter term to call out attacker tools explicitly. However, both terms are correct, and the community uses them interchangeably.

According to the Pyramid of Pain, TTPs are associated with behavioral characteristics and are the hardest to change. Tools are software applications, such as malware, utilities, and other software that a specific threat actor uses as part of their attack operations. Tactics describe how a threat actor operates at various phases of the cyberattack lifecycle and how the activities relate to one another. An example of a tactic used to escalate privileges on a compromised system is when a threat actor can use credential dumping software to harvest credentials from volatile memory and uses those credentials for lateral movement. Procedures describe a sequence of actions a threat actor executes during each phase of the cyberattack lifecycle. For example, during the lateral movement phase, an adversary may leverage harvested administrative credentials to access remote systems via services that accept remote connections, such as Secure Shell (SSH) on Unix-like systems.

Categorizing Indicators

Not all IOCs are equal. Analysts may have different levels of confidence in the information that they gather as part of the CTI lifecycle. One way to categorize the information is in terms of fidelity.

High-Fidelity Indicators   *High-fidelity indicators*, also known as *hard indicators*, are artifacts and other information that has concrete links to the investigated case and that provide additional contextual information about the potential threat. The use of a known C2 domain registered with an email address attributable to a specific threat actor is an example of a high-fidelity indicator. Incident responders typically ingest high-fidelity indicators into security tools for monitoring and investigative purposes. Incident responders also use this information to scan the compromised network to identify additional, unknown compromised systems and to identify attacker activity in the compromised environment.

Low-Fidelity Indicators   *Low-fidelity indicators* and behaviors, also known as *soft indicators*, are information that may be indicative of attacker activity but that is not strong enough on its own. The IP address of a virtual private network (VPN) exit node that a threat actor used to access a compromised service is an example of a low-fidelity indicator. In some cases, low-fidelity indicators may result in a high rate of false-positive events. Incident responders need to correlate and corroborate low-fidelity indicators with other incident information before drawing specific conclusions, such as the compromise of a system.

Another critical consideration is to classify IOCs into specific categories, such as network, host, or behavioral indicators. Grouping indicators and assigning them a fidelity level allows responders to search and filter for data of interest easily, as well as to identify specific information for further investigative steps and CTI enrichment.

It is also worth mentioning that the SANS Institute and many practitioners classify IOCs as follows:[5]

Atomic   Discrete data points that may indicate adversary activity on their own. According to the SANS Institute, those indicators may not always exclusively represent an activity associated with a threat actor. For example, if a threat actor compromises a legitimate website and uses it to launch their attack, an outbound network connection to that website is not necessarily indicative of a compromise by itself.

Computed   Computed indicators are calculated based on data obtained through forensic analysis. For example, an analyst may compute a hash value associated with a malware binary or create a signature to detect a network-based exploit.

Behavioral   Behavioral indicators closely resemble TTPs described in the previous section. They are composed of specific behaviors and characteristics attributed to a specific threat actor. For example, a threat actor may use a specific tactic to maintain persistence in the compromised environment, such as installing malware as a Windows service or placing a web shell script on a publicly accessible web server and using it as an entry point into the compromised network.

Finally, it is of crucial importance to document the indicators alongside their source and link them to the investigation. As investigations grow and include multiple, simultaneous workstreams, accurate and comprehensive documentation is what allows stakeholders to remain informed about how the threat actor operates in the compromised environment.

It is also worth noting that enterprises can choose to participate in intelligence sharing communities to gain access to CTI that otherwise might not be available to them. This information can be of vital importance during incident investigations. By participating in intelligence sharing programs, enterprises can draw on the collective knowledge and capabilities of their members. Examples of entities that create intelligence sharing programs include government agencies, cybersecurity vendors, and industry-specific CTI centers. These entities usually make CTI available for consumption in the following formats:

- IOCs
- TTPs

- Advisories
- CTI reports

Some platforms and websites make specific CTI available to the cybersecurity community at no cost, such as IBM X-Force Exchange or VirusTotal. These services also offer premium access to organizations that require access to advanced features.

Another option is to partner with a specific CTI vendor that can assist with strategic, operational, and tactical intelligence packages. In my personal experience, partnering with CTI vendors during incident investigations has been invaluable in understanding and scoping enterprisewide intrusions.

Malware Analysis

Malware analysis is an integral part of incident response investigations and requires breadths and depths of understanding of various technical disciplines. Attackers leverage malware and other software tools to gain unauthorized access to a computer network, move laterally, steal data, or encrypt data for ransom, among other things.

Malware has significantly evolved over the years from primitive, self-contained binaries to highly modular malware that often implements obfuscation techniques, such as encryption or polymorphism, to make it difficult to detect and analyze it. Sophisticated malware often relies on a complex infection chain that includes downloaders and droppers, payloads, and a C2 infrastructure. Furthermore, some malware types leverage legitimate applications as part of the infection chain. For example, many malware infections start with the execution of macros embedded in Microsoft Excel files.

With the evolution of the threat landscape, sophisticated attackers often rely on malware providers who offer malware-as-a-service on the dark web. Historically, it was common to attribute attacks based on the malware alone. With the malware-as-a-service model, attribution based purely on malware is rare.

This section discusses common malware types and malware analysis techniques that analysts leverage as part of the incident response lifecycle.

Classifying Malware

Several ways to classify malware exist, such as behavior or infection vector. Malware taxonomy is a process of classifying malware based on specific characteristics and attributes. The following list briefly discusses common malware types that threat actors leverage during enterprise intrusions.

Viruses   A *virus* is a malicious piece of code that attaches itself to a legitimate program or a file in order to spread from computer to computer and execute its logic. Another name for a virus is a *file infector.*

Network Worms   A *network worm* is a stand-alone malware that uses a programmatic approach to spread from computer to computer using mechanisms such as file sharing protocols and peer-to-peer networks.

Backdoors   *Backdoor malware* allows an attacker to bypass access control mechanisms and gain unauthorized access to a computer system. An example of backdoor malware is a web shell that an attacker places on a compromised web server. A term closely associated with backdoor malware is *Remote-Access Trojan (RAT).* A RAT is a remote administrative tool that has backdoor capabilities and typically allows an attacker to gain, often root-level, access to a system and remotely control the system.

Information Stealer   An *information stealer* is a class of malware that steals information by using techniques such as using keylogging, using desktop recording, enumerating local systems and remote data stores for specific types of data, and scraping memory for unencrypted sensitive information.

Ransomware   *Ransomware* is a type of malware that holds data or access to a computer system hostage until the victim pays a ransom. Three primary techniques exist to achieve this goal: data encryption, data distraction, and user lockout. *Data destruction* refers to inevitably threatening to destroy the data if the victim does not pay, typically to create a sense of urgency.

Destructive Malware   Malware authors develop *destructive malware* to render infected systems inoperable and make recovery challenging. Stuxnet[6] is a primary example of destructive malware.

Another way of looking at malware is in terms of how attackers use it and its purpose. *Commodity malware* is a category of malware that is widely available for purchase or free download and does not require any customization. Threat actors typically leverage commodity malware in opportunistic attacks by employing a "spray and pray" strategy. Dridex[7] is an example of commodity malware.

In contrast, *targeted malware,* also referred to as *bespoke malware,* is very precise malware that threat actors leverage while targeting specific users or a specific entity. Malware authors often write targeted malware for very specific purposes after performing an extensive reconnaissance to maximize the chances of achieving their objectives. Targeted malware is often associated with advanced persistent threat (APT) groups, such as nation-state threat actors. Stuxnet is a primary example of targeted, destructive malware.

An important point to cover before discussing specific malware analysis techniques is fileless malware and "living off the land" techniques. Traditional malware requires attackers to place a binary file on disk, which leaves forensic artifacts behind. Fileless malware, on the other hand, lives entirely in computer memory and does not leave evidence on a disk volume. This technique makes it much harder to detect with traditional tools, such as antivirus, and requires memory forensics to uncover evidence of its execution.

Living off the land is a technique that attackers often use alongside fileless malware. Attackers increasingly rely on legitimate administrative tools that they find in the compromised environment to progress through the cyberattack lifecycle. This technique is appealing because system administrators often whitelist tools that they require for day-to-day tasks. Furthermore, the use of legitimate tools as part of an attack makes it challenging for incident responders to identify malicious activity.

Static Analysis

Depending on the objectives of an investigation, analysts can perform basic or advanced static malware analysis or a combination of thereof.

Basic static analysis is the process of examining an executable file to determine whether the file is malicious and to provide fundamental information about it. During basic static analysis, analysts do not examine the actual code instructions. Instead, they gather and examine the file metadata, including hash, file type, and size. Analysts also search for strings that may provide information about the file's functionality, such as hard-coded IP addresses and URLs.

Static analysis may also check for obfuscation. Malware authors use this technique to obscure meaningful information to make it harder to analyze their malware. In some cases, basic static analysis may yield enough information to generate a signature.

To understand a malware sample fully, analysts may resort to *advanced static analysis*, which focuses on disassembling malware at the code level and examining the actual instructions. Analysts typically use tools, such as a disassembler, to break down a compiled malware binary file into machine-code instructions. By performing advanced static analysis, analysts can understand the full capabilities of the malware.

Depending on the size and complexity of the malware, reverse-engineering a malware sample can take days or even weeks. For this reason, analysts resort to advanced analysis when dealing with unknown malware, or they need to understand the malware capabilities fully to drive containment and eradication.

Dynamic Analysis

Dynamic analysis is the process of running a malware sample in a controlled environment in order to determine its behavior. One of the most common techniques that analysts leverage for dynamic analysis is a sandbox. A *sandbox* is a dedicated, isolated system with installed dynamic analysis software that collects telemetry when the malware executes.

Dynamic analysis typically focuses on the changes that malware makes to the system, such as creating new processes, making changes to the registry, network connections, or creating persistence mechanisms. The goal of dynamic analysis is to gather information necessary to identify the examined malware in the compromised environment.

Malware Analysis and Cyber Threat Intelligence

During incident response investigations, malware analysis and CTI go hand in hand. CTI often provides focus and direction for malware analysis. For example, if prior analysis yielded evidence of data theft, a reverse engineer may focus on looking for code instructions that may enumerate various repositories for data of interest.

At the same time, malware analysis can provide rich information on how a particular threat actor operates, including IOCs or tactics. This information, in turn, feeds into the CTI lifecycle. This process is iterative. The information that analysts glean from malware analysis initiates a full CTI enrichment process and servers as pivot points. The outcome of the enrichment process, in turn, allows analysts to identify additional malware that a threat actor may have used as part of their operations in the compromised environment.

Threat Hunting

Threat hunting is an approach to threat detection that combines a methodology, technology, skills, and CTI to detect attacker activity proactively that programmatic approaches, such as traditional antivirus software, may miss.[8]

Although threat hunting is primarily a proactive approach, incident responders also leverage threat hunting in situations where an organization discovers a suspicious activity but there are no specific IOCs to inform the investigation.

I led investigations where clients reported a suspicious behavior on their network or received a third-party notification about a potential compromise but did not identify specific IOCs. Without a "smoking gun," our team had to resort to threat hunting techniques to identify IOCs and scope the intrusions.

The premise behind threat hunting is that programmatic approaches to threat detection, such as traditional antivirus, network traffic inspection, or even statistical analysis methods, may not uncover all attacker activity. This approach is particularly applicable to attacks where threat actors employ stealthy techniques or evasion methods, or heavily rely on "living off the land" methods.

Prerequisites to Threat Hunting

Developing threat hunting capabilities requires commitment from senior management, dedicated resources, and an investment into appropriate technologies. The following list describes vital components that organizations must consider in order to enable threat hunting.

Framework   Organizations must develop a systematic analysis-driven approach to hunt for cyber threats effectively. Developing a process based on an established framework with dedicated resources is vital. Appropriate technology, skills, and CTI are crucial components of a sound methodology.

Technology   To hunt for evidence of compromise, analysts must collect the necessary network and endpoint data. Appropriate data must be available, accurate, complete, reliable, and relevant. There is no silver bullet technology to accomplish this task. Threat hunters typically leverage a combination of tools, such as EDR, Security Information and Event Management (SIEM), network-based detection systems, and others.

Skills   To become effective threat hunters, analysts must possess a wealth of skills across various technical disciplines. During threat hunting, analysts look for outliers in data sets and must be able to distinguish between normal versus abnormal activities on a computer network. Threat hunting also requires soft skills, such as critical thinking, analysis, or curiosity.

Cyber Threat Intelligence   CTI provides information about TTPs, and it is a vital component in threat hunting. High-quality CTI augments analysis in two ways: it helps identify low-hanging fruit through a programmatic approach, and it provides contextual information during manual analysis. In some cases, CTI delivers specific information that analysts may hunt for in their environments, such as information on how a specific threat actor operates.

Threat Hunting Lifecycle

Threat hunting is an iterative process with clearly defined phases. Moreover, organizations have two options at their disposal to perform threat hunting: data-driven and target-driven threat hunting.[9]

The data-driven approach involves collecting a specific data set and analyzing it for evidence of suspicious activity. For example, an analyst may choose to collect program execution artifacts from specific environments and look for evidence of malware and other suspicious tools.

In contrast, a target-driven approach allows organizations to determine whether a particular threat is present in their environments. For example, an analyst may compile a list of IOCs associated with a specific threat actor and leverage tools, such as EDR, to query endpoints for those indicators. Organizations with a mature threat hunting capability typically combine both approaches.

Figure 5.5 depicts a typical lifecycle approach that organizations can leverage to hunt for threats in their environment.[10]

Determine Purpose   Determine why a specific threat activity must occur, including any assumptions and limitations. Additionally, determine a specific outcome stemming from the activity. A clearly defined purpose provides general guidance and direction for hunting. For example, an organization may choose to perform threat hunting following a corporate merger and acquisition to gain assurance before connecting corporate networks.

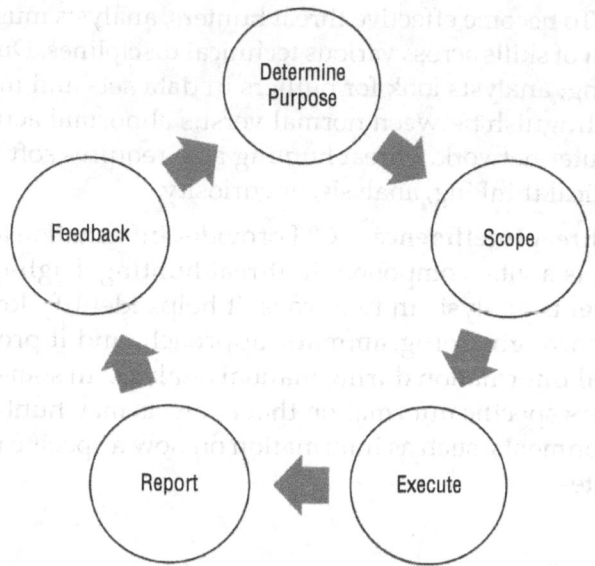

Figure 5.5: Threat hunting lifecycle

Scope   Scoping includes two activities: defining a specific environment or network segment for hunting and generating a hypothesis. The former identifies the technology in scope. The latter allows analysts to generate analytical questions to drive the hunting activity. CTI, situational awareness, and domain knowledge typically help analysts formulate a hypothesis.

Execute   The execution stage includes multiple iterations of data acquisition and analysis. The techniques that analysts employ depend on whether their hunting is data- or target-driven. The purpose of this phase is to collect data from systems in scope and use analysis techniques to prove or disprove the hypothesis developed during the scoping phase.

Report   Preparing a threat hunting report concludes the execution phase. Analysts should produce a formal report for large-scale threat hunting exercises, especially if senior leadership requested the activity based on risk concerns. Ongoing threat hunting activity does not typically require a formal, extensive report.

A formal report should clearly state the purpose and scope of a threat hunting activity before discussing the outcome and findings. A sound report also briefly articulates the analysis techniques that analysts employed and any limitations and obstacles.

Feedback   Feedback is a process that analysts employ to evaluate the previous stages of the lifecycle and to take corrective actions to improve the overall threat hunting methodology and framework. For example, analysts may evaluate the scoping phase to determine whether the scope was too narrow, just right, or too big. This evaluation can help ensure scoping future hunting activities more precisely. Consequently, feedback allows organizations to improve and optimize their threat hunting capability continuously.

Some threat hunting activities may lead analysts to discover evidence of a historical or ongoing network intrusion. In such cases, organizations must consider transitioning the hunting activity into an incident investigation. By declaring an incident, organizations can ensure that they dedicate the necessary resources to appropriately respond to the incident.

Reporting

Reporting is a critical but often forgotten part of the analysis phase. An adequate report summarizes an incident in a succinct yet complete manner, and it helps key stakeholders understand significant incident events. There are three types of reports that incident responders typically produce during enterprise incident response.

Technical Reports   *Technical reports* capture low-level technical information relating to a specific aspect of an investigation or analysis. An example of a technical report is a malware reverse-engineering report that captures the technical details and capabilities of a malware sample. The primary audience for technical reports is technical personnel who set the technical direction for an investigation and incident response analysts.

Periodic Management Reports   During large-scale, prolonged investigations, management may require *periodic reports* to understand the overall progress and findings during the investigation in order to make informed decisions about priorities. Periodic management reports should summarize investigative activities and vital findings in an easy-to-understand business security language and clearly articulate the next steps with defined timelines.

Investigation Report   An *investigation report* is a comprehensive report that focuses on an incident as a whole and helps key stakeholders understand significant incident events. Incident responders should produce a final investigation report after concluding an investigation. An investigation report typically consists of two major sections: an executive summary and a detailed incident discussion section.

The following paragraphs provide general recommendations that can help incident responders produce high-quality reports that communicate their findings to key stakeholders effectively.

Create a report template.   Create a template for reporting. Templates make the reporting style consistent and they save time. Also, reporting using a consistent style and a clear structure can help communicate findings in the long term, especially for internal reporting.

Focus on facts.   A well-written report provides an objective and impartial statement of the analysis effort and its findings. For this reason, report authors must focus on facts and avoid speculation or assumptions. Where speculation is unavoidable, the authors should clearly state that they speculate about specific events. Furthermore, authors must provide evidence, such as tables describing artifacts, to support their statements.

Know your audience.   A report for executive personnel has a very different focus compared to a report for technical audiences. Report authors must tailor the content and the presentation style for the intended audience to communicate their message effectively.

Write in formal language and active voice.   Formal language and active voice are the de facto styles for technical writing. Active voice adds impact to writing. Passive voice often leads to wordy and vague sentences and ambiguity. Active voice, on the other hand, makes writing more concise, actionable, and engaging. Active voice also helps move the narrative, improve flow, and generally improve readability.

To write in the formal style, report authors must use objective, impersonal, and precise language and avoid slang and informal expressions. Also, ensuring correct grammar, clear transitions, and logical flow between different sections of a report is vital.

I cannot emphasize enough the importance of reporting. Organizations may require investigation reports for a variety of purposes, including compliance, cyber insurance, or for anticipated litigation. Furthermore, reports are more reliable than human memory and outlive investigations. After several months or even a few years, a report may constitute the only reliable information available about a past incident.

Evidence Types

Systems and software applications often generate significant volumes of artifacts that incident responders may leverage during their investigations to determine attacker activity in a compromised environment.

Some of the artifacts are byproducts of normal system operations that happen to have forensic value. For example, the Windows operating system implements performance and software compatibility mechanisms that generate artifacts relating to program execution. These artifacts are an invaluable source of information on malware and other tools that a threat actor executed on a compromised system.

Furthermore, system administrators configure security policies that cause systems and applications to generate artifacts in response to specific events. For example, authentication logs provide information, such as user accounts that successfully and unsuccessfully attempted to log in to a computer system.

Before diving into a detailed conversation about digital evidence, it is crucial to understand the difference between artifacts and evidence. An *artifact* is a piece of data that a system or software application produces in the course of its operations. For example, an event log showing a successful authentication attempt is an artifact. In contrast, an artifact that is relevant to an investigated case because it either supports or refutes a hypothesis becomes *evidence*. For example, if an analyst identifies a program execution artifact associated with attacker malware, that artifact becomes digital evidence.

System Artifacts

Operating systems generate several types of artifacts that allow analysts to establish attacker activity on a compromised system. Chapter 3 discussed data acquisition in detail. Depending on the acquisition method, incident responders can collect persistent and volatile artifacts from systems of interest.

Persistent Artifacts

Persistent artifacts constitute data that resides in persistent storage, such as a hard drive, and outlives the process that created the data. For example, systems generate and write event logs to a persistent storage volume. If an administrator reboots the system that generated the event logs, the data is still available on the storage volume. The following list discusses typical persistent artifacts that systems generate in the course of their operations.

Filesystem Artifacts   A filesystem provides analysts with a catalog of all the files that exist on a disk volume. In some cases, a filesystem also contains residual metadata associated with recently deleted files. Analysts use filesystem artifacts to establish evidence of attacker-created files, such as malware, or evidence of data staging during data theft cases. In some cases, analysts can also recover deleted data if the system did not overwrite it with other data.

Program Execution   Threat actors often run malware, utilities, and other software on compromised systems as part of their operations. Operating systems may record artifacts related to their execution that enable analysts to establish what malware and software application a threat actor ran and, in some cases, recover their corresponding binary files for detailed analysis.

Account Usage   Account usage artifacts provide analysts with information about successful and unsuccessful login attempts and other security-related events that systems and applications generate in response to a security policy. Analysts leverage this information to establish evidence of activities, such as unauthorized access to systems, lateral movement, or privilege escalation.

External Devices   Whenever a user connects an external device to a system, the system may generate persistent configuration data for the device. This information is invaluable for investigating cases, such as data theft by an insider threat or malware infections through external storage media.

Browsing History   Forensic artifacts associated with browsing history allow analysts to determine what websites users accessed, evidence of social engineering attacks, or what files users downloaded, including malware. The artifacts vary from browser to browser.

File and Folder Opening   Systems generate file and folder opening artifacts for various reasons, such as recording the size of Explorer windows in the case of Microsoft Windows. File and folder opening artifacts provide an insight into the files and folders with which a threat actor interacted, browsing history, access to files on a remote media, or execution of software through the graphical user interface (GUI). In some cases, this artifact category can also help determine evidence of files that no longer exist in the filesystem.

Network Activity   Persistent network activity artifacts allow analysts to establish what networks an examined system connected to and, in some cases, even establish the physical location of those networks.

This list is by no means exhaustive. It is important to emphasize that artifacts may vary from system to system. For example, production Linux systems that support core applications typically do not have a GUI subsystem installed. For that reason, the systems do not generate browsing history artifacts.

Volatile Artifacts

In contrast to persistent artifacts, *volatile artifacts* constitute data that resides in system memory and is typically short-lived. The data ceases to exist when a user or administrator powers down the system or the process that created the data terminates. Analysts typically acquire volatile data through live response or by acquiring a forensic image of the system memory. The following list discusses typical volatile artifacts that systems generate in the course of their operations.

Process Data   In simple terms, a *process* is a program that is loaded into memory and currently executing on a computer system. A listing of running processes can help identify evidence of malware and other utilities that a threat actor may leverage as part of their operations. As part of collecting process information, analysts may be interested in attributes such as the full path of a binary file, the command line used to launch the process, loaded modules, security context, or how long the process has been running.

Network Connections   By listing and enumerating currently open connections, analysts may discover evidence of lateral movement or malware beaconing out to an attacker C2 infrastructure. In some cases, analysts may also identify suspicious programs that typically do not communicate over a network.

Mapped Drives and Shares   Information about mapped drives and shares can help analysts establish evidence of suspicious activities, such as lateral movement or data staging. This information is particularly useful for administrative shares that threat actors may use for lateral movement and deploying malware.

Logged-on Users   During an investigation, analysts may want to collect information about the currently logged-on user. Users can log into a system locally or remotely. In both cases, the information may provide context to other artifacts, such as running processes or access to specific files.

Clipboard Contents   Each time a user copies data from one application to another application, the operating system copies that data into the clipboard. In some cases, analysts may recover data that a threat actor copied, such as harvested credentials or files of interest.

Open Files   Enumerating open files allows analysts to identify files that remotely logged-on users accessed. This information is especially useful in cases when a threat actor uses harvested administrative credentials to access remote systems and enumerate them for valuable information.

Service Information   Services are background running processes. Service applications are often started at system boot, but administrators can also start them manually. Information about services is key to investigations because malware often runs as a service to maintain persistence and survive system reboots.

As in the case of persistent artifacts, this list is by no means comprehensive. The purpose of this section is to demonstrate the type of evidence that analysts may uncover during forensic examination of compromised systems. It is also worth mentioning that certain artifacts reside in memory first before the operating system writes them to persistent storage.

Network Artifacts

Network data is an invaluable source of evidence during incident investigations. It often augments host forensics and helps prove or refute a hypothesis surrounding an investigated incident. In some situations, network data is the only source of evidence that analysts have available.

Several use cases exist for acquiring and analyzing network telemetry as part of an incident investigation. The following list presents some common use cases:

Scoping   By importing IOCs associated with attacker activity into network monitoring tools, incident responders can identify additional compromised systems that they did not discover through endpoint analysis.

Identifying Evidence of Lateral Movement   Network telemetry helps establish evidence of lateral movement by correlating and tracking network connections associated with compromised systems, including the timing and duration of those connections.

Determining Data Theft   When correlated with evidence of data staging, network telemetry can provide corroborating evidence of data theft, such as network connections to an attacker-controlled infrastructure or evidence of data transfers. *Data staging* refers to the staging of data in a centralized location before transporting it out of the compromised environment.

Gaining Additional Visibility into Attacker Activity   By monitoring network connections and correlating network telemetry with endpoint-based artifacts, incident responders can better understand how the attacker operates in a compromised environment. This may include identifying additional C2 infrastructure associated with deployed malware, identifying the timing when the attacker is typically active on the network, or determining how the attacker performs reconnaissance within the compromised environment. Furthermore, event-based detection tools allow responders to determine whether the attacker uses network-based exploits or abuses network protocols as part of their operations.

Identifying Web-Based Indicators   Collecting data from tools such as proxy servers and web gateways allows incident responders to establish evidence of access to malicious domains or determine whether a user downloaded a malicious document from a rogue website.

Security Alerts

Alerts triggered by host and network security tools are often the first indication of a cybersecurity incident. Although alerts by themselves may not be enough to determine attacker activity in a compromised environment, they often help analysts to establish a hypothesis and create initial leads to drive further investigation. There are typically two types of security tools that enterprises deploy: host and network. The following list discusses typical information that analysts can glean from security alerts.

Evidence of Malware   Antivirus software and EDR alerts are often the first symptoms of an active threat in the enterprise environment. Endpoint detection tools are so ubiquitous in the enterprise that most organizations have some capability to detect a threat on their network.

C2 Communication   Most modern malware these days leverages a C2 infrastructure to receive instructions, download additional malware, or even exfiltrate data. Host- and network-based security tools can often alert on this activity, especially if they have CTI feeds integrated from a reputable source.

Vulnerability Exploitation   Many security tools use signatures of well-known attacks and heuristic capabilities to detect attempts to exploit vulnerabilities. These alerts can help analysts establish early evidence of attacker activity and lateral movement.

Data Theft   Solutions such as data loss prevention (DLP) can alert analysts on attempts to steal data from a compromised environment. Insider threat activities often trigger DLP alerts. In the case of an external attacker, DLP alerts typically trigger when the attacker progressed through the cyberattack lifecycle and attempts to extract data from compromised systems.

Unauthorized Access to Resources   Some access control and management tools monitor access to resources, such as database tables, and may alert on unauthorized access attempts to those resources.

Remediating Incidents

Remediation is the final step of the incident response lifecycle. *Remediation* encompasses the containment, eradication, and recovery phases. Each of these phases is necessary to protect crucial assets while an investigation is under way, eradicate the threat actor from the compromised environment, and recover technology into a fully operational state, respectively. Remediation is a complex process that typically starts at the onset of an investigation. It requires establishing a dedicated team and precise planning to be successful.

This section discusses vital considerations that victim organizations need to take into account when remediating large-scale breaches, including establishing a remediation team, planning, and execution. It is worth noting that in many enterprises, recovery is a function of information technology. For this reason, this section primarily addresses the containment and eradication phases of remediation.

Remediation Process

Chapter 2 briefly discussed the incident response lifecycle in detail. In this chapter, I focus on the overall process to remediate cyber breaches, as depicted in Figure 5.6.

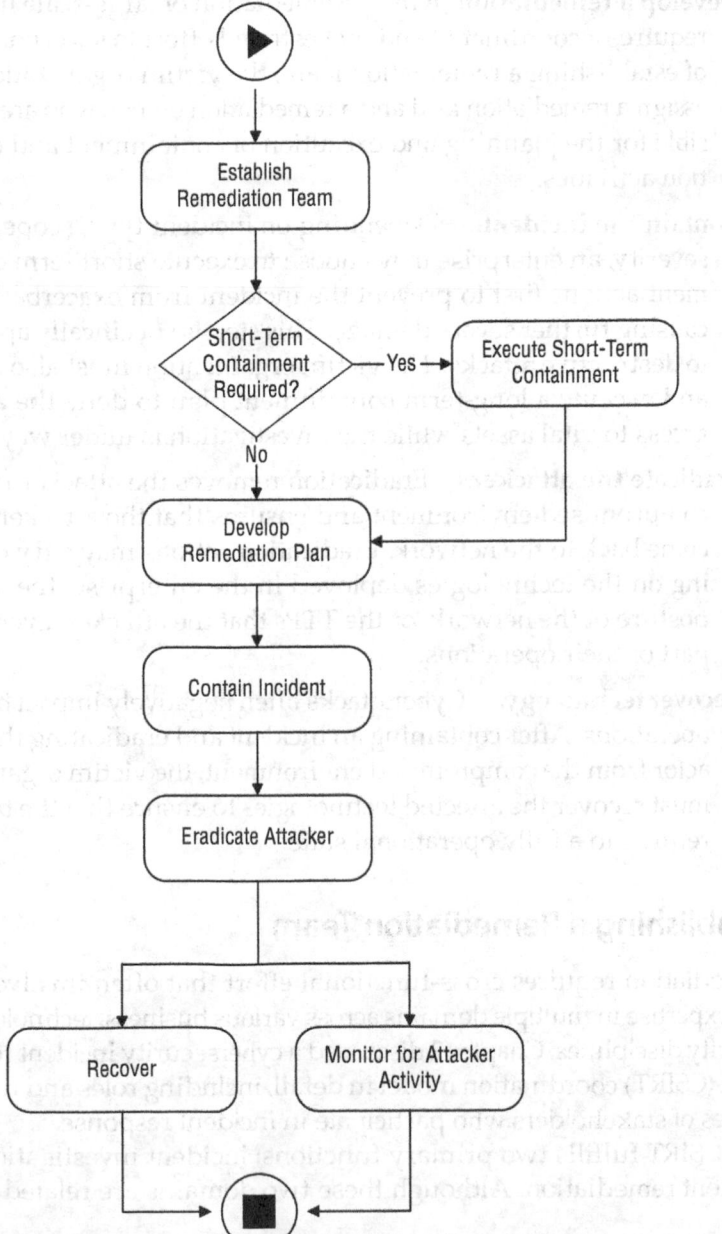

Figure 5.6: A remediation process workflow

Establish a remediation team. Remediation requires skills and expertise in various technical and nontechnical domains. At the onset of an investigation, the victim organization must establish a remediation team and start planning containment and eradication of the attacker from the compromised environment.

Develop a remediation plan. Remediation of large-scale incidents requires a coordinated and orchestrated effort to succeed. As part of establishing a remediation team, the victim organization must assign a remediation lead and a remediation owner, who are responsible for the planning and execution of containment and eradication activities.

Contain the incident. Depending on incident type, scope, and its severity, an enterprise may choose to execute short-term containment actions first to prevent the incident from exacerbating and causing further severe damage. This step is specifically applicable to destructive attacks. The victim organization must also develop and execute a long-term containment plan to deny the attacker access to vital assets while the investigation is under way.

Eradicate the attacker. Eradication removes the attacker from the compromised environment and ensures that the attacker cannot come back to the network. Eradication actions may vary depending on the technologies deployed in the enterprise, the security posture of the network, or the TTPs that the attacker leveraged as part of their operations.

Recover technology. Cyberattacks often negatively impact business operations. After containing an incident and eradicating the threat actor from the compromised environment, the victim organization must recover the affected technologies to ensure that the business returns to a fully operational state.

Establishing a Remediation Team

Remediation requires cross-functional effort that often involves skills and expertise in multiple domains across various business, technology, and security disciplines. Chapter 2 discussed a cybersecurity incident response team (CSIRT) coordination model in detail, including roles and responsibilities of stakeholders who participate in incident response.

A CSIRT fulfills two primary functions: incident investigations and incident remediation. Although these two domains are related to each other, they often require different skills and experience. The former focuses primarily on analysis and answering vital investigative questions, whereas the latter focuses on specific actions necessary to contain the investigated incident and eradicate the threat actor from the compromised environment.

This section briefly discusses two roles that are critical and distinct to remediation: remediation lead and remediation owner. Chapter 2 discusses other business, technology, and third-party roles that may participate in remediation as part of a CSIRT.

Remediation Lead

During smaller incidents, a single individual can assume the roles of an incident manager and a remediation lead. However, during large-scale and complex incidents, organizations need to designate a dedicated individual to lead the remediation effort. In such cases, an incident manager focuses on the overall investigation, whereas a remediation lead is responsible for planning and executing containment and eradication. The following list briefly describes the skills that an effective remediation lead must possess.

Technology Skills and Experience   A *remediation lead* is a senior technical person with breadth and depth of skills and experience across various technical disciplines. The person does not have to be an expert in every technology. However, a remediation lead must have a sufficient understanding of the technologies in scope to work effectively with technical subject-matter experts. For example, a remediation lead with a system administration background also needs to understand disciplines, such as networking, applications, and cloud computing, to plan and lead the remediation effort effectively.

Soft Skills   In addition to technical expertise, a remediation lead must possess soft skills, such as planning, attention to detail, and ability to communicate with technical and nontechnical audiences, including senior management. Execution focus and authority are also vital skills. Planning remediation is often a complex undertaking, and the remediation lead must have the necessary authority and project management skills to lead technical teams and execute remediation while managing business expectations.

Remediation Owner

A *remediation owner* is a senior business stakeholder who closely works with the remediation lead and holds the overall responsibility for the remediation. In many cases, a remediation owner is synonymous with the role of an incident officer, described in Chapter 2.

The remediation of large-scale incidents often results in interruption to business operations and causes anxiety and stress for senior leaders. A remediation owner provides strategic oversight of remediation and works closely with other senior leaders in order to ensure that remediation planning includes business priorities. For example, an organization might choose to switch to an alternate site or system to support core business functions during a disruptive remediation. The remediation owner must work closely with the remediation lead to ensure that technical priorities align with business priorities.

A crucial responsibility of a remediation owner is to assign authority to the remediation lead and communicate the authority downstream to ensure that technical teams prioritize remediation over day-to-day responsibilities. If there is a conflict of priorities, then the remediation owner must resolve it.

Sometimes remediations run into unexpected complications. For example, a victim organization may need additional budget to hire consultants, conflicting priorities, exceeded timelines, and others. The remediation lead typically works with the remediation owner to resolve any complications. Figure 5.7 depicts how information flows between vital stakeholders responsible for incident response, including remediation.

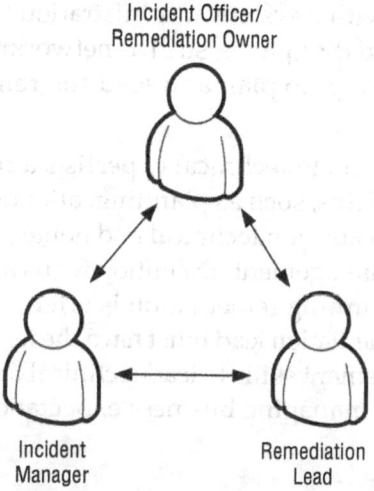

Incident Officer/
Remediation Owner

Incident
Manager

Remediation
Lead

Figure 5.7: Coordination between crucial roles

Remediation Planning

The remediation of a large-scale breach is a complex undertaking and requires cross-business collaboration and coordination. For this reason, planning and project management are vital components of remediation. In some cases, an organization may choose to assign a dedicated project manager to remediation to allow the remediation lead to focus on the overall planning and preparation for execution.

Business Considerations

As part of containment and eradication planning, the remediation lead must identify and consider business needs and priorities and ensure that technical staff have the necessary resources available. The following list briefly describes business considerations that organizations need to take into account before planning and executing containment and eradication.

Executive Buy-In   The first step in planning containment and eradication is executive buy-in. The remediation of large-scale incidents often interrupts business operations and requires additional resources, such as funding to hire external consultants or procure technology. A remediation owner must work with other senior leaders to obtain their buy-in, and secure the necessary resources required to remediate an incident.

Communications   Remediation typically leads to inquiries from employees and external entities regarding interruptions to business operations and other activities. For this reason, the remediation lead and owner need to work closely with corporate communications and corporate legal counsel to ensure appropriate messaging. In some cases, an organization may choose to release a statement proactively.

Execution Timing   Business priorities often conflict with eradication and containment. For example, an organization may have planned a major product or service launch, or payroll runs during specific days. The remediation lead and the remediation owner must work with crucial business stakeholders and consider business priorities before deciding on the execution timing.

Business Partners   Most medium- to large-sized enterprises leverage a complex ecosystem of business partners to operate their business. In some cases, containment and eradication may impact vital business partners and the service level agreements (SLAs) that the organization has in place with them. Consequently, the organization must include and work with business partners during remediation to minimize the potential impact to their business.

Budget   Remediation often requires additional budget to procure technology, hire external consultants, and compensate employees for additional labor. For this reason, the remediation lead and the remediation owner must work with finance to ensure that the necessary resources are available.

Technology Considerations

Containment and eradication often require changes to the technologies that support business functions. The following list briefly describes technology considerations when planning containment and eradication.

Procuring and Deploying Additional Technology   In many cases, an organization may need to procure and deploy new technologies as part of the containment and eradication effort. For example, to prevent the execution of attacker malware or exploits, the organization may need to deploy an EDR tool to its environments. Technology deployment requires planning and testing to prevent a potential negative business impact.

Enhancing Monitoring Capabilities   As part of incident response, organizations often need to enhance their monitoring capabilities to ensure that incident responders can gain additional visibility into attacker activity. The enhancements are also necessary to monitor for any evidence of the attacker after executing eradication. Examples of monitoring enhancement include increasing logging verbosity on specific technologies, shipping event logs to a log management server for long-term storage and correlation, developing attack signatures, or building SIEM correlation rules.

Upgrading Legacy Technology   Threat actors often exploit vulnerabilities in insecure, legacy technologies that vendors no longer support. Often, the only feasible option to prevent further exploits and damage is to decommission or upgrade legacy technologies to more up-to-date and secure solutions. If this is not feasible in the short term, then an organization needs to deploy compensating controls to reduce this risk. In either case, the remediation lead must closely work with technology stakeholders and ensure that the organization takes this requirement seriously.

Logistics

Including logistics as part of remediation planning helps to ensure that the necessary resources, support, and services are available to the remediation personnel. The following list briefly discusses logistical matters that organizations need to consider when executing containment and eradication.

Facilities   The remediation team needs to set up a command center or war room to provide a centralized location for coordinating containment and eradication activities, as well as to make rooms available for technical and management personnel. Another consideration is accommodation. Executing a remediation plan may take several hours and, in some cases, even days. Making accommodation available for remediation personnel is necessary to ensure that they can rest and refresh.

Communications   The remediation team must have available the necessary communications equipment and other tools available to communicate effectively during the execution phase. Setting up separate conference bridges for personnel working remotely or instant messaging channels is crucial. Also, the remediation lead must plan and set cadence for technical and management updates during the execution.

Food   Food is often a forgotten but essential consideration for remediation that may take an extended time. The remediation lead needs to ensure that food, drinks, and other refreshments are available to the remediation team, especially for personnel who cannot leave their tasks or assignment.

Assessing Readiness

I cannot emphasize enough how vital it is to conduct a comprehensive investigation and determine the full scope and extent of a breach before executing the containment and eradication phases of the incident response lifecycle. As part of their operations, threat actors may plant backdoors on numerous systems to maintain persistence in the compromised environment. If eradication does not cover the full scope of a breach, it is just a matter of time before the threat actor comes back and continues the attack.

Moreover, the remediation team must understand and take into account attacker TTPs and the associated IOCs to ensure that containment and eradication are comprehensive and effective. Forensic and CTI analysts derive this information during their investigation and refer to it as *actionable intelligence*. In practical terms, this information is necessary to inform containment and eradication. Gathering actionable intelligence is another reason why a comprehensive investigation is vital before eradicating a threat actor from the compromised environment.

The remediation of large-scale incidents is a complex task, and the planning typically starts in the early phases of the investigation. However, an organization must first understand the full scope of the incident before deciding on execution timing. The only exception to this rule is when an attacker becomes destructive, and the organization must immediately prevent any further damage.

Consequences of Alerting the Attacker

Incident responders and the remediation team should make every possible effort to prevent the attacker from becoming aware of the investigation. Depending on the attacker and their level of confidence, they may react in different ways. Their response may also be detrimental to the investigation. In some cases, where the attacker compromised systems that support communications tools, such as email or instant messaging, the incident response team must consider moving incident communications to an out-of-band communication channel. The following list briefly describes some frequent implications of alerting an attacker.

Becoming Dormant   An attacker may become dormant and remain hidden in the environment for a period of time, only to become active again after remediation. A victim organization may reimage end-user workstations and rebuild servers as part of remediation. However, after becoming active again, the attacker may plant additional backdoor malware and compromise additional user accounts to reinforce their presence in the environment. Incident responders often use the term "rinse and repeat" to describe this scenario.

Change in Operations   According to the Pyramid of Pain described earlier in this chapter, attackers can change how they operate. This point is particularly applicable in cases where an attacker becomes aware of an active investigation. For example, an attacker may recompile malware to change the corresponding hash value of the malware binary. An attacker may also employ defense evasion or antiforensic techniques, such as clearing log files or obfuscation. These actions can cause a loss of visibility into attacker activity and extra work for the incident response team.

Becoming Destructive   In some rare cases, attackers may engage in destructive activities upon discovering an active investigation. Examples of destructive activities include encrypting data for a ransom, deleting files, deploying destructive malware, or defacing web pages.

Developing an Execution Plan

An *execution plan* contains a detailed definition of the activities that a remediation team must execute as part of the remediation effort, including a listing of resources and a schedule. An effective plan typically focuses on containment and eradication activities. Recovery can take days, weeks, or even months in the most severe cases, and it often requires separate planning. The disaster recovery (DR) function typically handles this task. The following list discusses other considerations and highlights the main components of a containment and eradication plan.

Execution Scheduling   The remediation lead must develop a detailed execution schedule of containment and eradication tasks. The schedule should consist of high-level task categories accompanied by low-level activities with clearly assigned owners and validation criteria as required. In some cases, it is useful to organize those tasks into separate workstreams.

A vital part of the plan is an execution sequence of the activities mentioned earlier with clearly defined start and end times. Furthermore, it is a good practice to create milestones to demonstrate progress, as well as to include technical and management updates in the execution sequence.

Procedures   Some containment and eradication activities can be quite complex by themselves and may require a tested and documented procedure to ensure that the remediation personnel execute all of the necessary steps. For example, installing a security tool on a system may require specific configurations that the remediation team must test and document before remediation. Subject-matter experts are typically responsible for creating low-level procedures for activities in their respective domains.

Inventory   The execution plan must contain an inventory of all assets that are in scope of the remediation, compromised accounts, malware hashes, malicious domains, attacker IP addresses, and other information that is necessary to execute the remediation.

An inventory is another reason why scoping an incident is crucial before executing eradication.

Resource Allocation   A sound plan must assign and schedule personnel to work on specific tasks. Building a roster with resource allocation to every task within each work stream is crucial. Also, each work stream must have assigned a lead with the appropriate skills and level of authority. A resource allocation plan is especially vital when a containment and eradication may require shift work.

Containment and Eradication

Containment focuses on protecting critical assets, whereas *eradication* allows the victim organization to remove the attacker from the compromised environment. The following sections examine these two phases.

Containment

The remediation team determines and executes containment actions to deny the attacker access to vital assets in order to minimize impact and prevent further damage. Containment does not remove the attacker's access to the compromised environment. Instead, it limits the attacker's ability to achieve their objective. For example, if an attacker gains access to a system that handles highly sensitive data, the remediation team may put measures in place to prevent further access and data theft. The measures may include multifactor authentication (MFA), access control lists (ACLs), and other access control mechanisms that limit access to the system or network segment.

The remediation lead must plan containment measures with key technology stakeholders and consult with management about the plan before execution. It is important to emphasize that the involvement of third-party organizations, such as external vendors and technology outsourcing partners, often adds a layer of complexity to this process that the remediation lead must take into account.

Containment often requires changes to how users and administrators access certain technologies. The remediation lead must identify and prioritize, with the help of management and business stakeholders, mission-critical assets that the victim organization must protect. Furthermore, the remediation lead also must work with technical groups to understand technical constraints and the potential impact of implementing containment measures such as MFA.

Some containment actions are short-term and designed to prevent immediate damage. For example, during a ransomware outbreak, the victim organization may take immediate actions, such as isolating network segments from the rest of the network to limit the spread of the malware. The premise behind short-term containment is to "stop the bleeding."

In contrast, the remediation team executes long-term containment actions as temporary fixes. The term "long-term" may be misleading in this context. What it really means is that the organization makes temporary changes after "stopping the bleeding" before planning long-term, strategic controls to secure the environment. For example, the victim organization may implement a temporary jump server and lock down access to an environment that hosts highly sensitive data. This measure may prevent the attacker from accessing the environment while allowing the organization to investigate the incident and create an eradication plan. The following list includes examples of typical containment actions:

- Deploying a jump server to limit access to specific environments
- Implementing MFA to prevent access to environments with compromised credentials
- Network segmentation to limit lateral movement
- Micro-segmentation to protect specific systems or applications from unauthorized access
- Restricting access to the Internet from internal networks
- Restricting access to environments or applications to specific users

Eradication

The purpose of eradication is to remove the attacker from the compromised environment. The remediation team executes eradication during an agreed-on window, which typically lasts several hours.

One crucial consideration in remediating large-scale breaches is network isolation. In severe cases where an attacker gained a significant footprint in the enterprise environment, the victim organization may need to disconnect their internal networks from the Internet entirely. This approach is necessary to ensure that the attacker cannot react in response to eradication, and the organization can execute the plan and verify all steps before reconnecting the internal network back to the Internet. This approach is the most effective, but it also has a significant impact on business operations. For this reason, this approach is used relatively infrequently.

An alternative approach is to isolate the network segments in scope for the remediation. However, the victim organization must have confidence that the attacker did not compromise systems in any other environment. As with the previous approach, the remediation team must execute eradication activities before reconnecting the network segments to the Internet and other internal networks.

No network isolation typically works for small incidents that have no significant impact on business operations. Even in such cases, it is a good practice to isolate or disconnect the affected systems from the network. However, remediating large-scale incidents without network isolation is often a counterproductive effort that puts eradication at risk.

One vital consideration in eradication is execution timing. The incident response team must fully understand the scope and extent of the breach before executing eradication. The remediation team relies on the actionable intelligence that incident responders deliver to plan eradication. Another consideration is timing. If possible, the remediation team should plan the eradication window outside the attacker's standard operating hours to minimize the possibility of the attacker attempting to interrupt the eradication.

The following list provides examples of typical eradication activities that the remediation team may execute:

- Removing or disabling compromised user, service, and administrative accounts
- Resetting account credentials
- Removing backdoors and cleaning up other malware
- Patching vulnerabilities exploited by the attacker
- Blocking C2 IP addresses and domains
- Hardening systems and installing security tools
- Hardening and securing authentication and access control mechanisms and services, such as Microsoft Active Directory

Monitoring for Attacker Activity

Once the victim organization executed the eradication plan, there is one more thing to do: monitor for attacker activity. In some cases, even a thorough investigation may not uncover all attacker backdoors and entry points into the network, or every possible IOC associated with the attacker. More advanced attackers plan for being discovered and take the necessary measures to maintain persistence in the compromised environment. In other cases, an attacker may re-compromise the network to continue their attack. Attackers often invest significant resources into their operations and may not give up that easily, even after successful eradication.

For the reasons mentioned here, organizations must import the IOCs discovered during the analysis phase into their security tools and monitor for attacker activity for several weeks before closing the investigation. Even after the formal incident closure, the victim organization should still monitor for any indicators as part of day-to-day operations.

Summary

Incident responders leverage a lifecycle-based approach to investigate incidents. The first step is to generate an incident hypothesis and establish objectives to ensure that business priorities drive the investigation. The next step is to acquire and preserve the necessary data to support the investigation. Incident responders typically acquire data from host and network systems, event logs from enterprise services, and data generated by security tools.

Data analysis is a complex, iterative process that includes domains, such as digital forensics, malware analysis, and CTI. Digital forensics focuses on the analysis and recovery of digital data to answer investigative questions. CTI augments forensic analysis by providing contextual threat information necessary to scope and remediate an incident. As part of an investigation, incident responders may also analyze malware to understand the threat. Analysts leverage static and dynamic analysis techniques to achieve this objective. The final step in the analysis process is to produce an analysis report tailored to the target audience.

Enterprises can employ threat hunting techniques to identify evidence of a historical or ongoing compromise. This approach is necessary when an organization detects a suspicious activity or receives a third-party incident notification but has no specific incident information available, such as IOCs, to establish leads and generate a hypothesis. Organizations can leverage a threat-centric and data-centric approach to threat hunting.

The final phase of an incident investigation is remediation. Victim organizations must start planning containment and eradication activities as soon as an investigation commences. Containment allows organizations to deny the attacker access to crucial assets. In contrast, eradication removes the attacker from the compromised environment. After containing and eradicating the attacker, the final step is to restore technology to a fully operational state.

Notes

1. Scott J. Roberts, and Rebekah Brow, *Intelligence-Driven Incident Response*, O'Reilly Media, Inc, 2017.

2. Roberts and Brow, *Intelligence-Driven Incident Response*.

3. Central Intelligence Agency (CIA), "Psychology of Intelligence Analysis, Analysis of Competing Hypotheses," 2008, www.cia. gov/library/center-for-the-study-of-intelligence/ csi-publications/books-and-monographs/psychology-of-intelligence-analysis/index.html.

4. Enterprise Detection and Response, "The Pyramid of Pain," January 17, 2014, detect-respond.blogspot.com/2013/03/the-pyramid-of-pain.html.

5. SANS Digital Forensics and Incident Response Blog, "Security Intelligence: Attacking the Cyber Kill Chain," 2019, www.sans.org/blog/ security-intelligence-attacking-the-cyber-kill-chain.

6. European Union Agency for Cybersecurity (ENISA), Stuxnet Analysis, www.enisa.europa.eu/news/enisa-news/ stuxnet-analysis.

7. Cybersecurity and Infrastructure Security Agency (CISA), "Alert (AA19-339A): Dridex Malware," 2020, www.us-cert.gov/ncas/ alerts/aa19-339a.

8. VMWare Carbon Black, "What Is Cyber Threat Hunting?," www .carbonblack.com/resources/definitions/what-is-cyber-threat-hunting.

9. InfoSec Institute, "Threat-Hunting Techniques: Conducting the Hunt," resources.infosecinstitute.com/category/enterprise/ threat-hunting/threat-hunting-process/threat-hunting-techniques/conducting-the-hunt/#gref.

10. SANS Institute, "A Practical Model for Conducting Cyber Threat Hunting, 2018," www.sans.org/reading-room/whitepapers/threat-hunting/paper/38710.

6

Legal and Regulatory Considerations in Cyber Breach Response

Laws and regulations affect how organizations conduct cyber breach investigations. In many jurisdictions, cyberattacks are considered a criminal act. Cyber hacking can also lead to legal exposure and civil litigation for victim organizations. For this reason, it is vitally important to include legal and regulatory considerations in building a cyber breach response program. The appropriate handling of digital evidence and data privacy is a crucial consideration in this process.

This chapter discusses, from a high-level perspective, the legal and regulatory considerations that organizations need to take into account when building a cyber breach response program. Although this chapter primarily uses the U.S. legal system to provide examples, most of the concepts are applicable under other legal regimes and in jurisdictions outside the United States. Consequently, leaders and other stakeholders responsible for incident response in their organizations must consult with their legal counsel to establish appropriate requirements for their jurisdictions.

Keep in mind that this chapter, and the entire book, is not a substitute for professional legal guidance or legal advice. I have strived to make the information presented in this chapter accurate and actionable at press time. Furthermore, the information presented constitutes generic guidance, and it may become obsolete over time. Consequently, I do not assume and hereby disclaim any liability to any party for any errors, disruptions, damages, or other negative consequences resulting from applying the concepts discussed in this chapter.

Understanding Breaches from a Legal Perspective

Over the years, various jurisdictions have enacted laws that criminalize computer crimes, such as hacking, ransomware, or identity theft. Moreover, some jurisdictions and standardization bodies created regulations that require organizations to implement controls to protect themselves against predictable threats. With the increasing risk associated with cyber threats, many organizations also choose to purchase cyber insurance to cover costs associated with a potential cyber breach.

Victim organizations can report cybercrimes to and work with law enforcement during a cyber breach investigation. Attributing an attack is a vital activity in prosecuting a threat actor. However, with cross-jurisdictional challenges, even successful attribution rarely leads to successful prosecution.

This section discusses cyber breaches from a legal and regulatory perspective, including working with law enforcement and cyber insurance providers.

Laws, Regulations, and Standards

Unauthorized access to computer systems and data, denial-of-service (DoS) attacks, and other malicious or destructive activities involving computer systems can cause a severe impact on victim organizations and lead to legal exposure. In many jurisdictions, there is no single all-encompassing cybersecurity statute. For example, the legal system in the United States relies on a complex ecosystem of state and federal statutes, common law precedent, regulatory agency rules and guidance, implied standards of care, and other legal frameworks to prosecute computer crimes. This section briefly mentions a few such laws, regulations, and standards, to emphasize the role of legal and regulatory considerations in incident response.

United States

The following list briefly discusses a few examples of laws specific to the United States that attorneys leverage to prosecute cyber criminals:

Computer Fraud and Abuse Act The *Computer Fraud and Abuse Act (CFAA)* is a statute that addresses and penalizes certain forms of intrusions and behavior. The law imposes both criminal and civil penalties for individuals who access computer systems without authorization, or those who exceed their authorization while bypassing security controls. The statute applies to computer systems that are protected by security controls. If a victim organization does not appropriately protect a computer system or has no terms of use that put people accessing the system on notice, it is often difficult to use the CFAA to prosecute a threat actor who caused harm to the system under this statue. CFAA is one of the most commonly used laws in prosecuting computer crimes in the United States.[1]

Electronic Communications Privacy Act The *Electronic Communications Privacy Act (ECPA)* is another federal statute that attorneys use to prosecute computer crimes. The ECPA prohibits illegal interception or the disclosure of wire communications without authorization, including communications sent over the Internet. The law also protects stored communications, such as email. Access to a computer system without authorization constitutes a crime under the ECPA. Many states have their own versions of the ECPA that they use in conjunction with the federal statute when pursuing liability for computer crimes. Unlike the CFAA, attorneys often use the ECPA (and its state progeny) in invasion-of-privacy cases and data-misuse civil cases against private individuals and companies.[2]

Federal Rules of Civil Procedure and Federal Rules of Evidence The *Federal Rules of Civil Procedure (FRCP)* and *Federal Rules of Evidence (FRE)* provide guidelines concerning civil litigation and criminal cases in federal courts in the United States. FRCP and FRE address the gathering and admissibility of digital evidence in federal courts. States have their own rules of procedure and evidence, though they often closely follow the federal rules. Legal counsels often consult those rules to guide the collection of electronically stored information (ESI) for anticipated civil litigation. The section on collecting digital evidence discusses FRE as they relate to incident investigations.[3]

European Union

The European Union (EU) considers data protection and privacy to be fundamental rights. On May 25, 2018, the EU introduced the *General Data Protection Regulation (GDPR)*, which replaces the Data Protection Directive 95/46/EC that governed data privacy in the EU before the introduction of the GDPR. The purpose of the GDPR is to harmonize data privacy laws across the EU member states and give their citizens more control over their personal data.

Under the GDPR, organizations must ensure that the collection and processing of personal data is lawful and takes place under strict data protection principles, rights, and conditions. The regulation requires organizations to apply security controls to protect personal data from unauthorized access and other activities that can negatively impact the confidentiality, integrity, and availability of the data. The GDPR applies to any organization that operates within the EU and organizations outside the EU that offer services and goods to businesses and consumers within the EU.

The GDPR has significantly affected cyber breach response in recent years. Under the regulation, companies holding data about individuals must often notify supervisory authorities in their respective countries within 72 hours of becoming aware of certain types of data breaches. Organizations that suffer a data breach and that fail to comply with the GDPR, and surrounding regulations, can face fines up to €20 million, or 4 percent of the worldwide annual revenue of their previous financial year, whichever is higher. The state of California has recently enacted a law similar to the GDPR (the California Consumer Privacy Act, Cal. Civ. Code 1798.100), and other states are likely to follow suit.

Standards

The *Payment Card Industry Data Security Standard (PCI DSS)* and *System and Organization Controls (SOC)* are two examples of voluntary standards that organizations adopt to demonstrate good cybersecurity practices.

The Payment Card Industry Security Standards Council (PCI SSC), formed by major credit card processing brands, created PCI DSS.[4] The standard aims to ensure that organizations that handle payment card data maintain a secure environment to minimize the risk of data theft and fraud. The standard outlines 12 requirements centered around the following broad goals:

- Secure network
- Secure cardholder data

- Vulnerability management
- Access control
- Network monitoring and testing
- Information security

The council has no legal authority to compel organizations to comply. However, organizations may face significant fines imposed by card brands and other costs if found noncompliant. Examples of costs include reimbursing the cost that payment card brands incur to replace cards or hiring an outside firm to conduct an investigation. Furthermore, data breaches resulting from noncompliance may lead to civil litigation and substantial legal costs. For those reasons, many organizations that handle payment card data choose to comply with the standard.

In contrast to PCI DSS, the American Institute of Certified Public Accountants (AICPA) created SOC reporting that service providers can use to audit and validate internal controls. Service providers leverage SOC reports to provide assurance to their customers about business and operational controls surrounding their services.

SOC 1®—SOC for Service Organizations: ICFR

SOC 2®—SOC for Service Organizations: Trust Services Criteria

SOC 2®—SOC for Service Organizations: Trust Services Criteria for General User Report

Furthermore, AICPA developed SOC for Cybersecurity to enable service providers to communicate information about their cybersecurity risk management program. From an incident response perspective, this framework allows service providers to offer assurance that they have the necessary processes and controls in place to detect, respond to, mitigate, and recover from cybersecurity incidents.[5]

Materiality in Financial Disclosure

The U.S. Security and Exchange Commission (SEC) released a rule that requires publicly traded companies to disclose information that a reasonable investor would consider important in making investment or voting decisions.[6] Consequently, publicly traded companies in the United States must assess the impact of significant cybersecurity incidents to determine if there is a substantial likelihood that the incident information would influence investing or voting decisions of its shareholders. If that is the case, an organization must disclose the materiality in its financial statements. Materiality is the threshold above which missing or incorrect information in financial statements has an impact on investment and voting decisions.[7] Yahoo! is an example of a publicly traded company that failed to properly investigate and timely disclose its 2014 data breach that misled its investors. Consequently, the SEC charged Altaba, formerly known as Yahoo!, a $35 million penalty.[8]

Cyber Attribution

Cyber attribution is a challenging but often a possible task. There is no single process to attribute a cyberattack. Cyber threat intelligence (CTI) researchers often rely on extensive digital forensics, research about past attack patterns, malware analysis, and other techniques to attribute a cyberattack to a specific group. Moreover, analysts may also evaluate their findings and establish a confidence level of their judgment before deciding to attribute a cyberattack. The following sections briefly discuss cyber attribution and its applicability in incident response.

Motive, Opportunity, Means

Cybercriminals and other threat actors conceptually operate in a similar way to more traditional criminals. During traditional criminal investigations, investigators seek to establish "motive, means, and opportunity" to persuade the fact finders of the defendant's guilt during a criminal trial. Although these are not elements of any criminal law, they are often necessary to tell a convincing narrative to a judge or jury.

Motive refers to the internal and external conditions, which lead the defendant to commit the crime. *Means* proves that the defendant had the ability to commit the crime. *Opportunity,* on the other hand, is the defendant's ability to follow through with their intentions.

The concept of "motive, means, and opportunity" equally applies to cyber breach investigations. Threat actors target organizations for a specific reason. An attack may be opportunistic in nature or targeted, but there is always a motive for the attack, such as financial gain or economic espionage. Threat actors must also possess the necessary means to execute their attack. The means may include the necessary skills, tools, command and control (C2) infrastructure, and other capabilities. Finally, an opportunity arises if the victim organization has vulnerabilities and other weaknesses in its security posture that allow a cyberattack to succeed.

Proving a crime in the physical world is a challenging task. This task is even more challenging in the cyber world due to issues such as the following:

- Challenges with acquiring and preserving digital evidence
- Insufficient cyber threat information sharing within the cybersecurity and law enforcement communities
- Cross-jurisdictional nature of cybercrime
- A legal community that is still learning how to handle cybercrime and cyber espionage–related cases

The cross-jurisdictional nature of cybercrime is arguably one of the most challenging tasks when attributing and prosecuting cybercrime. Chapter 1 discussed nation-state threat actors and advanced cybercrime. Threat actors within these two categories often operate from jurisdictions that do not willingly cooperate with other jurisdictions, such as the United States or member countries of the EU. For example, the threat group APT38 conducts financial crime on behalf of the North Korean regime.[9] Even in the case of high-confidence attribution, European or U.S. courts cannot prosecute groups such as APT38 in the majority of cases.

Attributing a Cyber Attack

The CTI community uses the concept of *attribution* to establish a relationship between a victim and a specific entity believed responsible for the attack. According to the Office of the Director of National Intelligence, five key elements permit attribution of a cyberattack:[10]

Tradecraft   *Tradecraft* constitutes the behavioral patterns that threat actors exhibit when conducting a cyberattack. Behavior is closely associated with the tools, tactics, and procedures that threat actors use as part of their operations. According to the pyramid of pain discussed in Chapter 5, behavior is the most challenging indicator to change. For this reason, tradecraft is crucial to cyber attribution.

Infrastructure   Threat actors often build and maintain the network and server *infrastructure* required to establish and maintain C2. Threat actors can build a custom C2 infrastructure, lease it from third parties, or compromise a legitimate organization to leverage their servers as a pivot point as part of the cyberattack lifecycle.

Malware   *Malware* is the malicious software that threat actors leverage as part of their operations. Threat actors can build custom malware for targeted attacks, use widely available commodity malware, or leverage a third-party malware provider.

Intent   *Intent* is the commitment and reason for which a threat actor carries out an attack, such as intellectual property theft or a desire for a financial gain.

Indicators from External Sources   *Indicators from external sources* include information and data shared by the security community, researchers, law enforcement, and other organizations that track information about specific threat actors.

In forensic science, Locard's exchange principle holds that every time a criminal interacts with another entity, there is an exchange of physical materials. Similar to the physical world, by interacting with a computer system a threat actor often leaves a trail. The primary difference is that digital evidence tends to be more volatile than physical evidence.

There is no simple technical process to attribute a cyberattack. Consequently, the CTI community relies on multiple sources of data. Common activities that allow analysts to attribute a cyberattack include the following:

- Forensic analysis of compromised systems, and the determination of indicators of compromise (IOC)
- Open source and proprietary intelligence research
- Reviewing similar past cases and generating hypotheses
- Assessing and correlating data from multiple sources, as well as looking for common data points, patterns, and relationships

Attribution matters in the legal realm because the process of attributing a cyberattack helps gather evidence that prosecutors may use to open a criminal case and prosecute a threat actor. Prosecution becomes more frequent as international collaboration and CTI sharing increases, as well as when the legal systems within various jurisdictions gain more experience with cases related to cybercrime and cyber espionage.

Engaging Law Enforcement

Engaging law enforcement is one of the early decisions that organizations need to make when responding to a cyber breach. Reporting cyber breaches to law enforcement is not mandatory in many jurisdictions. Organizations need to carefully evaluate the benefits that law enforcement agencies bring to the table versus an added layer of management, complexity, and potential reputational harm. A good practice is to establish a bidirectional relationship with law enforcement agencies and enroll in cyber intelligence sharing programs as part of building a cyber breach response program. The benefits of working with law enforcement agencies include the following:

- CTI sharing. Information shared with law enforcement may help other organizations protect themselves against similar attacks.

- In some jurisdictions, law enforcement agencies may compel third parties to disclose the data necessary to progress an investigation, such as event logs or copies of compromised systems.

- If a threat actor operates out of a jurisdiction friendly to the victim's country, law enforcement may prosecute the actor if sufficient evidence exists and appropriate agreements are in place between the two countries.

- Reporting serious breaches, such as data theft, and working closely with law enforcement may look favorable in the eyes of regulators, the public, and outside parties.

- Law enforcement may reach out to foreign counterparts to obtain intelligence and assistance.

- Involvement from law enforcement may delay breach reporting requirements.

In some cases, working with law enforcement agencies may also have some downsides that organizations need to consider. These may include the following:

- Increased complexity of an investigation and management overhead.

- Local law enforcement agencies may not have the required level of expertise to help victim organizations investigate an incident.

- Law enforcement may open an investigation and abstain from sharing any information until the investigation completes.

As part of establishing a cyber breach response program, senior management, in consultation with legal counsel, should establish criteria for engaging law enforcement. In advance of an incident, organizations should at least consider whether to report breaches to law enforcement should there be a reasonable degree of confidence that a cyber-criminal group or a nation-state actor was behind an attack.

Cyber Insurance

Many enterprises purchase commercial general liability insurance coverage that protects them from claims, such as bodily injury, property damage, personal injury, and other incidents. In recent years, insurers have started to offer supplemental cybersecurity insurance policies to cover a wide range of incidents resulting from cyberattacks.

Cyber insurance typically covers a wide range of harms, such as unauthorized disclosure of private information, reputational damage, disruption to business operations, corruption of electronic data, and loss of intellectual property. Cyber insurance policies often include many caveats that relieve the insurer from covering all the damages resulting from a cyberattack. For this reason, stakeholders who make decisions relating to the purchase of cyber insurance must carefully examine a policy to determine the level of coverage and any caps. For example, some policies may have a cap on the expenditure associated with hiring external investigators and legal fees. In some instances, insurers may also refuse to cover losses if they determine that there was severe neglect, such as noncompliance with standards and regulations.

An alternative to cyber insurance is self-insurance. An enterprise may instead choose to set aside funds to cover expenses in the event of a significant cybersecurity event. These funds would be immediately available, and they do not require a hefty monthly premium for a policy that does not guarantee to cover all costs resulting from a cyberattack.

Collecting Digital Evidence

As the magnitude and cost of cyber breaches continues to rise, the amount of digital evidence also exponentially increases. The topic of digital evidence is broad, complex, and dependent on jurisdiction-specific legal protocols and requirements.

Traditionally, organizations relied on forensic duplication to acquire digital evidence. With the increasing scope of breaches and the need to accelerate the acquisition and analysis process, incident responders typically combine traditional forensic acquisition with live response methods. Regardless of the collection method employed, establishing a sound and defensible evidence-handling protocol is vital to ensuring that incident responders acquire and preserve digital evidence adequately and that the evidence is admissible in court.

What Is Digital Evidence?

Digital evidence, also referred to as electronic evidence, is any computer-generated data that is relevant to a legal case. The data may include email, files and electronic documents, event logs, forensic artifacts that systems produce in the course of their operations, or even a timeline of attacker activity that forensic analysts generate based on the outcome of their analysis.[11]

The volatile nature of some types of digital evidence sometimes makes it challenging to preserve. Unlike with physical evidence, it is relatively easy to alter or even erase digital evidence. For example, forensic artifacts that reside in system memory are often short-lived. The data may cease to exist when the process that created the data terminates or a user powers down the system. For this reason, incident responders must collect forensic data as soon as possible and handle it with extra care to ensure that its integrity remains intact.

Digital Evidence Lifecycle

The *Electronic Discovery Reference Model (EDRM)* is a reference framework that provides a conceptual overview of the lifecycle of digital evidence.[12] The model primarily focuses on the electronic discovery of ESI and provides a basis for developing a legally defensible protocol for collecting digital evidence. In spite of its primary use in electronic discovery, the EDRM is extremely helpful in understanding the lifecycle of all digital evidence, including the evidence that incident responders collect during the investigation of cyber breaches.

The EDRM is an iterative model that includes provisions to accommodate changing and evolving requirements relating to digital evidence. As incident responders progress their investigations, some of the phases may occur multiple times. This approach aligns with the incident response process that Chapter 5 discusses. The model also provides a feedback loop mechanism that allows incident responders to revisit earlier phases to accommodate changing requirements. Figure 6.1 depicts the EDRM. The following sections provide a brief explanation of each of the stages.

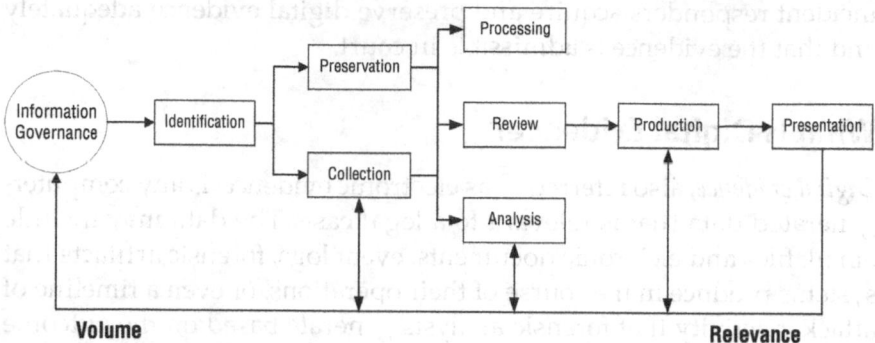

Figure 6.1: EDRM Phases

Information Governance

In the context of incident investigations, *governance* is the process by which senior management exerts control over how an organization conducts investigations. Enterprises typically establish governance through a steering committee as part of building a cyber breach response program. This process includes enacting appropriate policies, establishing legal and regulatory requirements, and allocating resources necessary to respond to incidents. As part of this process, enterprises must establish a data acquisition and preservation protocol to ensure that digital evidence is admissible in court in case of anticipated litigation.

Identification

The first step in the lifecycle is to *identify* the sources of potential digital evidence. In incident response investigations, this process involves identifying sources of events that may be indicative of attacker activity. Examples of sources of data may include compromised servers and end-user workstations, events generated by security tools, or firewall logs that show network connectivity to an attacker C2 infrastructure. Incident responders typically identify sources of digital evidence by looking for IOC in the compromised environment.

Preservation

Preservation relates to taking the appropriate actions to protect digital evidence in a forensically sound manner against alteration or destruction. The preservation methods that responders employ largely depend on the technology that holds evidence. Preservation is a critical step in ensuring that digital evidence is defensible in legal proceedings. Organizations must pay particular attention to preservation where there is a reasonable expectation for litigation. According to the EDRM, preservation may involve the following activities:

- Isolating systems from the network
- Calculating hashes for data integrity purposes
- Documenting the chain of custody
- Preserving event logs in an external storage medium

Collection

Collection is the acquisition of digital evidence identified and preserved during the previous two steps. Incident responders typically collect evidence through forensic imaging and live response techniques. In cases where a threat actor has gained a significant footprint in the compromised network, incident responders often deploy technology to systems in scope to perform live response collection at scale.

Organizations need to build a forensically sound acquisition process that includes provisions for data integrity and a procedure to document a chain of custody for both live response and forensic imaging. Furthermore, it is of vital importance that incident responders create multiple copies of the acquired data, verify its integrity by comparing cryptographic hash values, and work with copies only rather than the original data.

Processing

Computers store data in a binary format that is not easily readable by humans. Furthermore, various file types have different binary structures, and sometimes only software written to work with those files can read them. Before commencing analysis, analysts have to *process* electronic data into a format that they can understand. In the case of forensic images, both commercial and open source tools are available that can parse binary data into a human-readable format. Some live response tools extract and parse data as part of the same task, whereas others only extract data in its native format. Processing often includes one or more of the following methods:

- Parsing
- Normalization
- Format conversion
- Removing noise
- Indexing and cataloging
- Tagging

Reviewing

The final step before commencing analysis is to *review* the data and identify any additional sources of digital evidence. Several reasons exist why incident responders should review data before commencing analysis. Examples include the following:

- Establishing relevancy and selecting specific artifacts required to meet the objectives of the investigation, such as filesystem artifacts to determine data staging.
- Excluding specific types of data from analysis, such as email messages that may be protected by the attorney-client privilege.
- Excluding data that may raise data privacy concerns. This activity may be necessary if an employment contract does not explicitly allow access to private information stored on a corporate asset associated with the custodian.

In cases where an enterprise anticipates litigation resulting from a cyber breach, corporate legal counsel may retain an incident response team to work under the attorney-client privilege and provide guidance concerning the handling of digital evidence.

Analysis

Analysis encompasses an in-depth examination of data to answer crucial investigative questions and provide actionable intelligence. Analysis techniques vary depending certain factors, such as volume of data, format, available tools, and the objectives of the analysis. For example, insider threat cases may require analysis techniques that closely align with electronic discovery. In contrast, network intrusion cases may have a broader scope and rely heavily on CTI. Examples of analysis techniques that responders employ include the following:

- Identifying data points that are outside the normal system baseline
- Correlating data across systems
- Looking for relationships and patterns
- CTI enrichment
- Reconstructing events to determine how the attacker interacted with compromised systems
- Reviewing program execution artifacts to identify evidence of malware and unauthorized access
- Malware analysis
- Creating a timeline of events
- Frequency analysis
- Recovery of deleted files

Analysis is not an isolated task. There is a feedback loop from analysis to the identification phase. Findings during analysis may drive additional data collection requirements, as described in Chapter 5.

Production

The purpose of this step is to take analysis findings and present them in a format and style that is appropriate for the target audience. During incident investigations, analysts typically present their findings in a report format with an executive summary followed by more detailed sections, often of a technical nature. It is also not uncommon for incident responders to *produce* reports for legal purposes, especially if there is a reasonable expectation of litigation. Consequently, report authors must ensure that their reports are accurate and factual. Where possible, report authors should also abstain from expressing opinions and providing subjective interpretation of findings in formal reports, especially if the report is for legal purposes. Chapter 5 discusses reporting in more detail.

Presentation

The final step in the lifecycle of digital evidence is *presentation*. This step encompasses identifying, preparing, and presenting digital evidence to the target audience. In the case of litigation or a criminal trial, attorneys and prosecutors present the exhibits during a legal proceeding. As part of this step, attorneys and lawyers also conduct legal analysis to determine whether the evidence is admissible in court and defensible—that is, the evidence is authentic, and a proper chain of custody exists. The presentation phase may also involve interviews with expert witnesses, testimony, and the presentation of the exhibits in the courtroom or during a deposition.

Admissibility of Digital Evidence

Rules governing the admissibility of digital evidence are very diverse across jurisdictions, and technical innovation continually challenges them. Furthermore, cross-border gathering of digital evidence and proving its authenticity remains problematic. The purpose of admitting digital evidence in courts is to prove a fact at issue. Direct and circumstantial evidence is crucial to this process.

Victim organizations that anticipate a legal action resulting from a cyber breach, such as a civil lawsuit, often invoke legal protocols that allow them to keep communications relating to an investigation confidential and to prevent potentially harmful information from being discoverable.

This section discusses the admissibility of digital evidence in court based on the common law in the United States and how victim organizations can work with legal counsel to reduce legal risk associated with cyber breaches.

Federal Rules of Evidence

As discussed in the section on laws, regulations, and standards, the FRE and the FRCP[13] addressed the issue of digital evidence by setting guidelines on admission of digital evidence in civil and criminal federal courts in the United States. Generally, to be admissible, digital evidence must be relevant, and any of the rules of evidence must not exclude it. Broadly speaking, the rules of evidence seek to admit evidence if it would be helpful to the judge or jury, reliable, and authentic, and they bar the entry of evidence that might be unhelpful, unreliable, or fraudulent. The following list explains each of these rules:

Relevance   For digital evidence to be *relevant*, it must tend to make a fact at issue in the case more or less likely to be true. For example, evidence that a person's home IP address is present in the connection logs of a compromised server is relevant to whether that person actually attacked the server. In contrast, evidence that the person had MP3 files of The Beatles is usually not relevant to whether the person breached the server. Relevance is specific to the situation in a particular case, and information irrelevant in one context may be relevant in another. For example, if evidence on the server indicated the attacker set up fake user accounts with passwords that were obtained from lyrics to The Beatles songs, then the presence of the MP3 files on the person's home computer would then be relevant.

Helpfulness   Evidence must be *helpful* to the finder of fact. Since technical evidence, including digital evidence, is often beyond the ken of the ordinary judge or juror, attorneys often submit additional explanatory evidence to provide context and explanatory power to the original evidence. For example, if an attorney presents digital exhibits during a legal proceeding, expert witness testimony may accompany the evidence to correct any confusion and help the judge or jurors understand the meaning of the digital evidence.

Reliability   Evidence *reliability* refers to the trustworthiness of the evidence. Evidence is trustworthy when it is accurate, objective, and factual and preferably comes from a credible source. For example, if a server produces accurate and consistent event logs based on the configured security policy, the event logs are trustworthy as evidence of attacker activity.

Authenticity   Digital evidence is *authentic* when it "is what it purports to be." For example, attorneys may wish to tender into evidence an electronic file that they claim is an email between two entities. To establish authenticity, the attorney would need to prove that it actually is an email exchanged between those entities and that no third party forged or tampered with the exchange.

Evidence of authenticity can include testimony of an expert witness with knowledge of its creation, collection, and retention or a documented chain of custody. Another example of authenticity is sufficient documentation of the evidence-handling protocol, or evidence that shows that the tools the forensic analysts used produced accurate and consistent results.

Types of Evidence

Several types of evidence exist, each with its own characteristics and complexities. However, from a legal perspective, there are two categories of evidence that attorneys and prosecutors can use to prove a fact at issue: direct evidence and circumstantial evidence. This section briefly discusses the topic of digital evidence from a legal perspective and its admissibility in the courtroom.

Direct Evidence

Direct evidence is typically the most potent evidence, since it does not require any inference to prove a fact or an event; the evidence alone is the proof.[14] Traditionally, direct evidence constituted eyewitness testimony. For example, "I saw John stab Jim with the knife" is direct evidence that John stabbed Jim with the knife. Direct digital evidence often constitutes video and audio recordings, or photographs. Event logs supported by an expert witness testimony is also a primary example of direct evidence that attorneys and prosecutors present in court to prove that an attacker used a computer at a particular IP address to exploit the compromised system.

Circumstantial Evidence

In contrast, *circumstantial evidence,* also known as *indirect evidence,* requires an inference to connect between the piece of evidence and the desired fact.[15] "I saw John standing over Jim with the knife, and the knife was bloody" is indirect evidence that John stabbed Jim, because it requires an inference. For example, "People standing over others while holding a bloody knife often have stabbed the person" needs an inference to go from the evidence that "John standing over Jim with a bloody knife" to the fact that "John stabbed Jim." The following list provides examples of circumstantial digital evidence pertaining to an insider threat investigation:

- Evidence of unauthorized access to corporate assets or accessing other assets that the employee does not require to perform day-to-day duties
- Performing unrequired work outside business hours, especially if unsupervised
- Attempts to entice colleagues and other personnel to provide access to certain assets

- Critical or unfavorable messages about the company posted on social media platforms
- Antisocial behavior, paranoia, and other behavioral characteristics associated with insider threats

Circumstantial evidence can be as persuasive as direct evidence, especially if other evidence exists that reinforces the inference linking the evidence to the fact.

Admission of Digital Evidence in Court

Digital evidence is evidence stored or transmitted in digital form. Prosecutors and attorneys typically admit digital artifacts during a court proceeding as "documentary" evidence. Documentary evidence is a category used to describe a form of evidence that historically came from written documents. These days, *documentary evidence* generally means any evidence that attorneys or prosecutors do not present to the court through oral testimony by a live or previously deposed witness. Digital evidence typically includes any media that records or stores documentation—for example, printed emails, images, or audio and video recordings.

By contrast, "oral testimony," sometimes referred to as *testimonial evidence*, is evidence presented by a witness under oath in court or at a deposition. Oral testimony often accompanies digital evidence, such as the oral testimony that a forensic expert witness provides.

Evidence Rules

The FRE[16] governs the introduction of evidence at civil litigations and criminal trials, including digital evidence. This section briefly discusses the rules that are relevant to digital evidence.

Hearsay Rule

Hearsay is an out-of-court statement offered to prove the truth of the matter asserted, and it is often, but not always, inadmissible in court.[17] Spoken words, documents, and other records typically constitute hearsay evidence. For evidence of this sort to be admissible, it must meet one of the exceptions to the hearsay rule or be exempt from the rule. There are many such exceptions and exemptions, such as a dying declaration or a business record exception.

The purpose of the hearsay rules is to try to separate unreliable out-of-court statements from reliable out-of-court statements. The rule attempts to preserve the right of a party to subject the other side's evidence to examination to determine its trustworthiness and credibility. In practical terms, it means that a forensic expert witness must testify in court as opposed to the court relying on statements that the expert made out of court where the opposing party could not question the expert as to their basis for making the statement.

Business Records Exemption Rule

The *business records exception* to the hearsay rule[18] allows the admission of records in court if the admitting party can demonstrate that the business created the records in the ordinary course and scope of its business activity. Under this rule, the party must demonstrate the following:

- The record was made by a person with knowledge of the information within it.
- The record was made at or near the time of the recorded event of interest.
- The business has a regular practice to make such records.
- The record was made in the regular course of business.

From a cyber breach response perspective, this rule means that artifacts, such as event logs that organizations routinely collect, can be admissible as digital evidence in court. In demonstrating that the logs meet the business records exception, the party may need to tender testimony or other evidence that a system recorded the event logs as part of its routine operation and that the presented event logs are those recorded during the event. For this reason, a chain of custody is of vital importance.

Best Evidence

Best evidence[19] is an often misunderstood, and frequently misused, legal principle that prefers that attorneys and prosecutors submit originals or copies of documents and other pieces of documentary evidence in court rather than have witnesses come in and orally testify as to the contents of the documents. The best evidence rule prevents subjective interpretations from being substituted for the contents of the documents themselves.

As it pertains to digital evidence, parties involved in a legal proceeding often focus on the admissibility of the evidence in court and whether the evidence falls within the scope of the business records exception. Computers store data in a binary format, and parties must often take additional steps to present the evidence in a readable form. Although this sometimes raises challenges brought under the best evidence rule, the FRE and court precedent have now mostly addressed concerns that changing the format for presentation purposes violates the rule. Today, as long as the human-readable format accurately represents the digital format, courts do not bar its admission due to objections under the best evidence rule.[20]

Working with Legal Counsel

Enterprises face increasing risk resulting from cyber breaches, such as fines imposed by regulators, class action lawsuits, and brand reputation damage. As part of establishing a cyber breach response program, senior management should establish a strong and mutual relationship with corporate legal counsel. The involvement of legal counsel during the investigation of a cyber breach may help the enterprise manage legal risk and shield breach-related communications and documentation from disclosure in anticipated litigation.

In my personal experience of leading investigations into cyber breaches, engaging legal counsel following a breach saves many headaches in later stages of the investigation, especially if the breach may have data privacy implications. Corporate counsel typically works with senior management to determine whether to engage external counsel to provide assistance, or even lead the investigation. In many situations, it is appropriate for the counsel to assume a supervisory role and lead the investigation to demonstrate the legal nature of the breach. The involvement from legal counsel may include any of the following:

- Instructing both technology and business stakeholders on communication protocols and marking of written communication and documentation
- Retaining an external digital forensics and incident response firm to provide expertise and assist with the investigation
- Reviewing digital evidence and making decisions regarding disclosures
- Retaining outside counsel to lead the investigation during more severe breaches
- Setting legal priorities and direction for the investigation

The following subsections discuss protocols and privileges that legal counsel may invoke to facilitate an internal investigation.

Attorney-Client Privilege

The *attorney-client privilege* protects confidential communication between an attorney and the attorney's clients to obtain legal advice. The attorney-client privilege applies to any communication, including verbal and written communication between corporate counsel and the organization's employees, as well as third parties retained by the counsel. For the principle to hold, the communication must be confidential and for the purposes of seeking or providing legal advice.

The attorney-client privilege is a powerful legal tool that can shield information and documentation from discovery. Moreover, the principle can help organizations reduce the legal risk associated with cyber breaches by encouraging the free flow of information to legal counsel, who requires that information to help the company navigate legal risk.

Enterprises can intentionally or unintentionally waive the privilege. For example, confidentiality is a crucial element required to maintain the attorney-client privilege. If incident responders distribute the privileged communication too widely, courts may hold that the organization did not reasonably maintain confidentiality, thus waiving privilege for the communication. Organizations may also waive privilege voluntarily to disclose privileged communication if they wish.

Attorney Work-Product

The *work-product doctrine* is another tool that protects certain types of information from disclosure. Work-product protections apply when there is a reasonable expectation of legal action as a result of a cyber breach. The doctrine protects documents and other artifacts gathered in the course of preparing for such legal action from disclosure to third parties.

The doctrine can often protect documents and artifact analyses by incident responders, attorneys, consultants, and other experts on behalf of legal counsel pursuant to the counsel's work in preparing for litigation during or after a cyber breach. The vital concern in the work-product doctrine is litigation. For the doctrine to hold, an organization must have a reasonable expectation that the breach can result in civil litigation or a criminal trial.

Non-testifying Expert Privilege

One facet of the attorney work-product doctrine has become codified in the FRCP as a protection for non-testifying experts. During cyber breach investigations, legal counsel may seek assistance from external consultants to provide expertise in certain areas, such as compliance or digital forensics. When the legal counsel hires consultants with no anticipation to testify in court as experts in the case, these consultants are referred to as *non-testifying (or consulting) experts*. The work of a non-testifying expert cannot be subject to discovery by the opposing party unless the party can demonstrate "exceptional circumstances" demanding that disclosure. In practical terms, reports and other artifacts that external consultants produce to support cyber breach investigations at the behest of an attorney are not likely to be discoverable in most cases.

The attorney-client privilege, work-product doctrine, and non-testifying expert privilege are powerful tools, often asserted together, that legal counsel leverages to prevent the disclosure of sensitive analyses and other potentially damaging artifacts in civil litigation and criminal trials.

Litigation Hold

A *litigation hold*, also known as a *preservation order* or *hold order*, is a notification that corporate counsel sends to custodians, instructing them to preserve documents and other ESI. Legal counsel typically issues a litigation hold where there is a reasonable expectation of civil litigation or a criminal trial, and the information is relevant to the case. It is crucial to emphasize that a litigation hold notice overwrites any data retention policies that an organization may have in place.

A corporate lawyer typically issues a legal hold notification as soon as the organization anticipates litigation. The purpose of a legal hold is to avoid spoliation of evidence. *Spoliation* is the intentional or unintentional destruction of evidence relevant to a legal case. Unintentional spoliation typically occurs through neglect. For example, if an organization performs an internal insider threat investigation, the corporate counsel may issue a litigation hold notice to relevant personnel to avoid spoliation of evidence in case of anticipated litigation or even a criminal trial. This requires the relevant personnel to retain data, such as forensic images and other ESI relevant to the case, for a specific time.

In some instances, the corporate counsel may have to extend the litigation hold to third parties who may hold evidence that is relevant to the case. In this type of situation, typically the legal counsel engages the third party's legal counsel within the boundaries of the local law.

Establishing a Chain of Custody

Chain of custody has been historically associated with law enforcement, government intelligence services, and criminal law, often relating to computer crime cases. In recent years, the concept of chain of custody has been increasingly important in civil litigations. Furthermore, regulators increasingly emphasize maintaining a chain of custody during cyber breach investigations. A chain of custody is especially important in the investigation of cyber breaches that may result in data privacy or regulatory concerns, such as an unauthorized disclosure of data. Consequently, organizations must create appropriate policies and procedures and train incident response personnel in the chain of custody practices. This section discusses a chain of custody as it relates to the forensic acquisition of digital evidence and logical collection of files.

What Is a Chain of Custody?

Digital evidence is as relevant as physical evidence, and it can have an equal or more significant impact during legal proceedings. Due to its volatile nature, the handling of digital evidence requires extra care compared to physical evidence. In cyber breach response investigations, a *chain of custody* is the chronological documentation of digital evidence. A chain of custody is used to prove that no one has altered or tampered with the evidence from the point of acquisition to the time that parties present the evidence in court. In other words, organizations maintain a chain of custody to prove the integrity of digital evidence. If an organization does not adequately preserve evidence, or if there is a missing link, the opposing party may challenge the evidence, or the court may rule it is not admissible.

For traditional forensic acquisition, a chain of custody documentation includes information about the acquisition, transfer, analysis, and preservation of digital evidence. It also includes records concerning each individual who handled the evidence, the date and time of the transfer, and the purpose of the transfer. In contrast, for live response acquisition and logical collection, organizations must produce a defensible protocol to prove the authenticity and integrity of digital evidence. Adequate and sufficient documentation is a crucial component of the process.[21]

Establishing a Defensible Protocol

Incident responders typically leverage a combination of traditional forensic acquisition and live response techniques in cyber breach investigations. Occasionally, analysts may also perform a logical collection of files of interest using the native filesystem. Regardless of the acquisition method, organizations need to ensure that they can defend the acquired evidence against spoliation claims.

Traditional Forensic Acquisition

Forensic acquisition and preservation are the gold standard in legal proceedings. If acquired adequately, courts consider a forensic image as "best evidence." A *forensic image* is a bit-by-bit copy of the contents of a storage device. In addition to active data, forensic acquisition captures free, unallocated, and slack disk space. With the right tools, forensic analysts can recover active data and deleted data that still resides in unallocated space, including metadata about files that no longer exist.

Furthermore, forensic acquisition of volatile data such as random-access memory (RAM) preserves the state of a system at the time of acquisition. Memory analysis allows forensic analysts to recover data that the examined computer system has not saved to persistent storage and to determine activities that do not leave detectable artifacts of disk volumes. Chapter 3 discusses this topic in greater depth.

Different acquisition methods are available to incident responders. The choice of method primarily depends on the system or media that responders intend to acquire:

Imaging: A bit-by-bit copy of data contained on a device

Media cloning: A bit-by-bit copy of data contained on one storage media to another one

Incident responders need to take several considerations into account to acquire data in a forensically sound manner:

- Sanitize a storage device or the destination media for the acquired data before commencing acquisition.
- Use hardware and software write blockers to prevent writing to the source device during the acquisition process.
- Use tools that capture a complete bit-by-bit copy of the acquired media. In the case of software tools, use software that runs as a driver in kernel mode. Some types of malware, such as rootkits, can evade software that runs as a user-mode process.
- Execute trusted binaries from controlled media, and verify that the binary runs with the required privileges to ensure that the software captures all data.
- Acquire data according to the order of volatility described in Request for Comments (RFC) 3227.

To ensure a chain of custody, organizations must create appropriate policies and procedures that sufficiently detail the acquisition process and what information incident responders must capture to ensure that the collected evidence is defensible. The following list contains information that organizations typically document as part of the acquisition and evidence handling process:

- Unique case number
- Date and time
- Personnel who acquired the data
- The acquisition methodology, including tools
- Device information such as brand, model, and serial number
- Operating system details
- Location where the evidence was acquired
- Photographs of physical evidence
- Hashes of the evidence files for data integrity verification purposes
- Information concerning the personnel that handled the evidence, including date of transfer, identity, signature, and purpose

Live Response and Logical Acquisition

In addition to traditional forensic acquisition, incident responders often leverage live response acquisition and logical collection as part of cyber breach investigations. Chapter 3 discussed live response in detail. For this section, it is worth mentioning that live response involves the acquisition of forensic artifacts from a system that is running.

In contrast, *logical collection*, also referred to as *non-forensic collection*, is the most prevalent method that enterprises leverage in electronic discovery. Logical collection involves collecting active data utilizing the native filesystem in which the data resides. As a result, logical collection does not capture data from unallocated or slack space, as in the case of forensic acquisition, and may miss relevant metadata. In spite of its primary use in electronic discovery, incident responders may occasionally perform a logical collection of ESI as part of a cyber breach investigation. For example, analysts may acquire and analyze specific files accessed by an attacker to determine if those files contain protected information.

A sufficiently documented chain of custody is crucial in establishing a defensible protocol for live response acquisition and logical collection. In the United States, the Federal Rule of Civil Procedure addresses the handling of ESI. The rule places emphasis on collecting data in a defensible manner. Rule 26, "Duty to Disclose; General Provisions Governing Discovery," is most directly related to how enterprises should conduct electronic discovery. For this reason, in the majority of civil litigations, courts do not anticipate forensic acquisition of digital data.[22] Instead, civil litigations emphasize the collection process. Arguably, provisions with this rule equally apply to live response acquisition. Consequently, organizations must establish a defensible protocol for live response and logical collection to ensure that digital evidence is defensible against spoliation claims.

Documenting a Defensible Protocol

The EDRM, discussed earlier in this chapter, forms a foundation for building a defensible protocol for live response and logical acquisition that incident responders may leverage in their investigations. The following sections briefly discuss crucial considerations that organizations need to take into account to create a protocol that they can defend in a courtroom.

Documentation

I cannot overstate the importance of documentation in establishing a defensible protocol for traditional forensics, live response, and logical acquisition. Accurate and comprehensive documentation sets the standard for each step in the lifecycle of digital evidence. It provides sufficient information on what data an organization collected and the evidence handling procedure that the organization followed.

Chain of custody is critical to this process. An adequate chain of custody provides chronological documentation of custody changes throughout the lifecycle of the digital and physical evidence.[23] It allows organizations to establish that the evidence they collected for anticipated litigation (or even a criminal trial) is authentic and that no one has tampered with it. A chain of custody is especially important for digital evidence because it can easily change compared to physical evidence. For this reason, organizations must handle digital evidence carefully and produce detailed documentation to avoid allegations of tampering or misconduct.

In the case of logical collection and live response acquisition, chain of custody heavily focuses on documenting the collection and evidence handling process. The sophistication of the collection methodology or the skills and experience of analysts handling the evidence can also directly affect the admissibility of the evidence in court. The following list provides examples of information that organizations typically document as part of producing a defensible protocol:

- Labeling convention to identify uniquely collected items, artifacts, and the media for storing the collected data
- Collection methodology and the tools used for collection of each ESI type and for forensic artifacts
- Secondary collection methods if the primary means fail
- Exception handling documentation and escalation criteria for any unanticipated issues and concerns during the collection process
- Types of ESI and forensic artifacts collected for each custodian or system
- Chain of custody requirements
- Standard templates for documenting the results

Accuracy

Failure to ensure that the data collection is accurate and complete, or other negligence in the collection process, can lead to data spoliation. It is vital that organizations build quality management into the collection process to account for all data sources and custodians, to preserve the necessary metadata associated with the collected items, and to verify their integrity.

Auditability and Reproducibility

To establish a defensible protocol, organizations must produce consistent and reproducible results. Consequently, the protocol must include sufficiently outlined steps that any person with appropriate skills and experience can follow to repeat and produce identical results. Accurate documentation containing a sufficient level of detail is critical to auditability.

Collection Methods

Collection methods vary depending on the type and scope of ESI and forensic artifacts. To enhance the defensibility of a collection process, organizations should consider building technical procedures for traditional forensics, live response, and logical acquisition. The procedures should have provisions to allow enterprises to demonstrate that the specific methods collect the necessary items from all the identified sources and custodians and preserve data integrity.

Data Privacy and Cyber Breach Investigations

This chapter would not be complete without a brief discussion of the issue of data privacy in cyber breach investigations. Data privacy is a complex topic that greatly varies from jurisdiction to jurisdiction, and in some cases, breach investigations and data privacy may be at odds. For this reason, organizations need to establish a lawful basis for accessing personal data on corporate assets for security purposes.

This section discusses common data privacy concerns about which organizations need to be cognizant, and it gives examples of how enacting appropriate policies may alleviate some of the concerns.

What Is Data Privacy?

According to the UK Information Commissioner's Office (ICO), personal data is information relating to an identified or identifiable individual, such as name, unique identification number, or even a cookie issued by a website. Organizations can identify an individual directly from the information or indirectly by linking various pieces of information.[24]

In the United States, the term *personally identifiable information (PII)* is more prevalent. It refers to information that entities can use to distinguish or trace the identity of an individual alone or, when combined with other information, is linkable to a specific individual.[25]

Data privacy is the right to have control over how organizations collect and use personal data. With technological innovation and organizations steadily increasing their digital footprint, the subject of data privacy is becoming complex. Moreover, people are becoming increasingly aware of data privacy and are concerned with how organizations handle their personal data. Various jurisdictions have enacted data privacy laws and regulations to ensure that organizations implement data protection measures to safeguard personal data from unauthorized access. For this reason, inappropriate handling of personal data can result in legal risk and noncompliance with laws and regulations.

Handling Personal Data During Investigations

Most organizations provide employees with computer equipment necessary to fulfill their job duties. Unless employees are working in heavily secured government facilities, it is unrealistic for most enterprises in the private sector to prohibit the personal use of business equipment completely. Excessive use of corporate equipment for personal purposes can lead to potentially significant amounts of personal data stored on the equipment, such as workstations, smartphones, or even corporate email.

Although forensic tools and methods steadily evolve and mature, analysts still rely on human judgment and manual procedures to exclude specific types of data from forensic examination, such as personal data of custodians. Forensic techniques and tools heavily focus on the technical aspect of an investigation. For example, acquiring a full forensic image preserves all data, including personal data of the custodian.

In some instances, forensic analysts unavoidably require access to private information during investigations. This access may lead to data privacy violations if an organization does not have appropriate controls in place to allow security personnel access to personal data stored on corporate equipment for investigative purposes. This point is especially applicable to organizations that operate in jurisdictions with strict data privacy laws, such as the EU. Consequently, it is vital that organizations enact appropriate policies and create procedures as part of their cybersecurity program to ensure that cyber breach investigations do not result in data privacy violations and lawsuits.

Enacting a Policy to Support Investigations

One effective safeguard against data privacy violations is to design and implement a well-thought-out privacy policy. A well-crafted policy considers laws and regulations, risk appetite, and the security culture of an organization. To ensure that cyber breach investigations do not violate data privacy, the policy must regulate the personal use of business equipment and include provisions to facilitate security monitoring and access to personal data on corporate assets for the purposes of investigations.

A privacy policy should take into account data privacy laws and regulations specific to the jurisdictions where the organization operates. It is vital that security professionals enact such a policy in consultation with corporate legal counsel.

Organizations can regulate access to personal data stored on corporate equipment for investigative purposes as part of a governing security policy. Another approach is to create an issue-specific policy and include provisions within the policy to allow security personnel access to personal data on corporate assets for security monitoring and investigations of security incidents. Organizations can also include specific privacy provisions in employee contracts before commencing employment.

It is crucial to emphasize that local data privacy laws and regulations largely influence privacy provisions within a security policy. For example, in some jurisdictions, such as the United States, employee privacy expectations are limited. On the other hand, EU countries have enacted strict data privacy laws that organizations must consider when enacting security policies.

To ensure that a security policy complies with laws and regulations, and that it aligns with other corporate documents, cybersecurity leaders must collaborate closely with other organizational functions, such as legal and human resources, when enacting a security policy.

Cyber Breach Investigations and GDPR

This chapter is not about specific laws and regulations. However, the GDPR introduced by the EU on May 25, 2018, has a global scope and has affected the way that enterprises conduct cyber breach investigations. For this reason, it is worth briefly discussing the GDPR in the context of cyber breach response.

The forensic data that incident responders acquire and analyze may contain data subjected to the GDPR. Consequently, organizations must address GDPR concerns as part of building a cyber breach response program to remain compliant and avoid violations that may result in significant fines.

Understanding the role under which an organization falls concerning the GDPR in the context of incident response is crucial to ensuring compliance. There are a few key terms set by Article 4 that enterprises must understand before implementing specific controls to comply with the regulation.

Personal Data   In terms of the GDPR, *personal data* means any information relating to an identified or identifiable natural person ("data subject"); an *identifiable natural person* is one who can be identified in particular, directly or indirectly, by reference to an identifier such as a name, an identification number, location data, an online identifier, or to one or more factors specific to the physical, physiological, genetic, mental, economic, cultural, or social identity of that natural person.[26]

Data Controller   In terms of the GDPR, a *data controller* means the natural or legal person, public authority, agency, or other body that, alone or jointly with others, determines the purposes and means of the processing of personal data; where the purposes and means of such processing are determined by EU or member state law, the controller or the specific criteria for its nomination may be provided for by EU or member state law.[27]

Data Processor   In terms of the GDPR, a *data processor* means a natural or legal person, public authority, agency, or other body that processes personal data on behalf of the controller.[28]

Processing   In terms of the GDPR, *processing* means any operation or set of operations that is performed on personal data or on sets of personal data, whether by automated means, such as collection, recording, organization, structuring, storage, adaptation or alteration, retrieval, consultation, use, disclosure by transmission, dissemination or otherwise making available, alignment or combination, restriction, erasure, or destruction.[29]

It is vital to emphasize that terms mentioned here are specific to the GDPR. Jurisdictions outside the EU may have different definitions of similar terms. For example, as mentioned earlier, regulators in the United States use the term PII.

Data Processing and Cyber Breach Investigations

Cyber breach investigations, especially digital forensics, fall under the definition of processing under the GDPR. Senior managers responsible for incident response need to establish appropriate controls to ensure that their organizations conduct incident investigations in compliance with the regulation. For this reason, the senior managers must closely work with data privacy professionals, such as the data privacy officer (DPO) or legal counsel, to determine regulatory requirements and ensure that the implemented controls satisfy those requirements.

The GDPR sets seven principles concerning the processing of personal data that affect cyber breach investigations:[30]

Lawfulness, fairness and transparency: Identify an appropriate lawful basis for processing, taking into account how the processing may affect the concerned individuals and being open and transparent about the processing.

Purpose limitation: Ensure that organizations process personal data for the original purpose for which they collected the data.

Data minimization: Ensure that the data is adequate for the stated purpose, relevant, and limited to what is necessary.

Accuracy: Take reasonable steps to ensure that the data organizations collect is correct and remains correct.

Storage limitation: Keep the data for the required period of time only.

Integrity and confidentiality: Ensure that appropriate safeguards are in place to protect the data.

Accountability: Ensure that the controller adheres to all privacy principles set in the GRPR.

Establishing a Lawful Basis for the Processing of Personal Data

Enterprises must ensure that they have a lawful basis for the processing of personal data acquired to conduct a cyber breach investigation. This principle includes the following lawful basis for processing:[31]

Consent: The subject of the data must provide consent for the processing.

Contract: Processing is necessary to fulfill a contract.

Legal obligation: Processing is required to comply with a law or a regulation.

Vital interest: Processing is necessary to protect or save a life.

Public interest: Processing is necessary for a task in the public interest or by exercising official authority.

Legitimate interest: Processing is necessary for the legitimate interest of the controller or third party.

Organizations must establish an appropriate basis for processing based on the nature of their organization and their relationships to the individuals whose personal data is subject to processing. For example, a law enforcement agency in an EU member country may use the "vital interest" basis to process personal data to investigate computer crimes lawfully. Private sector organizations, on the other hand, may use the "consent" basis established through a policy or an employment contract, as mentioned earlier.

A *lawful basis* is the foundation of the processing of personal data that incident responders acquire to conduct an investigation. The following list presents examples that can help organizations, especially in the private sector, establish a lawful basis for processing of personal data as part of conducting a cyber breach investigation.

Contracts Employees can give explicit consent in their employment contracts, allowing the employer to monitor and collect personal data for security monitoring and responding to cyber incidents.

Legal Obligations Under the GDPR, organizations have a legal obligation to notify a supervisory authority about breaches of personal data. Each EU member has an authority that supervises the compliance with the GDPR. Organizations must investigate security events to determine if a data breach occurred, including data concerning employees. Arguably, this scenario qualifies as a "legal obligation" basis for processing personal data.

Security Policy An effective security policy regulates the use of personal data on business equipment and may be an effective safeguard against the GDPR violations. By agreeing to comply with such a policy, employees give their employers consent to monitor and collect their personal data for monitoring and investigative purposes.

Legitimate Interest Most organizations have a legitimate interest in collecting and processing personal data as part of their cybersecurity program to safeguard vital assets and prevent breaches of personal data in the first place.

Territorial Transfer of Personal Data

In some instances, the processing of security data as part of an investigation may take place outside the EU. This situation may occur for various reasons, such as the following:

- The data controller operates the "follow-the-sun" model to provide global cybersecurity monitoring and support.

- The data controller conducts business activities in multiple markets, including the EU, but their incident response team operates out of a non-EU country.

- The data controller hires an external incident response firm that operates outside the EU.

- The data controller leverages tools, such as endpoint detection and response, that send security data to a cloud environment hosted in a non-EU country.

Under the GDPR, if territorial transfer of personal data occurs, then the data processor must comply with the GDPR as would any organization within the EU. Furthermore, the processor must have a designated representative in the EU, unless exempted.

There is an exception to this rule. The processor does not have to comply with the GDPR if the processing is occasional or does not occur on a large scale, or if the processing includes special categories of data or is related to criminal convictions and offenses. Senior managers responsible for incident response in their organizations must seek guidance from a qualified data privacy professional or legal counsel to determine whether an exception may apply to a particular case, such as when hiring an incident response firm to assist with a specific case.

Summary

This final chapter briefly discussed legal and regulatory considerations that organizations need to take into account when establishing a cyber breach response program.

Various jurisdictions criminalize specific uses of computers for malicious activities, such as fraud or data theft. One of the early decisions that victim organizations need to make is whether to notify law enforcement. In case of anticipated legal action, victim organizations must also invoke their legal protocols and closely work with legal counsel to minimize potential legal exposure resulting from a cyber breach.

Adequate acquisition and preservation of digital evidence is crucial in instances where a cyber breach may lead to civil litigation or even a criminal trial. The rules governing the admissibility of digital evidence in legal proceedings vary from jurisdiction to jurisdiction. For this reason, enterprises must work with their legal counsel to ensure that their acquisition and preservation protocols are sound from a legal perspective.

A well-documented chain of custody is of vital importance. Traditional forensic imaging is the gold standard in acquiring and preserving digital evidence. However, organizations can also admit evidence gathered through live response or logical collection as long as the evidence handling protocol is sound and defensible.

Finally, this chapter concluded with a brief discussion about the GDPR. Organizations whose activities fall within the scope of the GDPR must establish a lawful basis for the processing of personal data that incident responders may acquire as part of cyber breach investigation to comply with this regulation.

Notes

1. Office of Legal Education Executive Office for United States Attorneys, OLE Litigation Series, "Prosecuting Computer Crimes," `www.justice.gov/sites/default/files/criminal-ccips/legacy/2015/01/14/ccmanual.pdf`.

2. U.S. Department of Justice, Justice Information Sharing, "Electronic Communications Privacy Act of 1986 (ECPA)," `www.it.ojp.gov/PrivacyLiberty/authorities/statutes/1285`.

3. Cornell Law School, Legal Information Institute, "Federal Rules of Civil Procedure," `www.law.cornell.edu/rules/frcp`.

4. PCI Security Standards Council, "Requirements and Security Assessment Procedures Version 3.2.1," May 2018, `www.pcisecurity standards.org/documents/PCI_DSS_v3-2-1.pdf?agreement=true& time=1584935353756`.

5. System and Organization Controls: SOC Suite of Services, `www.aicpa.org/SOC`.

6. Find Law, "SEC Release on Materiality in Financial Disclosure," `corporate.findlaw.com/finance/sec-release-on-materiality-in-financial-disclosure.html`.

7. Accounting Tools, "Materiality," May 14, 2019, `www.accountingtools.com/articles/2017/5/8/materiality`.

8. U.S. Securities and Exchange Commission, Press Release, "Altaba, Formerly Known as Yahoo!, Charged with Failing to Disclose Massive Cybersecurity Breach; Agrees to Pay $35 Million," `www.sec.gov/news/press-release/2018-71`.

9. FireEye, Threat Research, "APT38: Details on New North Korean Regime-Backed Threat Group," October 3, 2018, `www.fireeye.com/blog/threat-research/2018/10/apt38-details-on-new-north-korean-regime-backed-threat-group.html`.

10. Office of the Director of National Intelligence, " A Guide to Cyber Attribution," September 14, 2018, `www.dni.gov/files/CTIIC/documents/ODNI_A_Guide_to_Cyber_Attribution.pdf`.

11. EDRM, Glossary, "Electronic Evidence: Definition(s)," `www.edrm.net/glossary/electronic-evidence`.

12. EDRM, "EDRM Model," `www.edrm.net/resources/frameworks-and-standards/edrm-model`.

13. Cornell Law School, Legal Information Institute, "Federal Rules of Civil Procedure," www.law.cornell.edu/rules/frcp.

14. Cornell Law School, Legal Information Institute, "Direct Evidence," www.law.cornell.edu/wex/direct_evidence.

15. Cornell Law School, Legal Information Institute, "Circumstantial Evidence," www.law.cornell.edu/wex/circumstantial_evidence.

16. Cornell Law School, Legal Information Institute, "Federal Rules of Civil Procedure," www.law.cornell.edu/rules/frcp.

17. Cornell Law School, Legal Information Institute, "Hearsay," www.law.cornell.edu/wex/hearsay.

18. Cornell Law School, Legal Information Institute, "business records exception," www.law.cornell.edu/wex/business_records_exception.

19. Cornell Law School, Legal Information Institute, "Best Evidence Rule," www.law.cornell.edu/wex/best_evidence_rule.

20. Cornell Walker, "Computer Forensics: Bringing the Evidence to Court," www.infosecwriters.com/Papers/CWalker_Computer_Forensics_to_Court.pdf.

21. Merrill Legal Solutions, "Maintaining the Chain of Custody in Civil Litigation," White Paper, pdfserver.amlaw.com/legaltechnology/Merrill_Chain_of_Custody_White_Paper.pdf.

22. Merrill Legal Solutions, "Maintaining the Chain of Custody in Civil Litigation," White Paper, pdfserver.amlaw.com/legaltechnology/Merrill_Chain_of_Custody_White_Paper.pdf.

23. EDRM, "Chain of Custody: Definition(s)," www.edrm.net/glossary/chain-of-custody.

24. ICO, "Guide to Data Protection, Guide to the General Data Protection Regulation (GDPR), Key Definitions, What is personal data?," ico.org.uk/for-organisations/guide-to-data-protection/guide-to-the-general-data-protection-regulation-gdpr/key-definitions/what-is-personal-data.

25. NIST, Computer Security Resource Center, Glossary, "(PII)," csrc.nist.gov/glossary/term/personally-identifiable-information.

26. GDPR, Article 4(1), eur-lex.europa.eu/legal-content/EN/TXT/PDF/?uri=CELEX:32016R0679.

27. GDPR, Article 4(7), eur-lex.europa.eu/legal-content/EN/TXT/PDF/?uri=CELEX:32016R0679.

28. GDPR, Article 4(8), eur-lex.europa.eu/legal-content/EN/TXT/PDF/?uri=CELEX:32016R0679.

29. GDPR Article 4(2), eur-lex.europa.eu/legal-content/EN/TXT/PDF/?uri=CELEX:32016R0679.

30. ICO, Guide to Data Protection, Guide to the General Data Protection Regulation (GDPR), "The principles," ico.org.uk/for-organisations/guide-to-data-protection/guide-to-the-general-data-protection-regulation-gdpr/principles.

31. ICO, Guide to Data Protection, Guide to the General Data Protection Regulation (GDPR), "The principles," ico.org.uk/for-organisations/guide-to-data-protection/guide-to-the-general-data-protection-regulation-gdpr/principles.

Index

A

A. P. Møller - Maersk, xxv
Accept option, in risk
    response, 180
access control lists (ACLs),
    238
account usage artifacts, 224
accountability, 275
Accountable, in RACI chart,
    159
accuracy, of data, 190, 270,
    275
Acquire Additional Data
    step, in analysis
    lifecycle, 201–202
acquisition method, 199
Act step, in Deming cycle,
    185
actionable intelligence, 175,
    235–236
active voice, writing in, 222
admissibility, of digital
    evidence, 258–265
advanced persistent threats
    (APTs), 2–3
advanced static analysis,
    217
adversary. *See* threat actors
adverse event, 9
agent-based collection,
    134–135
agentless collection,
    134–135
alerting the attacker,
    236–237

alerts, 9–10, 132
Align TTPs to Target
    phase, of cyberattack
    preparation framework,
    6
Altaba, 248
Amazon Web Services
    (AWS), 116, 117, 119
analysis
    automating tasks, 101
    in incident response
        playbook workflow,
        174–175
    performing, 200–222
    processing data before,
        100
    of requirements, 34
Analysis/Analyze phase
    in EDRM, 254, 256–257
    in lessons-learned
        process, 181–182
Analyze Data step, in
    analysis lifecycle,
    200–201
Analyze Information
    step, in seven-step
    improvement process,
    187, 191
antivirus software,
    128–129
application group, 88
application logs, 130–131
architectures, for log
    management, 135–137
artifacts, 223

Assess Findings and Create
    Plan step, in seven-step
    improvement process,
    187, 191–192
assessing readiness,
    235–236
Assessment step, in
    strategic planning,
    23–24
asset management, 156
assigning roles and
    responsibilities, 82–90
atomic indicators, 213
attack vector, 209–210
attacker. *See* threat actors
attorney work-product,
    264
attorney-client privilege, 86,
    263–264
attribution, cyber, 248–250
audience, knowing your,
    222
audit events, 131
audit logs, 126
auditability, of data, 270
authenticity, Federal Rules
    of Evidence (FRE) and,
    259
authority, establishing,
    75–77
automating, 100, 101
availability, of data, 189–190
Avoid option, in risk
    response, 180
AWS VPC flow logs, 119